Eternal Blessedness for All?

Eternal Blessedness for All?

A Historical-Systematic Examination
of Friedrich Schleiermacher's
Reinterpretation of Predestination

Anette I. Hagan

James Clarke & Co

To Hughie. For everything.

James Clarke and Co
P.O. Box 60
Cambridge
CB1 2NT

www.jamesclarke.co
publishing@jamesclarke.co

ISBN: 978 0 227 17430 2

British Library Cataloguing in Publication Data
A record is available from the British Library

First published by James Clarke and Co, 2014

Copyright © Anette I. Hagan, 2013

First Published, 2013

This edition is published by arrangement
with Pickwick Publications

Contents

Contents

PART THREE: Schleiermacher's Account of Election in Context

Foreword

ONE OF THE MOST significant theologians of modernity, Friedrich Schleiermacher continues to generate intense scholarly activity. Often judged to be revisionist, liberal, and romantic in its orientation, his thought has for long been interpreted through a reading of the *Speeches* and the opening sections of the *Glaubenslehre*.

More recently, however, the breadth and complexity of Schleiermacher's work have become more evident. This has coincided with the range of his writings being accorded closer study, more of these now appearing in English translation. Schleiermacher wrote extensively on hermeneutics, literature, and Reformed dogmatics, specialisms that are not often comprehended in a single system of thought. In addition, he preached regularly throughout most of his life, his sermons being an integral element of his theological output. He has to be understood, therefore, as a theologian of the German Protestant Church and as someone who sought the unity of its Reformed and Lutheran strands in the early nineteenth century.

Anette Hagan's volume pays close attention to Schleiermacher's intensive engagement with the doctrine of predestination. This is a topic that he discusses not only in the *Glaubenslehre* but in a key essay that reveals his interaction with the Lutheran tradition. Predestination has been a neuralgic theme in the Reformed tradition for several centuries, many of the most divisive disputes in the late sixteenth and seventeenth centuries being generated by revisions to its most controversial aspects. Historically, it was also one of several contested issues that deeply divided the Reformed and Lutheran traditions after the Reformation.

In recent times, many Reformed theologians have tended to circumnavigate these waters as if the effort of steering a safe passage through them is either too hazardous or not worth expending the effort. Schleiermacher, however, faced the problems head-on, arguing that much of what the seventeenth-century Reformed tradition had to say about predestination was correct. This is a somewhat surprising verdict and confirms those contemporary readings of his work that cast him as a multi-faceted and novel thinker. Yet while siding with the determinist leanings of the Reformed tradition, Schleiermacher reworks it in a more explicitly universalist direction. The separation between belief and unbelief is divinely ordained but only as temporary. It is destined to fade through time as the Christian faith spreads across space. Ultimately God's good intention is a universal restoration that must inevitably be accomplished; hence the division of human beings into two groups is not final or eschatological, but one that is destined to vanish.

By working through Schleiermacher's original writings on this theme and his impressive engagement with the Reformed and Lutheran theologians of his own day, Dr. Hagan is able to display the importance of his work as a theologian of the church who is at once both Reformed and ecumenical. What emerges is a valuable study of one of the most significant renderings of the doctrine of election since the Reformation.

David Fergusson

Preface and Acknowledgments

THIS BOOK HAS GROWN out of my dissertation for a Master of Theology by Research, which was accepted by New College, University of Edinburgh, in 2009. It has since undergone a thorough revision and has almost trebled in length.

My interest in Friedrich Schleiermacher was first awakened and fostered by Prof. Dr. Eilert Herms, one of Germany's foremost Schleiermacher experts, whose lectures and seminars I attended between 1990 and 1993 as part of my first degree at the University of Mainz, Germany. It was there, too, that I became interested in the doctrine of predestination, and I even chose it as the subject for my final divinity exam. I then moved to Edinburgh, where I undertook postgraduate work in English Language and later in Information and Library Studies, but with hindsight it is clear that my interest in systematic theology had not disappeared. In 2007, while working as a rare books curator at the National Library of Scotland, I finally decided to take up my old quest and to do some structured research on the topic of predestination. It was Prof. David Fergusson, Principal of New College, the supervisor of my masters program, who suggested that I should concentrate entirely on Schleiermacher for the dissertation, and who asked all the pertinent research questions. I wish to express my heartfelt gratitude for his encouragement, his inspiration, and his continuing support, which has extended well beyond the confines of the degree course.

The next step on the road to this book was making the acquaintance of Prof. Terrence Tice, the doyen of all things Schleiermacher in the Anglo-American world of theology; this contact was also mediated through Prof. Fergusson. Prof. Tice has been the most tireless, enthusiastic, inspiring, and helpful companion on the way to this book that anybody can imagine, and I cannot thank him enough for all he has done to further the project. His email epistles are legion, and his encouragement and fine sense of humor have gone a long way to keeping me focused on the project. This is also the place to express my sincere thanks to his wife Dr. Catherine Kelsey, who provided invaluable technical support for file transfer operations—not to mention their generous hospitality on a visit to Denver in 2009!

Dr. Allen G. Jørgenson, Assistant Professor at Waterloo Lutheran Seminary at Ontario, Canada, very kindly sent me a manuscript copy of the translation into English of Schleiermacher's essay on election, which he had undertaken along with Prof. Iain C. Nicol. I am most grateful to have had access to this magisterial translation even before its publication.

Dr. Paul Nimmo of New College, Edinburgh, acted as external examiner for my MTh thesis, and has since become a most engaging conversation partner regarding *Schleiermacheriana*. I wish to thank him sincerely for all his time and wonderfully constructive criticism, and for the rounds of laughter we've had.

I am also grateful for the inspiration and support offered by PD Dr. Kirsten Huxel, whom I first met in Prof. Herms' Schleiermacher seminar at Mainz. Our friendship has flourished on the basis of the theological interests we share.

Many friends and colleagues have kept asking about the progress of the book and made me feel better when the going was tough next to my full-time job. Among them, I would like to single out Scott McKenna, parish minister of Mayfield Salisbury Church in Edinburgh. Scott's ceaseless enthusiasm for this project and his belief in my ability to pull it off have proved to be a real tonic, and I am hugely grateful for the fun and banter of our friendship.

Most importantly though, I want to thank my husband Hughie. This book would have been impossible to conceive and write without him. He quietly assumed (almost) all the household chores, spent uncountable evenings trying to cheer me up when the task ahead seemed insurmountable, and often kept us both sane with his fantastic sense of humor. Not only that, Hughie also came to be my sounding board regarding the content and structure of the book, and many sections were designed or revised as a result of one of our ding-dongs—and he's not even a Protestant! It gives me great satisfaction that he must now be one of the most knowledgeable Roman Catholics in matters Schleiermacher and predestination, and I can only hope that he revels in that distinction.

1

Introduction

ACCORDING TO ITS ORIGIN, election denotes the epitome of divine favor: the bestowing of God's grace initially on the Israelites. As a result of a shift in perspective from God's determining will for a nation in this world to his foreordination of the eschatological fate of individuals election came to be perceived as a dark enigma, a decree associated with the hidden God even before creation. Now predestination was interpreted in the context of a neutral stocktaking that positioned believers and non-believers side by side and tried to explain the empirical observation that some have faith and others do not by way of election or non-election. At that stage, the relationship between God and human beings came to be seen as a causal relationship according to the motto "nothing happens without a reason."

Augustine of Hippo (354–430) was the first Western theologian to systematize predestination and present it as a doctrine. He employed the notion of omnipotent divine causality to explain the principle of election that God elects whom he wants to elect. Christian mainstream has generally followed Augustine's understanding of predestination as divine foreordination that separates human beings into those that will ultimately be saved and those that will not. Augustine himself stopped short of endorsing the notion of foreordained perdition, and instead referred to the reprobate as those passed over by election. A millennium later, the two major exponents of the Protestant Reformation, Martin Luther (1483–1546) and John Calvin (1509–1564) then unequivocally endorsed double predestination: the divine decree to both salvation and perdition.

During the Reformation, the notion of predestination served as reassurance for the struggling and persecuted Protestant congregations that their very existence was due to a divine decree, and not to human decisions, and that, as a consequence, human impotence would be unable to cause it to fail. The Reformed tradition then tended to adhere to Calvin's original teaching, albeit with some variations and indeed exceptions, whereas the Lutheran mainstream[1] moved away from Luther's original interpretation to a diametrically opposed position. Philipp Melanchthon (1497–1560) introduced the humanist ideal into the debate. His emphasis on free will and ethical improvement eventually drove a wedge between those who followed Luther's original teaching and those who sided with Melanchthon. The former retained Luther's focus on the divine decree and the irresistibility of grace, whereas the latter focused on human beings, on freedom of the will, and on personal responsibility. As a result, the strict causal relationship between God and human beings, which Luther had insisted on, was weakened to make room for the power of the human will to accept or reject faith. Lutheran orthodoxy favored Melanchthon's understanding and came to champion a single divine decree to salvation.

In the early nineteenth century, the Reformed theologian Friedrich Daniel Ernst Schleiermacher (1768–1834) decisively reworked the theory of predestination. He championed the notion of universal restoration, yet he was careful to propound it as a proper doctrine of faith. Upholding the causal relationship between God and human beings endorsed by Luther and by the Calvinists, he nevertheless moved away from the traditional perspective that ultimately distinguishes the elect from the reprobate. His solution to the ancient dilemma of the separation into two groups consisted in explaining that separation as a temporary state of development. Allowing for the *post mortem* working of grace, he argued that the kingdom of God would be completed eschatologically through the universal restoration of all human beings.

This study explores the historical and ecumenical situation in which Schleiermacher's views on predestination took shape. It provides a close examination of the confessional and doctrinal sources Schleiermacher employed and a detailed discussion of his major texts on predestination. It attempts a critical assessment of these works and locates Schleiermacher's interpretation in its systematic-theological context as well as in the universalist tradition. As such, it focuses on original sources and contemporary responses to Schleiermacher's position. No evaluation of the critique of Schleiermacher's interpretation of predestination by the representatives of neo-orthodoxy, such as Emil Brunner, or of dialectical theology, in

---

1. There were variations and exceptions in the Lutheran tradition as well.

particular Karl Barth,[2] is attempted here. Instead, this study is intended to provide a critical assessment of Schleiermacher's interpretation of predestination in its original context.

The first section of this study explores the historical background as well as the theological, ecumenical, and political situation in which Schleiermacher's thinking on predestination took shape. To this end, it first provides an overview of the confessional developments in Western Europe from the Reformation to the early seventeenth century. It then focuses on Schleiermacher's part in the negotiations and debates that brought about the Prussian Church Union of 1817, one of the first unions of the Lutheran and Reformed Churches in the German states. Predestination was one of the issues that had traditionally separated the two Protestant Churches. Schleiermacher argued in favor of preserving doctrinal differences and debating them in academic circles while insisting that such differences should simply be ignored for practical purposes such as joint communion celebrations. He thus had to defend his position on two fronts: against those who opposed any kind of church union and against those who demanded that a doctrinal agreement between Lutherans and Reformed, if not in fact a unitary confession, precede any implementation of a church union. To illustrate those positions, this study analyzes the published correspondence between Schleiermacher and two leading Lutheran theologians, the anti-unionist Christoph Friedrich von Ammon (1766–1850) and the pro-unionist Karl Gottlieb Bretschneider (1776–1848), who advocated doctrinal clarification in advance of union negotiations.

Against this background, the second section of this study examines Schleiermacher's development of the theory of election. It pays particular attention to the confessional and doctrinal texts he cited and referenced as his sources in his main publications on election, and to the treatment and positioning of the theory of predestination in those texts. Historical and biographical details regarding the symbolic books and their authors are provided to contextualize those sources.

This study then discusses Schleiermacher's two main texts on predestination: the essay "On the Doctrine of Election," first published in 1819, and the relevant propositions in the second edition of 1830 of his major dogmatics, *Christian Faith*. The essay, Schleiermacher's first publication on a dogmatic subject, was a direct response to a publication

---

2. For an exemplary comparison of Schleiermacher's and Barth's understanding, see most recently Matthias Gockel, *Barth and Schleiermacher on the Doctrine of Election*, 2006.

by Bretschneider. In it, Schleiermacher sets out to uphold the Calvinist doctrine against the Lutheran orthodox one, explicitly declaring himself a defender of Calvin in this matter. In about 30,000 words, he argued for the stringency of the Calvinist position while striving to counter the Lutherans' concerns regarding foreordained perdition. In a volte-face, he then reconceptualized predestination as universal restoration and proceeded to advocate that interpretation, hoping that this compromise would prove to be attractive to both Lutherans and Reformed. The analysis of Schleiermacher's essay is followed by a synopsis of different aspects of predestination held by Calvinists, Lutherans, and Schleiermacher in form of a table of comparison. An examination of the reception of Schleiermacher's essay both by his contemporaries and by some recent reviewers concludes that chapter.

Next, the propositions relating to election in Schleiermacher's main theological work, *Christian Faith*, and their position within the structure of that work as a whole are considered. Here, within a purely systematic-theological context and unconstrained by issues surrounding the Prussian Church Union, Schleiermacher still advocates the ultimate election of all to salvation, but he is reluctant to posit universal restoration as a proper doctrine. His discussion of election is embedded within the doctrine of pneumatology, which, in turn, constitutes part of the doctrine of ecclesiology.

The last chapter in Part II examines a number of Schleiermacher's sermons with a view to a comparison of his homiletic with his doctrinal output on election. The series of homilies he preached on Acts in 1820 provide the focus for discussion, because they were closest to his essay on election not only with regard to subject matter but also in terms of their time of production. A number of other relevant sermons, in particular but not exclusively on Acts, are also considered.

The last section of this study considers Schleiermacher's account of election in its systematic context. It first explores his treatment and positioning of those doctrines that are most closely related to predestination: providence, hamartiology, soteriology, and eschatology, and their relation to predestination. Schleiermacher's understanding of divine providence, in which human choices are imbedded in divine causality, his interpretation of the original state of perfection and his rejection of the fall, his emphasis on the role of Christ in election and redemption, and his exposition of the consummation of the church all bear direct relevance to his universalist theory of election. This discussion is followed by an account of the notion of universalism, its difficulties and advantages compared to particularist versions of predestination, and an attempt to position Schleiermacher in a typology of universalism.

The study closes with an evaluation of Schleiermacher's break with the traditional understanding of particular election. Against the Lutherans, he retained the Calvinist notion of an unconditional decree. In this context, a number of contemporary Lutheran publications are examined to clarify the Lutherans reservations and concerns regarding the Reformed doctrine of double predestination, whose unease is explained by their different understanding of human beings before God, or theological anthropology. Against the Reformed tradition, Schleiermacher dismisses the double decree as incompatible with Christian pious self-consciousness. His account of predestination posits a single, divine, all-encompassing decree to the creation and redemption of the entire human race.

Schleiermacher's family background was Reformed, he was ordained into the German Reformed Church and employed explicitly as a Reformed preacher and teacher. However, the German Reformed Church was never strictly Calvinist, and in some ways, for instance with regard to church government, it was closer to Lutheranism than to Calvinism. The German Reformed never endorsed the doctrine of double predestination. Their main symbolic book, the *Heidelberg Catechism* of 1563, makes no mention of the doctrine of predestination, and therefore plays no part in Schleiermacher's publications on the subject. One of the questions underpinning this study relates to Schleiermacher's outspoken endorsement of the Calvinist stance in a theological and political debate in which Calvinism was not even at stake, and the question for whom he actually spoke. A related issue is the success or otherwise of his attempt to convince his opponents of the validity of universal restoration.

This study makes use of a variety of texts in English, German and Latin; where translations into English were available I have employed them and referenced the translators accordingly. All other translations are my own; they are not particularly marked.

I use the term "Protestant" throughout to convey the German term *evangelisch*, which is coterminous with *protestantisch*. This choice is informed solely by the intention to avoid the ambiguity of the English term "evangelical," which has the additional connotation of "fundamentalist." A similar ambiguity does not exist in German, which distinguishes between the terms *evangelisch* and *evangelikal*.

PART ONE

Background and Context for Schleiermacher's Conception of Election

2

Theological Background

Protestant Confessions

THE CONFESSIONAL SITUATION OF early nineteenth-century Prussia, which provides the backdrop for the debates and publications to be discussed in this study, cannot be properly understood without some awareness of its historical theological development. This introductory chapter intends to give an account of the political events and theological debates that informed the formulation of the most important Protestant confessions, and it introduces the key players from the Reformation to the seventeenth century.

THE EARLY SIXTEENTH CENTURY

The first Protestant confession of faith to be officially regarded as a symbolic book is the Lutheran *Confessio Augustana* of 1530. However, this was by no means the earliest Protestant statement of confession. The first such documents were generated in the vicinity of the Zürich Reformation during the 1520s. By the end of the sixteenth century, more than forty confessions had been produced in Europe,[1] many of which achieved only regional importance. Among the earliest statements are the *Sixty-seven Theses* or *Conclusions of Zürich* (1523) penned by the leader of the Reformation in Switzerland, Huldrych Zwingli (1484–1531), a "humanistically trained exegete."[2] They were followed in 1526 by the *Eighteen Theses of*

---

1. See Plasger and Freudenberg, *Reformierte Bekenntnisschriften*, 9.
2. Muller, "John Calvin," 131.

Ilanz and in 1528 by the *Ten Theses of Bern*, edited by Zwingli, all of which tried to clarify the Reformed faith, but none of which received official recognition outside their regional sphere of influence.

In 1529, Martin Luther (1483–1546) published both his *Small* and *Large Catechism*; they represent the only summary of Protestant teaching by Luther in a single text. Motivated by his church visitations in Saxony Luther intended the two catechisms for instruction in the Protestant faith: the *Small Catechism* for the fledgling Protestant communities and their young people, the *Large Catechism* for ministers and preachers. Although they were not meant to be confessional statements, both catechisms would be included among the final collection of Lutheran symbolic books.

In 1530 the Holy Roman Emperor Karl V (r. 1519–1556) called an Imperial Diet to the south German city of Augsburg with the intention to end the religious controversies in his Empire by gathering everybody under the umbrella of Roman Catholicism. Much as his desire might have been theologically motivated, Karl V also needed a united Christian front for the impending war against the Turks. The Diet occasioned the production of several confessional statements. Elector[3] Johann Friedrich of Saxony (r. 1532–1554) asked the Wittenberg theologians to work out a statement of apology or defense of the Lutheran congregations for Electoral Saxony. In the absence of Martin Luther, who was still holed up in Castle Coburg and was therefore prevented from attending the Diet, Philipp Melanchthon (1497–1560) drafted a defense statement. He also produced a preface to this statement about ecclesiastical customs, which was to accompany the actual confession by way of an introduction. Both documents together constitute the *Confessio Augustana*. It set out to prove that doctrinally the Protestants agreed with the Catholic Church, and it played down their opposition against the papacy and transsubstantiation in favor of stressing their agreements. It was signed by the representatives of Electoral Saxony, Ansbach, Braunschweig-Lüneburg, Hesse, Anhalt, Reuchlingen, and Nuremberg.

---

3. In the Holy Roman Empire of the German Nation, there were traditionally seven Electors, also known as Duke Electors, Prince Electors, or Electors Palatine. Since 1257, these were the Archbishops of Mainz, Cologne and Trier, the Count Palatine of the Rhine, the Duke of Saxony, the Margrave of Brandenburg, and the King of Bohemia. In 1648, the Palatinate was added to this list, and in 1692 Hanover. The Electors formed the College of Electors, which had the sole right to elect the Roman-German King: this title traditionally symbolized the candidature for the Holy Roman Emperor. After the dissolution of the Holy Roman Empire by Napoleon in 1806, the title of Elector became obsolete.

The *Augsburg Confession,* as it also came to be known, was to be read out at the Diet and presented to the Emperor in written form. However, even before it was submitted, the Catholic delegation decided to commission a critique and refutation of it, trying to deflect from its criticism concerning the misuses of the Church in the last few articles by making the Lutherans out to be heretics. A committee of Catholic theologians drafted the *Confutatio,* and read it out at the Diet. The Emperor considered the *Augsburg Confession* to be thus refuted and demanded obedience to this judgment. The Protestants, however, did not consider themselves to be defeated. Although he was denied access to a written copy of the text of the *Confutatio,* Melanchthon drafted a theological evaluation, the *Apologia,* as a counter reply; the Emperor refused to accept it and the Protestant estates then left the Diet in protest.

Melanchthon proceeded to extend and improve his *Apologia,* an amended form of which was finally published in May 1531. Although it was originally a private document, the *Apologia* gained the status of a symbolic book in 1537 when it was signed by the Lutheran theologians of the Schmalkald League[4] and adopted alongside the *Augsburg Confession.* The latter, in turn, had attained the status of a symbolic book of the Protestant princes and estates when its preface was signed by Gregor Brück, the chancellor of Electoral Saxony. The *Augsburg Confession* in tandem with Melanchthon's *Apologia* became the most important Lutheran confession of faith. It served a dual function as a legal document and as a guide for spiritual teaching. Its first twenty-one articles stress the agreement with Scripture and the Catholic tradition, and only articles twenty-two to twenty-eight discuss controversial issues and call for the cessation of misuses. These misuses concern the two elements of communion, marriage of priests, mass, confession, food laws, monastic vows, and the power invested in the office of bishop. Much to Luther's dismay, the *Augsburg Confession* was silent on the issue of papal primacy.

Also in preparation for the Imperial Diet at Augsburg, the Strasburg reformer and former Dominican theologian Martin Bucer (1491–1551) had met with Luther and Melanchthon to discuss the possibility of a statement of faith that they could all subscribe to. When this proved to be impossible, chiefly because of their conflicting interpretations of communion, Bucer, with the assistance of Wolfgang Capito (1478–1541)

---

4. This was a defensive alliance of the Protestant princes and cities of the Holy Roman Empire. It was concluded at Schmalkald in 1531 in order to ward off potential Catholic attacks. The Schmalkald League would become "the most powerful Protestant political force in Europe" until the late 1540s. MacCulloch, *Reformation,* 174.

produced the *Confessio Tetrapolitana* (1530) for the four Upper German cities Strasburg, Memmingen, Konstanz, and Lindau for presentation to the Emperor. The *Tetrapolitana* was never officially recognized as a symbolic book. For the Swiss Protestants, their leader Huldrych Zwingli only managed to submit his private confession, the *Fidei Ratio ad Carolum Imperatorem* (1530), in order to clarify the Swiss Reformed position.

After the Diet, Bucer met repeatedly with Melanchthon with the intention to overcome the alienation between the south German cities and the Wittenberg Reformers. Their debates culminated in a statement agreed in Kassel in 1534. This was adopted in the *Wittenberg Concord* (1536), which contains compromise formulations that both sides agreed on, and acknowledges the *Augsburg Confession* and *Apologia* as well as a communion formula drafted by Melanchthon. As a result, doctrinal unity was achieved in Protestant Germany. At the same time, however, this unity meant that from then on Germany and Switzerland would go their separate ways in the further progress of the Reformation.

Also in 1536, Basel saw the production of the first common confession held among the German-speaking Reformed Swiss cities, the *Confessio Helvetica Prior*. Intended to help form a union with the Lutherans, the twenty-seven articles of this confession were penned by Zwingli's successor in Zürich, Heinrich Bullinger (1504–1575), as well as Oswald Myconius (1488–1552) and others under the unionist influence of Bucer and Capito. During the year 1536, the *Theses of Lausanne* and the *First Geneva Confession* were drafted in French-speaking Switzerland. It is worth noting that 1536 also marked the publication of the first edition of *Institutio Christianae Religionis* by John Calvin (1509–1564).

In 1537, Luther published the *Schmalkald Articles*, which were originally intended for presentation at the 1537 Council of Mantua. They sharply emphasize the Lutherans' confessional opposition to Rome—the same opposition which the *Augsburg Confession* had tried to cover up. The *Schmalkald Articles* were signed only by theologians attending the Schmalkald Convention of 1537, but they were eventually recognized as a symbolic book in 1580.

During the late 1530s, Melanchthon was working on a revision of the *Confessio Augustana*. He had been commissioned by the Schmalkald League to draft an official new edition of the *Augsburg Confession* for the impending doctrinal discussions. In 1540 he re-published it as the so-called *Variata*. From then on, the original version of 1530 was also known as the *Invariata*. Leaving the preface of the *Augsburg Confession* untouched, in the *Variata* Melanchthon took account of the recently developed understanding of the doctrine of communion, which brought it into line with the *Wittenberg Concord*, and he greatly extended the text of the original 1530 version. The contrast to the Roman Catholic Church and the Anabaptists also became much sharper. With regard to the church history, the original version, the *Invariata*, remained the standard confession of faith in the Lutheran Churches.

The *Variata* was eyed with great suspicion as a crypto-Calvinist document. As a corollary, it gained its importance from the fact that most Calvinist theologians (though not the Zwinglians) could actually subscribe to it. In fact, even Calvin himself signed the *Variata*. It was also the official document presented at the Colloquy at Worms in 1540 by the Schmalkald League.[5] With the *Variata*, Melanchthon had quietly distanced himself from Luther's view. He had moved relatively close to the Calvinist understanding of the presence of Christ during communion, in that he shared with it a strong sense of the mystery of Christ's presence. As a result, he was open to an agreement with Calvinist views. The *Variata* was to become particularly important after the Religious Peace of Augsburg of 1555.

This Religious Peace was preceded by another two important statements of confession: one was the *Consensus Tigurinus*, or *Zürich Confession*. It developed out of negotiations between Calvin and Bullinger to unite the Swiss Protestants, and set off a "burst of confessional activity among the Reformed."[6] Drafted by Bullinger in 1549 and published in 1551, it expressed an agreement regarding the doctrine of communion between Calvinist Geneva and Zwinglian Zürich and Bern. It favored the Zwinglian symbolic explanation of the presence of Christ at communion, but allowed a range of definitions of the sacrament. It was quickly accepted by both the French-speaking and the German-speaking Swiss Reformed churches. Safeguarding the Swiss Reformation inevitably meant a sharp break between Calvinism and German Protestantism, marked especially by Calvin's rapprochement with the Zwinglians in the *Consensus Tigurinus* (1549).[7]

The other confession published before the Peace of Augsburg (1555) was the *Confessio Doctrinae Saxonicarum Ecclesiarum Synodo Tridentinae*

5. See Kusukawa, "Melanchthon," 65.

6. Muller, "John Calvin," 135.

7. Calvin was originally very close to the German Lutherans, but the dispute between Melanchthon and Luther's direct followers, the Gnesio-Lutherans, as well as Calvin's increasing agreement with the Zwinglians led to a renewed dispute about communion, and eventually to bitter enmity. See Heussi, *Kompendium*, 315.

Oblata, or *Saxon Confession*, of 1551. It was drawn up by Melanchthon for the Roman Catholic Council of Trent (1545–1563) as a repetition and exposition of the *Confessio Augustana*. In effect, it represented an adaptation of the *Augsburg Confession* accounting for the changed state of affairs: unlike twenty years earlier, there was no hope of a reunion with the Catholic Church any more. At Melanchthon's suggestion, the *Saxon Confession* was signed by theologians rather than secular princes. The original manuscript, entitled 'Repetitio Confessionis Augustanae' is dated 1551. It was first published in Basel in 1552.

THE LATER SIXTEENTH CENTURY

In 1555, Emperor Karl V called a new Imperial Diet to Augsburg in order to settle the differences between Catholics and Protestants politically. The so-called Religious Peace of Augsburg, which was negotiated at that Diet, meant that all Protestants who signed the *Confessio Augustana* would be placed under imperial protection so as to enjoy freedom from religious persecution. Sacramentarians, especially Zwingli's followers, and more extreme Protestant groups such as the Anabaptists and Anti-trinitarians could not bring themselves to subscribe to the Lutheran *Augsburg Confession*. Calvinists adhered at least to Melanchthon's 1540 *Variata* version and claimed inclusion in the Peace, but their status remained precarious for nearly a century until the end of the Thirty Years' War in 1648 and the attendant Treaty of Westphalia.

The Peace of Augsburg also introduced the *ius reformandi*, the right of each sovereign to determine the confession (Catholic or Lutheran) of his territory, thereby abolishing the old law of heretics. The principle of *cuius regio, eius religio* stipulated that the territorial sovereign determined the denomination of his subjects, and it allowed subjects who belonged to a different confession from that of their sovereign to emigrate without any damage to their honor or to their possessions.[8] The reasons behind

---

8. Developments in Electoral Palatinate can serve to illustrate the power of this principle. Elector Friedrich III (r. 1559–1576) turned the Palatinate into a Calvinist territory in 1560. His eldest son and successor Ludwig IV (r. 1576–1583) reinstated Lutheranism and withdrew favor from Reformed clerics and academics, thus forcing them to emigrate or to take refuge in the small Reformed enclave of Neustadt. Neustadt was ruled by Ludwig's younger brother, Count Johann Casimir, who, in turn, was an enthusiastic Calvinist. After Ludwig's death, Johann Casimir ruled for his underage nephew, Ludwig's son Friedrich. When the latter became Elector Friedrich IV (r. 1583–1610), he enabled Johann Casimir as principle regent to extend the Reformed faith throughout the entire Electoral Palatinate. The returning ministers marked their

this principle were not of a purely political nature, however. The drive of nearly all European sovereigns to permit only one denomination in their territory was partly informed by the conviction that no territory could have a permanent basis if truth and untruth, true worship and idolatry were allowed to exist side by side. The mutual assurance of Catholics and Lutherans that they would not wage war against an imperial estate because of its confession lasted for more than six decades until the onset of the Thirty-Years War in 1618. It is important to note, nevertheless, that the Religious Peace of 1555 guaranteed the religious unity of individual territories, but it dissolved the religious unity of the Empire. The confessional era had begun in earnest.

The French and Dutch Reformed statements of confession were mainly a result of Roman Catholic oppression. The *Confessio Gallicana* or *Huguenot Confession* of 1559 was occasioned by persecutions, heretics' courts, and executions of Protestants under King Henri II of France (r. 1547–1559). In May 1559 a national synod of French Reformed Churches met secretly in Paris in order both to strengthen their confessional identity and to reach a consensus on some doctrinal differences, one of which concerned the doctrine of election. The moderator of the synod was François Morel, a pupil of Calvin. Calvin learned about the Synod very late. Fearing that its theological resolutions would not go far enough, he sent three delegates of the Geneva Church Council to Paris, who conveyed thirty-five articles of faith to the Synod. This draft confession had been prepared by Calvin and his pupil Antoine de la Roche Chandieu (1534–1591), and the Paris Synod approved it with only minor revisions. It was finally declared the binding confession of French Protestantism at the National Synod of La Rochelle in 1571. The *Confessio Gallicana* was disseminated throughout Germany by the Huguenot congregations living in Prussia.

Three more Protestant confessions followed in short succession: the *Scots Confession* in 1560, the *Confessio Belgica* in 1561, and the Anglican *Thirty-nine Articles* in 1563. The first two stood in the Geneva tradition and, together with the *Huguenot Confession*, formed "a trilogy of Calvinian theology."[9] The *Scots Confession* was commissioned by the Scottish Parliament as a summary of the articles of faith that the Protestant faction adhered to. It was drafted by six theologians including John Knox

---

celebrations with an iconoclastic campaign, much to the annoyance of the general populace.

9. Plasger and Freudenberg, *Reformierte Bekenntnisschriften*, 124.

(1510–1572) within four days, and passed by Parliament along with three other Acts to constitute Scotland as a Protestant nation.

The *Confessio Belgica* was composed by Guy de Bres (1522–1567) for the Reformed Churches in Flanders and the Netherlands on the basis of the *Huguenot Confession*. Its ratification by the Synod of Antwerp in 1566 marked the final acceptance of Calvinism in the Low Countries, and it made the *Confessio Belgica* the confessional standard for the Reformed Church in the Netherlands.

The *Thirty-nine Articles* of the Anglican Church in England do not represent a statement of confession as such, but a summary of doctrinal formulations. First issued in 1563 and accepted by the Church of England, the *Thirty-nine Articles* were a revision of the original *Forty-two Articles* of 1552. They moved away from the Calvinist tendency expressed in the *Forty-two Articles* and were passed by the Westminster Parliament in 1571.

The statement of faith that was to become the most important symbolic book for the German Reformed Church for centuries to come was the *Heidelberg Catechism* of 1563. Moderately Calvinistic, it was intended to serve as a kind of unionist confession in Electoral Palatinate, then the largest territory in the Holy Roman Empire. It strove to satisfy both Melanchthon's sympathizers, the Philippists, and the Reformed theology of western Europe.[10] In 1556, under Elector Ottheinrich (r. 1556–1559), the Palatinate had become Lutheran. Melanchthon, himself a native of Electoral Palatinate, had acted as chief counselor, impressing a moderate Lutheranism friendly to Calvinism upon the territory. The Lutheran *Augsburg Confession* was adopted as the doctrinal basis, whereas worship was remodeled after Reformed principles. Elector Ottheinrich also granted Calvinist refugees asylum in the Palatinate. Heidelberg, its capital city and university town, began to attract Protestant scholars of all denominations. As a result, it became a battleground where Lutheran, Philippist, Calvinist, and Zwinglian views collided. To settle some of the differences, Ottheinrich's successor Elector Friedrich III (r. 1559–1576), called The Pious, arranged a public disputation for June 1560 on the doctrine of communion. When the different Protestant groups subsequently demanded of him to unequivocally embrace one confession, he decided in favor of Calvinism, thus turning the Palatinate into the first German Reformed territory in 1561.[11] Elector Friedrich III commissioned the divinity professor and

---

10. See MacCulloch, *Reformation*, 254.

11. Calvinism was subsequently introduced in Bremen (1580), Nassau (1586), Anhalt (1596), Hesse-Kassel (1605) and Brandenburg (1614).

Melanchthon pupil Zacharias Ursinus (1534–1583), according to Mac-Culloch "the most prominent theologian of the Palatinate,"[12] probably along with the more Calvinist Kaspar Olevian (1536–1587) and other theologians, to draft a statement of the doctrines befitting this new orientation. As far as possible, this statement would bring together the divergent Reformed trends. The resultant *Heidelberg Catechism* deliberately included points that would unite Zwinglians, Calvinists, and Philippists. The doctrine of the sacraments hovered between Zwinglianism and Calvinism, and any discussion of predestination was deliberately omitted. After its adoption, the *Heidelberg Catechism* was read out in church over the course of each year, with one passage being treated each Sunday. It also served as an elementary text for the religious instruction of the youth, as the doctrinal norm next to Scripture for ministers, and as edification for families.[13] The Elector also ordered the *Heidelberg Catechism* to be incorporated in the Palatine Church Order. Soon after its publication, this "most catholic and popular of all the Reformed symbols"[14] spread throughout Germany and to the Netherlands, even superseding Calvin's *Catechismus Genevensis* of 1545. Not surprisingly, it was violently attacked by Lutherans for its alleged Zwinglian and Calvinist heresies, and the Palatinate was threatened with exclusion from the protection of the Peace of Augsburg. At the Synod of Dort in the Low Countries, which took place from 1618 to 1619, the *Heidelberg Catechism* attained the status of a Reformed symbolic book. Soon after its publication, it was introduced in Brandenburg, and it was still used for the instruction of the Hohenzollern princes, the Royal House of Prussia, in the late nineteenth century.[15]

The *Confessio Helvetica Posterior* or *Second Helvetic Confession* (1566) was the most important confession of the German Swiss Reformation. It was originally drafted in 1561 by Heinrich Bullinger, Huldrych Zwingli's successor in Zürich, as his private confession. He had intended it to be presented on his death to the Town Council of Zürich, but in 1566 it was printed and put into the public domain. The reasons for this were mainly political in nature. The introduction of the Reformed faith and of the *Heidelberg Catechism* in the Palatinate had attracted strong criticism from some Lutheran princes, because some parts of the *Catechism*, in particular its doctrine of communion, contradicted the *Augsburg Confession*. Strictly

12. MacCulloch, *Reformation*, 355.
13. See Plasger and Freudenberg, *Reformierte Bekenntnisschriften*, 153.
14. Schaff, *Creeds* I, 540.
15. See ibid., 548.

speaking, therefore, the Palatinate was in violation of imperial law. So, in 1566 the Holy Roman Emperor Maximilian II (r. 1564–1576) called an Imperial Diet, again to Augsburg. The Diet threatened Elector Friedrich III with exclusion from the protection of the Peace of Augsburg. In his defense statement, the Elector emphasized the agreement of the Palatinate Church with the Protestant Churches abroad. He had been aware of Heinrich Bullinger's private confession of 1561, which Bullinger had previously circulated within the Swiss Reformed cities. Friedrich III had it translated into German in order to present it at the Diet. Bullinger's confession then found broad acceptance in the Palatinate. It is not clear whether it was actually read out at the Diet, but the Elector's arguments and obvious piety ensured the Palatinate's further protection by the Peace of Augsburg, and secured further the unity among the German Protestant princes.

Bullinger's confession of faith did not attain the status of a symbolic book in the Palatinate, but it was signed by the Protestant cities in Switzerland. All Reformed German-speaking Swiss cities apart from, initially, Lutheran Basel, accepted Bullinger's confession, now entitled *Confessio Helvetica Posterior*. It was also given official recognition by the Reformed Churches of France, Scotland, Poland, Hungary, and the Netherlands, and it signified the final separation of the Reformed from the Lutheran Church. By the late 1560s, the Reformed tradition had, as Muller notes, "a well-defined doctrinal codification"[16] in the shape of national and regional confessional statements.

In 1577, the Lutheran church produced the *Formula of Concord* as its final statement of confession. This step was deemed necessary in the face of the competing positions that different Lutheran territorial churches had taken. After Luther's death in 1546, two distinct groups of his followers had begun to emerge: the Philippists, who followed Philipp Melanchthon and identified with his desire to unite Lutherans and Calvinists, and the Gnesio-Lutherans, or "Lutheran ultras,"[17] who remained faithful to Martin Luther's teaching.[18] Melanchthon himself had gradually diverged from Luther with regard to the doctrines of election, original sin, good works, christology, and communion, and he had gone public with his new convictions in the 1540 *Variata*. Certainly with respect to communion, the Philippists now approached the Calvinist understanding of the presence of

16. Muller, "John Calvin," 134.

17. MacCulloch, *Reformation*, 349.

18. The Gnesio-Lutherans upheld Luther's understanding of passive righteousness, God's grace, and human sinfulness. See Kolb, "Confessional Lutheran Theology," 71.

Christ at communion, and the Gnesio-Lutherans were not entirely wrong in regarding them as Crypto-Calvinists. It is also noteworthy that the German Reformed approached the Philippist understanding of a synergism of God's act and human cooperation, and that they never did accept the strict Calvinist interpretation of predestination as a double decree.

The sharp distinction between the two Lutheran factions was particularly visible in Saxony. Electoral Saxony, under Elector Albrecht and with the University of Wittenberg as its theological center was Philippist, whereas the Saxon Duchy, under Duke Ernst and with the University of Jena slowly advancing as its theological center was Gnesio-Lutheran.[19] In 1559, the Gnesio-Lutherans under their leader Matthias Flacius Illyricus (1520–1575), still a personal disciple of Luther, drafted the *Weimar Book of Confutation*. The Philippists responded to that a year later with the publication of the *Corpus Doctrinae Christianae*, which contained the three Early Church confessions and some of Melanchthon's writings. Initially a private collection of confessional statements, this work quickly gained respect. In 1567 it was officially accepted in Electoral Saxony.

LUTHERAN CONSOLIDATION

The *Augsburg Confession*, according to Hillerbrand the "most ecumenical of Lutheran confessional statements,"[20] had been designed to demonstrate the Reformers' agreement in many points with the Catholic tradition. Clearly, though, it was not suited to settle the disputes between Philippists and Gnesio-Lutherans. These disputes set the agenda for the *Formula of Concord*,[21] which strictly delimited the genuine Lutheran understanding from the Reformed one. According to its full title, the *Formula of Concord* represented "the general, true, correct and ultimate reiteration and explanation of several articles of the *Confessio Augustana*" that had been debated since its initial publication. It excluded more extreme statements of both parties, among them the *Variata* of the *Augsburg Confession* as an

19. See Heussi, *Kompendium*, 346.

20. Hillerbrand, "Legacy," 237.

21. The evolution of the text of the *Formula of Concord* is rather complex. It was based on the *Swabian Concord* of 1574, which was revised by Martin Chemnitz (1522–1586) and others to become the *Swabian-Saxon Concord* (1575). After more editorial work, the *Formula of Maulbronn* was drafted, and the following year a theological colloquy at Torgau produced the *Torgau Book* based on the *Swabian-Saxon Concord* and the *Formula of Maulbronn*. Eventually, the *Torgau Book* itself was revised and turned into the *Formula of Concord*. See Hägglund, *Geschichte der Theologie*, 215–16.

independent interpretation. Most notably, it played down the doctrine of predestination while affirming the real presence of Christ in communion. However, the dissociation both from Calvinism and from the Philippists is even sharper in the *Formula of Concord* than that from the Gnesio-Lutherans. As the result of numerous endeavors to produce a unitary confession for the territorial churches that had emerged as a result of the Lutheran Reformation, the *Formula of Concord*, compiled in 1577, did put a provisional end to intra-Lutheran disputes and set the standard for the teaching of orthodox Lutheranism. It was accepted by 213 of the Imperial estates, which also adhered to the original or *Invariata* version of the *Confessio Augustana* of 1530.

Three years later, in 1580, the *Book of Concord* was collated. It concluded the process of confessional development in Lutheranism and marked the end of Lutheran pluralism by bringing together all those statements of confession which the Lutheran Church had acknowledged as symbolic books: The *Nicene, Apostles'* and *Athanasian Creeds*, Luther's *Small* and *Large Catechisms*, the *Confessio Augustana* (*Invariata*) with its *Apologia*, the *Schmalkald Articles*, Melanchthon's 1537 tract *De Potestate et Primatu Papae* concerning the power and sovereignty of the Pope, and the *Formula of Concord* itself. It was signed by eighty-six imperial estates and by 8,000 to 9,000 theologians[22] and accepted by the majority of Lutheran territories in Germany. Lutheran ministers pledged allegiance to it in their ordination vows. A small number of territories (Holstein, Pomerania, the Archbishopric of Bremen, Braunschweig, Nuremberg, Anhalt, and Hesse) refused to accept the *Book of Concord* but retained their Lutheran identity nonetheless.

There were also a small number of territorial churches in which Philippism had dominated, that now turned toward Calvinism. Although the *Book of Concord* stabilized German Lutheranism internally, German Protestantism as a whole was weakened, for the *Book of Concord* guaranteed that the prospect of a union between Lutherans and Reformed would be out of the question. Regarded as the only valid interpretation, the *Book of Concord* offered a particularly anti-Calvinist interpretation and repudiated Melanchthon's 1540 *Variata*. Thus, whereas the thrust of pro-Reformed Philippist confessions (including the *Variata*, the *Wittenberg Concord* and the *Saxon Confession*) were developed out of disputes with the Gnesio-Lutherans, the *Book of Concord* emerged in the context of the struggle against Calvinism. It has remained the valid collection

22. See Heussi, *Kompendium*, 349.

of Lutheran symbolic books to this day and has never been amended or superseded.

On the Reformed side, a definitive collection of officially recognized statements of confession was never achieved. The *Harmony of Confessions of Faith of the Orthodox and Reformed Churches*, published in Geneva in 1581, served a specifically unionist purpose. Its intention was to demonstrate the agreement between the Reformed Churches and genuine Lutheranism, and to this end it included, among others, two of Melanchthon's confessions, the *Variata* and the *Saxon Confession*. It was extended in 1612 and again in 1654. Yet, despite its unionist intention, it entirely ignored the Zwinglian confessions as well as the German Reformed confessional tradition.

THE SEVENTEENTH CENTURY

In 1607, Reformed theologians in Heidelberg, which Christopher Clark has aptly called "the powerhouse of early seventeenth-century German Calvinism,"[23] drew up a confession summarizing what the German Reformed Churches believed. Although it achieved an almost normative authority in Reformed Germany, it did not gain official recognition. Nevertheless, it did become crucial for the history of confessions in Brandenburg and Prussia, and therefore ultimately for Schleiermacher.

In May 1614, on the advice of the Heidelberg professor Abraham Scultetus (1566–1625), Elector Johann Sigismund of Brandenburg (r. 1608–1619) published the *Confession of the Reformed Churches of Germany*. It contained a preface by Scultetus and a reprint of the 1562 *Confession of Heidelberg Divines*. The preface explained that a new edition of the confession of those whose teachings had become suspicious to the common people under the hateful term Calvinist had become necessary. It was intended to counter the general slandering of the Brandenburg Church reform for the purpose that Elector Johann Sigismund's subjects would understand his conversion to the Reformed faith and indeed grasp hold of the Reformed faith themselves. In order both to pacify his opponents and to explain that some of their perceptions of Calvinism were misleading, the Elector subsequently issued a private statement of faith, the *Sigismund Confession* (1614). Along with the *Heidelberg Catechism*, the *Sigismund Confession* has remained the decisive confession of faith within the German Reformed Church. Rather than endeavoring a re-statement of the

23. Clark, *Iron Kingdom*, 115.

whole Reformed faith, it dealt in detail with four articles of doctrine that formed the bones of contention for Lutherans: the person of Christ, baptism, communion, and predestination.[24]

Commissioned by the Elector as a commentary on the general *Reformed (Brandenburg) Confession*, the *Sigismund Confession* was drafted by Martin Füssel (1571–1626), the former Reformed superintendent of Zerbst in Anhalt and one of the Elector's court preachers. This *Sigismund Confession* declared the Elector's adherence to Scripture as the true master over all texts, and to the Ecumenical Creeds. It further acknowledged the *Variata* version of the *Augsburg Confession*, but it repudiated the *Formula of Concord*. Calvin and Zwingli were not named in the confession. The *Confession of Sigismund* was not understood as a statement of faith through which the sovereign exercised his *ius reformandi*, but as a private document in which the Elector attested to his conversion.

From 1618 to 1619, the assembly of the Dutch Reformed Church at Dort (Dordrecht) in the Low Countries took place. Convened by the States-General, it was the first and only super-national synod of older Calvinism. It was intended to bring the conflict between Calvinists and Arminians to an end. Besides the Low Countries, England, Scotland, and Switzerland; most German Reformed territories were also represented at Dort. The Huguenots did not send any representatives, and, referring to his private confession, Elector Sigismund, too, declined to take part in the Synod: he had taken a clear stance against the Calvinist doctrine of election. The Synod condemned the heresy of Jacob Arminius (1560–1609) and his followers, the so-called Remonstrants.[25] They held that human beings had the choice to come to faith, and that this human choice preceded God's election. God therefore elected those to salvation of whom he foreknew that in time they would accept the gift of grace. At Dort, the doctrine of predestination as an absolute double decree was elevated to a binding Calvinist dogma. A tangible result of the deliberations there was the publication of the *Canons of Dort* (1619). They restated the Reformed faith based on Calvin's *Institutio*, but they actually went beyond it in their logical pursuit of ultimate consequences of a number of doctrines, in particular that of predestination. The Synod also confirmed the *Confessio Belgica* (1561) and the *Heidelberg Catechism* (1563) as valid confessional statements of the Reformed Church of the Low Countries. Interestingly

---

24. See below p. 79.

25. So called because they represented an admonition or remonstrance to the Dutch Reformed Church.

enough, the *Confessio Belgica* strongly supported the doctrine of double predestination, while the *Heidelberg Catechism* was silent on the matter.

ATTEMPTS AT UNIFICATION

During the Thirty-Years' War (1618–1648), efforts were made to reunite the Christian faiths and to put an end to religiously motivated bloodshed. In 1631 Elector Johann Georg of Saxony (r. 1611–1656) invited around 160 Estates and several imperial cities to a Convention at Leipzig. As part of that Convention, Johann Bergius (1587–1658), chaplain of Elector Christian Wilhelm of Brandenburg, was able to arrange a theological colloquy. Its Reformed representatives included himself, Elector Christian Wilhelm, Landgrave Wilhelm of Hesse, and two Calvinist theologians. The Lutheran faction consisted of three divines and the Elector Johann Georg of Saxony.

Both parties to this Colloquy were propelled by their common fear of pressure from Rome. The Reformed party agreed to continue teaching the *Augsburg Confession* in their schools and churches but urged the retention of the *Variata* as well. The *Confessio Augustana* with Melanchthon's *Apologia* formed the basis of the Colloquy's deliberations. Both parties reached an agreement on twenty-six out of its twenty-eight articles, but they did not see eye to eye with regard to the doctrines of Christ and of communion. Although predestination had not featured in the *Augsburg Confession*, it formed part of the discussions at the Colloquy. Here it emerged that some of the Reformed party, in particular Johann Bergius, had more or less arrived at the Philippist understanding of the doctrine. In the event, however, the more strictly Calvinist view of Johannes Crocius (1590–1659) came to prevail and found its way into the final theological document, the *Relation*. The *Relation* was signed by the six divines but not by the Electors. The parties continued to disagree regarding the omnipotence of Christ's human nature and therefore communion, and on election. The Lutheran doctrine of *fides praevisa*, or foreknown faith, remained the stumbling block for the Reformed faction. While the Reformed party was willing to make common cause with the Lutherans against the Catholics, the Lutherans would go no farther than taking into serious consideration the Reformed party's proposal to treat them as brethren.

What turned out to be the most memorable statement to be passed at the Colloquy at Leipzig was the classical union phrase "in necessary matters unity, in doubtful matters liberty, in all matters charity."[26] In the *Leipzig Manifesto*, the political document that emerged from the Convention, the Protestant estates pledged to form a defensive alliance against Catholic aggression. The theological colloquy had provided the ideological basis for this agreement.

Another union conference, itself ultimately fruitless, was held after more than a quarter of a century of religious warfare, in Thorn in 1645. Thorn an der Weichsel, a town in modern-day Poland, had embraced Lutheranism in 1557. The Colloquy had been instigated by the Catholic King Wladislaus IV of Poland (r. 1632–1648) in order to bring the Polish Protestants back into the fold of the Catholic Church. It brought together twenty-six Catholic, twenty-eight Lutheran, and twenty-four Reformed representatives. Since the Protestant aristocracy had pushed through a *pax dissidentium*, or general religious peace, in 1573, Lutherans, Reformed, and Moravian Brethrens had officially enjoyed political and constitutional equality in Poland. However, the Catholic monarchy had largely ignored this peace and was now trying to return the country as a whole to Catholicism. Dissent among the Lutheran party and also between Lutherans and Reformed at this Colloquy only served to strengthened the Catholic faction.[27] Each party met in a separate room of the town hall and only negotiated with the others through deputies or by exchanging written documents. Only four out of twenty-six meetings were public. Each party kept minutes of their meetings, but they would only be printed some eighteen months after the publication of the official *Acta Conventus Thoruniensis* (1648). The first item of business was the preparation of a statement of faith by each faction. The resultant Catholic confession, which repeated the teachings of the Council of Trent, was read out in the first public meeting and was received among the official acts. The Reformed confession, the *Declaratio Thoruniensis*, managed to be heard but was omitted from the official acts, because the presiding chairman declared it to be a defamatory invective against the Catholic Church. The Lutheran confession was ready four days later. It essentially repeated the *Augsburg Confession* of 1530, a fact that incensed the Catholic party to such an extent that they they did not even allow the document to be read out in the public meeting.

The Colloquy of Thorn closed without accomplishing any kind of union and it succeeded only in emphasizing the existing differences. Still, as Philip Schaff points out, the Reformed statement of confession

---

26. Schaff, *Creeds* I, 558.

27. For the following see Tschackert, "Thorn," 747–48.

formulated at Thorn, the *Declaratio Thoruniensis*, remains "one of the most careful statements of the Reformed creed."[28] It accepts the 1540 *Variata*, the *Consensus of Sendomir* (1570), and the three Ecumenical Creeds.

Both the Lutheran and the Reformed confessions produced at Thorn were excluded from the official edition of the *Acta Conventus Thorniensus Celebrati a 1645*, even though it was signed by nobles and clergymen from Poland, Lithuania, and Brandenburg. Nevertheless, the *Declaration of Thorn* was adopted among the *Brandenburg Confessions*, also known as *Confessiones Marchicae*, which also comprise the *Confession of Sigismund* (1614) and the *Relation* of the Colloquy at Leipzig (1631). These confessions were only moderately Calvinistic, and the Canons of Dort "were respectfully received but never adopted by the Brandenburg divines."[29] The *Brandenburg Confessions* enjoyed a certain symbolic authority in Prussia until the Prussian Church Union of 1817.

The *Helvetic Consensus Formula* of 1675 was the last major Reformed statement of faith formulated in the seventeenth century. Drawn up by Johann Heinrich Heidegger of Zürich (1633–1699) to defend Calvinism against the doctrine of universalism propagated by the Saumurian School, it was characterized by its strict version of the doctrines of predestination and of verbal inspiration. It was added, as an appendix and exposition, to the *Second Helvetic Confession* of 1566 and introduced in the Reformed Church across Switzerland. However, it was generally recognized only until 1722, and in Basel only until 1686.

CONCLUSION

The Reformed faith in Germany approached Philippism and was therefore different from the Western European Calvinism of the Low Countries, Switzerland, France, and Scotland. Although the writings of Calvin and Bullinger rather than those of Melanchthon became the doctrinal norm, in terms of a church constitution Lutheranism made itself felt, for the German Reformed Church lacked a synodal constitution. This Lutheran influence first became obvious when Elector Friedrich III of the Palatinate, rather than a synod, ordered the *Heidelberg Catechism* to be incorporated with the Palatine Church Order. In matters of doctrine, the German Reformed doctrines differed from those of their Lutheran counterparts mainly with regard to communion but explicitly not with regard

28. Schaff, *Creeds* I, 562.
29. Ibid., 555.

to predestination. Also, Reformed and Lutheran attitudes to doctrinal statements generally diverged markedly. While the Reformed insisted that Martin Luther's words must not be canonized into a rigid dogmatic system —something Luther had never produced himself—Lutherans did exactly that. As a corollary, there has never been such a clearly defined collection of Reformed confessional statements as is presented in the Lutheran *Book of Concord*. Indeed, there has been no ultimate agreement about the very criteria that should be applied to qualify a text as a symbolic book.[30] The large number of Reformed confessions in tandem with the lack of universal validity of any of them reflect their geographical and chronological limitations. Although both the *Heidelberg Confession* and the *Second Helvetic Confession* gained validity across national borders, some other confessions such as the *Canons of Dort* were in time superseded or replaced. In the Reformed Churches there has never even been a consensus on the question whether or not one uniform confession is desirable. Moreover, as a matter of principle, the Reformed hold that their statements of confession can be revised. This is borne out by the underlying contention that better insights into Scripture can make new confessions necessary. In the course of the Enlightenment, confessional statements often collapsed under new criticism. Lutheran Churches reacted to this development by reiterating the ultimate validity of the *Book of Concord*, whereas the Reformed Churches adjusted themselves, as Jan Rohls observed, "by either totally abandoning their confessions, reworking them, or formulating new ones."[31]

The Reformed understanding that a faith community is not established through one common doctrine clearly underpins and indeed reflects Schleiermacher's attitude and argumentation in the debates about his essay on election. His Lutheran counterparts, like their sixteenth-century predecessors, did not share the Reformed openness for new confessions. The 1580 *Book of Concord* is still the binding doctrinal norm for the Lutheran Churches 430 years after its creation.

---

30. See Plasger and Freudenberg, *Reformierte Bekenntnisschriften*, 8.

31. Rohls, *Reformed Confessions*, tr. Hoffmeyer, 5.

3

Historical Developments in Prussia up to the Early Nineteenth Century

FRIEDRICH SCHLEIERMACHER'S ECCLESIASTICAL AND theological leadership was of signal importance to early nineteenth-century efforts to achieve a union between the predominant Lutheran and the minority Reformed Churches in Prussia. The following chapter deals first with the historical ecclesiastical reforms that took place in Prussia in the 300 years preceding the Prussian Church Union of 1817. It then examines the developments in church and state that culminated in that Union.

THE FIRST AND SECOND REFORMATION IN PRUSSIA

The Kingdom of Prussia, in which Schleiermacher lived and worked, was the result of a number of historical events and developments. At the turn of the sixteenth century, its original constituent parts, Brandenburg and the Duchy of Prussia, were two politically and geographically separate territories. The Duchy of Prussia, a Baltic principality, was controlled by the Teutonic Order as a Polish fief over which the King of Poland acted as feudal overlord. At that time, its territory comprised roughly that of modern East Prussia. Albrecht von Hohenzollern (1490–1568), the Grandmaster of the Teutonic Order, achieved the investiture of his dynasty, the Brandenburg Hohenzollern, with the fief of the Duchy of Prussia: when Prussia was secularized and turned into a Protestant Duchy in 1525, Albrecht became its sovereign, the Duke of Prussia. The inhabitants of Prussia had embraced the Reformation from the early 1520s, and it became one of the first territories to receive a Protestant church order. Geographically, Lutheran ducal Prussia, roughly the same size as Brandenburg, lay outside the Holy Roman Empire and was surrounded by Poland-Lithuania.

Brandenburg played a vital part in the Holy Roman Empire: it was one of its seven Electorates. It had been ruled by Hohenzollern princes since 1417, when Friedrich Hohenzollern purchased it from its then sovereign, Emperor Sigismund. In 1614 Brandenburg acquired the Reformed Rhine provinces Kleve, Mark, and Ravensberg some 700 miles west of Brandenburg. In 1657 Elector Friedrich Wilhelm of Brandenburg (r. 1640–1688), the so-called Great Elector, also obtained recognition of his sovereignty over the Duchy of Prussia from Poland. Henceforth, he ruled the Hohenzollern state, which became known as Brandenburg-Prussia, as both Margrave of Brandenburg and Duke of Prussia in personal union. He laid the foundation of the Prussian state, and his son Elector Friedrich III crowned himself King in Prussia in Königsberg in 1701. At the time of Schleiermacher's birth in 1768, Prussia was ruled by King Friedrich II (r. 740–1786), who also held the title of Elector of Brandenburg.

Brandenburg had first embraced the Lutheran Reformation in 1539. To start with, Elector Joachim I (r. 1499–1535) had sought to suppress any Lutheran stirrings both in his territory and within his family, and he had tried to place his sons under the obligation to preserve Brandenburg for the Catholic Church.[1] In 1539, after some initial hesitation, his son, Elector Joachim II (r. 1535–1571) publicly adhered to the *Confessio Augustana*. Nevertheless, Joachim II was keen to maintain an intermediate position in church politics. He thus left the Catholic liturgy and its rites mainly untouched, and he even kept the episcopal constitution intact until 1543. His moderate attitude was grounded in his concern for his family, and, perhaps even more so, for his territorial interests. The need for a new ecclesiastical constitution in Brandenburg became very obvious. As a consequence, the Elector became the head of state as well as the *summus episcopus* or supreme bishop, with a superintendent as the highest church official under the prince.

Under Joachim II's successor Elector Johann Georg (r. 1571–1598), Lutheranism attained undisputed sovereign authority. Doctrinally it was very strict, but the Catholic liturgical elements that Joachim II had left in place still remained. Any influx of Calvinist elements into Brandenburg was prevented by law. Elector Johann Georg signed the *Book of Concord*

---

1. See Kawerau, "Sigismund," 331.

and enforced its adherence among his subjects. His son and successor, Joachim Friedrich (r. 1598–1608), shared neither his father's religious convictions nor his pro-imperialist stance. In matters of doctrine he moved closer to Calvinism. Politically he associated himself with the Reformed Electoral Palatinate and the Calvinist Low Countries. He also made efforts to reform the still strongly Catholic liturgy.

Joachim Friedrich's son Johann Sigismund (r. 1608–1618) had been brought up under the guidance of the strictly Lutheran and anti-Calvinist court chaplain of Halle, Simon Gedicke (1551–1631), according to the teaching of the *Formula of Concord* (1577). In 1593 Johann Sigismund's grandfather, Johann Georg, even extracted a solemn pledge from the twenty-year old that he would always adhere to orthodox Lutheranism and the *Formula of Concord*. At the start of Johann Sigismund's reign, the entire territory of Electoral Brandenburg, except for the three largely Calvinist Rhine provinces, was Lutheran. However, Johann Sigismund had gained very favorable impressions of the Reformed faith through his social relations with governmental heads of the Low Countries, and with Elector Friedrich IV of the Palatinate and Landgrave Moritz of Hesse. In 1615, he engaged his son Georg Wilhelm (r. 1619–1640) to the Reformed Princess Elisabeth Charlotte of the Electoral Palatinate. But the dice had already been cast a year earlier: according to Johann Sigismund's *Erklerung die Religion betreffendt an die versamblete Landstende zu Berlin* ("Explanation Concerning Religion for the Assembled Estates in Berlin") of 6 April 1614, he had secretly converted to Calvinism. On Ascension Day 1613, which saw a visit of the Reformed Landgrave Moritz of Hesse in the capital Berlin, the service in the Castle Chapel was conducted according to the Reformed rite.[2] On 18 December, Johann Sigismund announced through his Reformed chancellor Bruckmann that he did not demand any authority over his subjects' consciences, but neither were they to dictate his faith to him. On Christmas Day 1613, finally, the Elector announced his conversion to the Reformed faith by publicly taking communion in Berlin Cathedral according to the Reformed rite. His brother Johann Georg, the Count of Nassau Ernst Casimir, the English ambassador, and some fifty others joined in, but not his wife Duchess Anna of Prussia, who remained resolutely Lutheran.

As Clark points out, Elector Johann Sigismund's conversion "placed the House of Hohenzollern on a new trajectory."[3] It secured him the

---

2. See Kawerau, "Sigismund," 332.

3. Clark, *Iron Kingdom*, 115.

political alliance of the Low Countries, Scotland, and France, but effectively placed him outside the provisions of the Augsburg Peace of 1555. His conversion also "drove a deep confessional trench between dynasty and people."[4] In an edict of 24 February 1614, he declared the four Early Church symbols, the *Variata* of the *Augsburg Confession*, and Melanchthon's *Apologia* to be the doctrinal basis for all pastors.[5] He established a Reformed church council, which was intended to execute his *ius reformandi*[6] through the exclusive employment of Reformed school and university teachers and church ministers, and through the ordination only of those who adhered to the Reformed catechism and the Reformed church order. The *ius reformandi* also granted Lutheran ministers freedom to leave the country. These measures were promptly met with sharp criticism and outspoken protests from the Lutherans, who represented the vast majority of the population of Electoral Brandenburg, "one of the most conservative Lutheran states in the Empire."[7]

Johann Sigismund's Reformed advisers drafted a proposal with the intention to transform Brandenburg into an entirely Reformed territory. Resistance to these plans formed at every level of society. Abraham Scultetus (1566–1625), Johann Sigismund's court preacher, advised the Elector to leave the parish churches in the Electorate untouched and to restrict his reform to his own court chapel and Berlin Cathedral. Margrave Johann Georg, Johann Sigismund's brother, promptly ordered the removal of images and liturgical implements from Berlin Cathedral, an action that provoked outright riots. The houses of two Reformed preachers, including Martin Füssel's, were being ransacked by infuriated Lutherans. Christoph Pelargus (1565–1633), the Lutheran superintendent of Brandenburg, happened to be a Philippist; he was not in favor of orthodox Lutheranism and therefore did not intervene. Orthodox Lutherans subsequently accused him of being soft on Calvinism.

Apart from family members and the court preachers whom the Elector had brought to Berlin, his Reformed supporters included only a few nobles and some lawyers, teachers, physicians, and professors, i.e., members of the professional elite. Jörg Baur's observation that the advancement of the Reformed faith was particularly successful at princely courts,

4. Ibid.

5. See Kawerau, "Sigismund," 333.

6. The principle of *cuius region, eius religio*, which meant that the sovereign of a territory decided his subjects' religious adherence, was first proposed at the Diet of Speyer in 1526. See MacCulloch, *Reformation*, 274.

7. MacCulloch, *Reformation*, 357.

among the nobility and in parts of the city patriciate,[8] was certainly true for Brandenburg.

Now the estates, dominated by Lutheran provincial nobles, exploited their taxation powers "to extract concessions from the deeply indebted Elector."[9] After four representations by the estates, who demanded that Lutheran ministers and professors be reinstated, Johann Sigismund had to back down. On 5 February 1615, he issued an edict in which he declared that those of his subjects that adhered to Lutheran doctrines and confessions must in no way be compelled to relinquish them. "Everybody in the county who so desires should adhere to Luther's teaching and the *Invariata*, as well as the *Book of Concord*."[10] He emphasized that, even though it was his right to introduce the Reformed faith in Brandenburg, he would not insist on it. Thus, although the Peace of Augsburg of 1555 had granted each sovereign the *ius reformandi*, Johann Sigismund effectively waived this right to impose his faith on his subjects. Instead, he decreed that both Protestant confessions would coexist in peace and harmony in Brandenburg. In this way, he established a sound basis for religious liberty. Nevertheless, in 1616 he turned the University of Frankfurt an der Oder into a Reformed seat of learning. As a consequence, those of his Lutheran subjects who wanted to study divinity simply went to the Lutheran University at Wittenberg.

Thus, in the face of the resistance the Elector and his Reformed advisers encountered, they abandoned their hope of a Second Reformation in Brandenburg. Instead, they settled "for a 'court Reformation' (*Hofreformation*), whose religious energies petered out on the fringes of the political elite."[11] Despite the religious freedom granted in Prussia, only small and scattered Reformed congregations began to form. The number of Reformed subjects was boosted considerably under the Great Elector Friedrich Wilhelm I (r. 1640–1688),[12] when Prussia welcomed some 20,000 exiled Huguenots into the country.[13]

The Lutheran Church remained the territorial church in Brandenburg-Prussia. As a consequence, there was no organic Reformed structure

8. See Baur, "Johann Gerhard," 105.

9. Clark, *Iron Kingdom*, 118.

10. Kawerau, "Sigismund," 336.

11. Clark, *Iron Kingdom*, 120.

12. Born in 1620, Friedrich Wilhelm was "the first Hohenzollern prince to grow up within an entirely Calvinist nuclear family." Clark, *Iron Kingdom*, 120. Johann Sigismund's wife Anna had remained a staunch Lutheran until her death in 1625.

13. See Schaff, *Creeds* I, 535.

above that of a parish. The supervision of the Reformed Church would remain in the hands of the Lutheran consistory until 1713, when King Friedrich Wilhelm I of Prussia (r. 1713–1740) ordained the establishment of the Reformed Church Directory as the supreme Reformed church organ for all his territories.[14] In effect, Elector Johann Sigismund's factual abolition of the *ius reformandi* in Prussia prepared the ground for the later union politics of the House of Hohenzollern.

EARLY UNIFICATION EFFORTS

Movements to unite the Reformed and Lutheran Churches in the Holy Roman Empire took place from the seventeenth century onwards, but they were almost exclusively initiated by Reformed theologians. I would conjecture that the Lutherans did not adopt unionist views because they did not have to. They formed the majority of German Protestants, they were protected by the Peace of Augsburg, and they regarded the *Book of Concord* as the ultimate symbolic book that need not and should not be amended in any way. It is therefore not surprising that church union endeavors usually occurred at the initiative of the Reformed. Also, the more open attitude of the German Reformed to confessions of faith, as well as their politically more precarious situation outside the protection of the Religious Peace goes some way toward explaining their greater willingness to form a united Protestant church.

Many of the early German Reformed theologians were so-called Irenicists. Standing in the humanist tradition of Erasmus of Rotterdam (1466–1536) and Philip Melanchthon (1497–1560), they stressed the confessional and doctrinal agreements between Lutherans and Reformed and de-emphasized the matters that divided them in the hope to overcome the existing divisions between Protestants. The development of irenical literature in the first half of the seventeenth century was mainly motivated by Catholic advances, to which Irenicists thought Protestantism should present a united front.

Noteworthy publications by Irenicists include David Pareus' *Irenicum*, published in 1614, which has been described by Bodo Nischan as "one of the most important pieces of ecumenical literature of the period."[15] Paul Stein, one of the court chaplains of the Reformed Landgrave Moritz of Hesse, published the three-volume *Evangelische Kirchen Brüderschaft*

14. See Dowart, "Church Organization," 286.
15. Nischan, "Reformed Irenicism," 7.

("Protestant Church Unity") of 1622. The most prominent Hessian Irenicist was Johann Crocius (1590–1659). Between 1615 and 1617, he also
played a part in assisting the Brandenburg Elector Johann Sigismund in
establishing the Reformed Church in his territory.

The most important Irenicist of the 1620s and 30s was probably
Johann Bergius (1587–1658), the court chaplain of Elector Christian
Wilhelm of Brandenburg and an outspoken advocate of Protestant unity.
Although Lutheranism did not generally support the Irenicist move-
ment, there was at least one prominent Lutheran exception: Georg Calixt
(1586–1656), a divinity professor at Helmstedt. Greatly inspired by the
Philippist tradition of his home—his father Johann had been a pupil of
Melanchthon—and his humanist education, he had a deep-seated antipa-
thy against Gnesio-Lutheran narrowness, and he rejected the *Formula of
Concord*. He came to believe that the full Christian truth was contained in
the confessions and councils of the first five centuries AD. Accordingly, he
wanted to reduce the *articuli fundamentales*, the articles of faith necessary
for salvation, in order to establish a consensus among all Christian faiths,
Lutheran, Reformed, and Catholic alike. His almost untenable position
was highlighted by his role at the 1645 Colloquy of Thorn.[16] He was invited by the Great Elector, Friedrich Wilhelm I of Brandenburg to support
the Reformed delegation from Brandenburg. As a Polish vassal, though,
the Elector was mainly interested in consolidating the Reformed position
against the Catholics in Poland, and under these circumstances the Irenicist Calixt was welcome to strengthen the Protestant faction even though
he was Lutheran. The Lutheran delegation, on the other hand, refused
to let him join their ranks because of his Philippist convictions, which
their leader Abraham Calov (1612–1686) dismissed as "Melanchthonian
half-heartedness."[17] In the end, Calixt counseled the Reformed without
relinquishing his Lutheran position. Not surprisingly, resistance against
this passionate union theologian was massive, and his cause failed. Even
though Irenicism did not actually lead to a church union, it represented an
important intellectual development within the seventeenth-century German Reformed Church,.

Doctrinal differences rather than issues of liturgy or church governance were the main reason for Lutherans to preserve their confessional
identity and remain separate from the Reformed. The seventeenth century,
which saw the heyday of Lutheran Orthodoxy, was particularly opposed

16. For the following see Mager, "Georg Calixt," 145f.

17. Ibid., 145.

to unification efforts. The Peace of Westphalia of 1648 had finally granted official recognition to the German Reformed Church. It had thus superseded the Peace of Augsburg and the political urge for a church union. In the eighteenth century, however, as Albert Hauck put it, Pietism started to rock the dominion of traditional orthodoxy, and the Enlightenment abolished it altogether.[18] As a result, the idea of a church union became more popular again. The community of the Moravian Brethren or *Herrnhuter*, founded by Graf Nikolaus Ludwig von Zinzendorf (1700–1760), was considered to be the first united Christian community. This was, of course, the community in which Schleiermacher grew up, and which would shape his life decisively.

In eighteenth-century Germany, only some individual initiatives toward a union of the two Protestant Churches were undertaken.[19] Key players included Daniel Ernst Jablonski (1660–1741), Jean Alphonse Turretin (1671–1737), and Christoph Matthäus Pfaff (1686–1760). Their support for a union originated in the ideas of the Enlightenment and its conviction that confessional separation was neither desirable nor necessary. The philosopher and polymath Gottfried Wilhelm Leibniz (1646–1716) made several, albeit unsuccessful, attempts at unification. In 1703, Leibniz, together with the Prussian court chaplain Daniel Ernst Jablonski, instigated a colloquium under King Friedrich I in Prussia, at which they tried to promote a church union through secret negotiations between the Royal Courts at Hanover and Berlin. However, the discussions failed because of Lutheran opposition. In 1717, efforts were made to align an initiative toward a union of the two Protestant Churches with the bicentenary of the Reformation. The bicentenary also brought confessional Lutheran theologians on the scene, who proceeded to attack the Reformed in a heated and partly vitriolic pamphlet war that extended from 1721 to 1723. Erdmann Neumeister (1671–1756) and Esdras Heinrich Edzard (1703–1733) emerged as two of the main Lutheran protagonists.

Then, from the late 1760s and increasingly after 1780, passionate discussions about the identity and the renewal of the Protestant Church were held in Germany. Not only theologians and the clergy took part in the debate, but also, as Friedrich Wilhelm Graf notes, educated non-followers of the church as well as critics of the Enlightenment, constitutional lawyers,

18. See Hauck, "Union, kirchliche," 254.

19. It is worth noting that church unions, in the sense of a unification of confessionally separate churches into one church without changes to original confessional adherence, are only known in Protestantism, and indeed chiefly in German Protestantism. See Hauck, "Union, kirchliche," 253.

philosophers, historians, and high-ranking administrative staff.[20] Their discussions took place within the context of the larger debate concerning Enlightenment issues.

In the last third of the eighteenth century, not only Enlightenment thought, but also Revivalist, or Pietist, movements helped prepare the ground theologically in favor of a union. Enlightenment theologians tended to consider doctrines as altogether irrational and anachronistic, arguing that human reason had to liberate itself from dogmatic patronization. The Pietists turned against confessionalism of any kind too,[21] albeit for different reasons; they focused on personal piety and acts of love rather than doctrines. Toward the end of the eighteenth century, therefore, the majority of the Prussian clergy appear to have been convinced that a union would be both theologically legitimate and politically compelling.

THE EARLY NINETEENTH CENTURY

In the early nineteenth century, the political conditions for a church union became very favorable indeed.[22] The former imperial law that had arisen from the Peace of Westphalia of 1648 had prescribed the confessional status of a territory. However, as a result of Napoleon's politics of conquest, religious relations in the French-occupied territories west of the Rhine were ordered anew. Now, parity between confessions was replacing the old prescribed confessional status, and ties between church and state were being loosened.[23] The secularization of the majority of the territories previously placed under church sovereignty followed the Final Recess of 1803. That Recess also specified that the sovereign was free to tolerate other co-religionists and to grant them full enjoyment of civil rights.[24] In the

20. See Graf, "Restaurationstheologie," 70.

21. See Stiewe, "Unionen IV," 324–26.

22. Outside Prussia, the following territories agreed to a church union: Nassau in 1817, Hesse between 1817 and 1822, the Palatinate as well as Hanau and Fulda in 1818, Baden and Waldeck in 1821, Bernburg in 1820, and Dessau in 1827. See Hauck, "Union, kirchliche," 257.

23. See Rohls, *Reformed Confessions*, tr. Hoffmeyer, 289.

24. The General Prussian Law of 1794 used the term 'church' only to denote the actual building where worship took place. For the faith community it employed the term 'religious party.' This usage reflects the tendency of church politics towards neglecting doctrinal differences. However, in the consciousness of the members of the congregations such differences were considered to be more important. See Besier, "Luthertum," 134.

wake of Napoleon's conquest of Russia and Austria in 1805, and of Prussia in 1806, the Holy Roman Empire of the German Nation was dissolved, and all sovereign rights were transferred. Due to the countless changes of territorial boundaries, by 1806 hardly any confessionally uniform territories had survived intact. In Prussia, the Hohenzollern Court had been Reformed since 1613, but the vast majority of congregations and of the army had remained Lutheran. However, the Reformed minority of the population was scattered throughout the provincial capitals, and their role in church government functions was guaranteed. In diaspora situations, members of the minority confession had access as guests to the services of worship of the majority confession without thereby having to convert.

After the final defeat of Napoleon's army at Waterloo in 1815, the Congress of Vienna drew up new territorial borders in Europe. Prussia now consisted of 278,042 square kilometers, divided into ten provinces: East Prussia, West Prussia, Posen, Brandenburg, Pomerania, Silesia, Saxony, Westphalia, Jülich-Kleve-Berg, and the Lower Rhine provinces. Each province had a president whose remit included the management of both ecclesiastical and educational affairs. In 1816, of the total 10 million inhabitants, ca. 5.7 million were Lutheran, 390,000 were Reformed, ca. 3.9 million were Catholic, ca. 124,000 were Jews, and the rest belonged to the Mennonites, the Moravians, and others such as the French Huguenots.[25] The ratio of the total population to the Reformed was thus twenty-five to one, and that of Lutherans to Reformed fifteen to one. With Silesia and the Lower Rhine provinces, territories with a Catholic majority now fell to the Prussian Crown. Moreover, in the provinces that had been acquired by Prussia in the west, the Reformed tradition was of considerable influence. Nevertheless, as Schleiermacher observed, "the size of the Reformed community in Prussia [was] of little or no economic consequence."[26]

With the ecclesiastical picture of Prussia being so diverse, it was surely in the interest of Prussian politics and its need for integration and domestic peace to surmount the confessional rift. The Acts of Confederation took confessional differences in the new territories into account. No longer did the variety of Christian denominations in the German Federation provide the basis for a difference in the enjoyment of the civil and political rights of its inhabitants. As Rohls states, "confessional parity was thus anchored in law."[27] In Prussia's neo-humanist, idealist civic culture,

25. See Goeters, "Anschluß," 82.

26. Schleiermacher, *Zwei unvorgreifliche Gutachten*, 53.

27. Rohls, *Reformed Confessions*, tr. Hoffmeyer, 289.

confessionalist views had lost their decisive impact. On a more emotional level, patriotic enthusiasm following the victorious end of the Prussian wars of liberation in 1813 and 1814 served to promote a feeling of solidarity and communal spirit among Prussians. In the ensuing period of continuous peace, the gate to ecclesiastical reform and a church union appeared to be wide open.

Within the Prussian Ministry of the Interior, an administrative union had already taken place over a few years up to 1806. In the course of bourgeois reforms introduced by Heinrich Friedrich Karl von und zum Stein and Karl August von Hardenberg between 1807 and 1814, the so-called Stein-Hardenberg Reforms, the Lutheran and Reformed ecclesiastical authorities had been amalgamated. Prussia was striving toward the centralized management of all matters concerning church, education, and health by the Ministry of Education and the Arts. In 1808, all ecclesiastical authorities were suspended, and their former remits were assigned to the central state administration. After 1815, matters of worship became the remit of the Minister of the Interior. The centralizing political tendencies of the Crown and its administration provided the backdrop for the King's promulgation of the Prussian Church Union of 1817.

Between 1790 and 1810, Prussian ministers and other educated people published numerous proposals for a church union, which might have given the impression that the majority of ministers had already inwardly consummated a union. There were other indications of favorable receptivity to some form of church union. For instance, since 1780 the number of mixed marriages between Lutheran and Reformed spouses had markedly increased, at least in Berlin. Further, Lutheran and Reformed preachers were exchanging pulpits, and attendance at worship in confessionally different churches had become something of a custom. The influential Reformed court and cathedral chaplain Friedrich Samuel Gottfried Sack (1738–1817), one of Schleiermacher's early mentors, had stated in his *Promemoria* of 13 July 1798: "The two Protestant Churches in the Prussian territories are already so closely united through the wise tolerance of their sovereigns that the difference between the two ecclesiastical systems has lost its former importance and does no longer cause an essential separation among them."[28] In the same document, Sack even requested that a common liturgy be drafted, since the existing liturgies deviated from each other "more in words than in essence."[29] Not only had differences

---

28. Wappler, "Reformationsjubiläum," 96.
29. Neuser, "Agende," 136.

in doctrine between Lutherans and Reformed lost their previous importance, but there were only minor liturgical differences between Lutheran
and Reformed as well. Even before 1817, worship prescribed for Lutheran
and Reformed soldiers displayed no confessional differences.[30] "In some
places one assumes the unification in faith has already been accomplished,
only that it has not yet yielded a declaration and a formal union,"[31] as Carl
Städlin observed in 1804. In his publication *Über die Vereinigung der
beiden protestantischen Kirchengemeinden in der preußischen Monarchie*
("Concerning the Unification of the Two Protestant Church Congregations in the Prussian Monarchy") of 1812, Sack declared that no reason
for the continued separation remained, and that the Church itself should
officially pronounce this verdict. In contrast to Schleiermacher, however,
Sack considered a confession of faith for the united church to be necessary.
He also demanded that all clergy of all parties take a vote on the union,
and that a majority vote be returned.[32]

SCHLEIERMACHER'S EARLY WRITINGS
ABOUT CHURCH UNION

Steeped in "Reformed and Pietist congregational Christianity,"[33] Friedrich
Schleiermacher played a prominent part in the debates about the Prussian
Church Union. He became one of the most influential promoters of its
establishment, and, according to Wilhelm Gaß (1813–1889), "one of the
spiritual fathers of the Union."[34] Wilhelm Gaß, the son of Schleiermacher's
close friend Joachim Christian Gaß (1766–1831) and editor of their published correspondence, characterized Schleiermacher's role succinctly:
"Schleiermacher was the dogmatist of the Union, and, since the two impartial reports of 1804, its public representative."[35] That reference is to two
reports published anonymously in 1804 under the title *Zwei unvorgreifliche Gutachten in Sachen des protestantischen Kirchenwesens zunächst in
Beziehung auf den Preußischen Staat* ("Two Impartial Reports Concerning
the Protestant Churches, Initially with Reference to the Prussian State").
These publications signal the starting point of Schleiermacher's academic

30. See ibid., 139.

31. Städlin, *Kirchliche Geographie und Statistik*, Tübingen 1804, 116f.

32. See Hauck, "Union, kirchliche," 256.

33. Von Thadden, "Schleiermacher und Preußen," 1100.

34. Gaß, *Briefwechsel*, 222.

35. Ibid.

activity. In them, Schleiermacher acted as the eloquent champion of the Prussian Royal Court and its leading clergy supporting the union. In the first report, entitled *Über die Trennung der beiden protestantischen Kirchen* ("Concerning the Separation of the two Protestant Churches"), he declared a union to be independent of dogmatic issues. There was no need for a doctrinal consensus. As Theodore Vial observed: "Most subjects no longer knew the dogmatic basis of the separation."[36] The union was to be founded entirely on the mutual admission of Lutherans and Reformed to communion, and on the revocation of confessional differences in the appointment of clergy.

Schleiermacher opposed the establishment of a third Protestant church, a union church characterized by a complete removal of dogmatic differences. Instead, he demanded a minimization of doctrinal differences—differences, he argued, that were "not preached from the pulpit and hardly taught at school."[37] Indeed, in a sermon he preached on the occasion of the unification of the Lutheran and Reformed congregations of Trinity Church, Berlin, on Palm Sunday 1822, he argued that although there were historical reasons for the two faiths to develop out of the Reformation, their departure was "a regrettable misunderstanding."[38] He called it a "pernicious delusion"[39] to act as if the dogmatic differences were of particular importance. In his Palm Sunday sermon he used more pastoral terms when he said that "those who are also externally divided but yet are at least internally separated from one another are again reunited in the exhortation and comfort that come from teaching and in the pure love of brethren for one another."[40] Union should be accomplished not only without doctrinal consensus, but without restrictions regarding freedom

---

36. Vial, "Schleiermacher and the State," 280.

37. Schleiermacher, *Zwei unvorgreifliche Gutachten,* 29.

38. Schleiermacher, *On Creeds, Confessions and Church Union,* tr. Nicol, 203. Indeed, in the postscript to §24 of *Christian Faith,* Schleiermacher insisted that "the original relation [between the Reformed and the Lutheran Churches] was such that, notwithstanding their different starting points, they might just as well have grown together into an outward unity." He continued: "Thus [this presentation of doctrine] starts from the assumption that the separation of the two has lacked sufficient grounds, inasmuch as the differences in doctrine are in no sense traceable to a difference in the religious affections themselves, and the two do not diverge from each other, either in morals and moral theory or in constitution, in any way which at all corresponds to those differences of doctrine." Schleiermacher, *Christian Faith,* tr. MacIntosh and Stewart, §24 postscript, 107.

39. Schleiermacher, *Zwei unvorgreifliche Gutachten,* 44.

40. Schleiermacher, *On Creeds, Confessions and Church Union,* tr. Nicol, 201.

of belief. In the 1831 preface to his nine 1830 Augustana sermons celebrating the tercentenary of the handing over of the *Augsburg Confession* in 1530, Schleiermacher still insisted that a consensus confession for the united church was unnecessary, and also that he had always vehemently opposed it out of concern for the well-deserved freedom attained without any consensus confession. Once full communion was established, there would be no need for separate Lutheran and Reformed administrative structures. As an example he mentioned the chaplaincy at the Charité Hospital in Berlin, which position he himself had held from 1796 to 1802, wherein the mutual representation of Lutheran and Reformed clergy was already lawfully practiced.

When Schleiermacher took up his professorship at the thriving University of Halle in 1804, King Friedrich Wilhelm III (r. 1797–1840) had created a post for him as the first Reformed lecturer at the hitherto solidly Lutheran divinity faculty. In a parallel development, the Lutheran theologian Gotthelf Samuel Steinbart (1738–1809) was called to the Reformed divinity faculty at the University of Frankfurt an der Oder. With the foundation of the University of Berlin in 1810 and the reorganization of other universities in Prussia (apart from Greifswald), the co-existence of both Protestant denominations within one divinity faculty became the norm. Schleiermacher himself regarded what Kurt Nowak called his "implantation into the Lutheran theological faculty"[41] as an exercise in the spirit of his two earlier reports. He was also appointed to the university chaplaincy, but he did not actively take up this position until 1806. The School Church, where university services were to take place, was being repaired when he arrived, and it was subsequently used for corn storage after Napoleon's troops had taken over Halle. In his correspondence with Joachim Christian Gaß, Schleiermacher reported that he had been able to preach on a couple of occasions, "but only in the Cathedral Church; in the Lutheran City Church they do not want to admit this heretic, though on occasions there is need enough."[42] Schleiermacher was not a faculty member to start with, but he served as Professor *extraordinarius theologiae et philosophiae* until a vacancy arose in February 1806, albeit not for long. In the wake of Napoleon's victory over Prussia at Jena and Auerstädt on 14 October 1806, French troops occupied Halle, and Napoleon closed down the University on 20 October 1806. Still, the very fact that Schleiermacher's employment at the divinity faculty had been orchestrated by the Prussian monarch, and

41. Nowak, *Schleiermacher*, 147.
42. Gaß, *Briefwechsel*, 22.

that it was motivated by the pro-union attitude he had demonstrated in his two impartial reports of 1804, was a clear indication of the government's policy to move toward one Protestant Church. In a royal decree of 10 May 1804, Friedrich Wilhelm III had actually stated that "the Faculty at Halle laudably obliges my intentions in this matter."[43] That policy, along with a number of other factors, would eventually culminate in the Prussian Church Union of the Lutheran and Reformed faiths in 1817.

THE PRUSSIAN CHURCH UNION OF 1817

The early nineteenth-century ecclesiastical reform in Prussia had three aspects:[44] first, a reform of the church constitution with the aim of replacing the existing bureaucratic absolutism with a synodal constitution; second, a reform of worship to introduce liturgical changes that would reflect the general spiritual progress and, at the same time, trim back the prevailing liturgical enlightened arbitrariness; and third, the actual union of Lutherans and Reformed. As early as 1808, Schleiermacher made a comprehensive reform proposal entitled *Vorschlag zu einer neuen Verfassung der protestantischen Kirche im Preußischen Staate* ("Proposal for a New Constitution of the Protestant Church in the Prussian State"). In it, he emphasized that all three aspects were inextricably linked, and that any reorganization would inevitably abolish the ecclesiastical differences between Lutherans and Reformed. The case would be no different with regard to doctrinal matters, because in Schleiermacher's view, the doctrinal differences that existed between different factions within each confession were much greater than those generally held between the two confessions. With regard to customs too, the rites in various geographical areas of the same confessional tradition were also very different, and in the consciousness of the common people, the denominational barriers had almost been eradicated at any rate. Bearing in mind that Schleiermacher's ideas here form part of his proposal for an altogether new church constitution, his ambition seems rather modest. The union would be achieved by implication, as it were. It should simply not be considered a conversion when a preacher or lay person belonging to one congregation and adhering to its rites transfers to a congregation of the other rite or alternates between both. Accordingly, §7 of the proposed constitution declared that "parochial

---

43. Stiewe, *Unionsverständnis*, 22.
44. For the following, see Wallmann, *Kirchengeschichte*, 208.

constraint is abolished and where several congregations exist in one town, everyone can adhere to whichever one he or she likes."[45]

Martin Stiewe has argued that the Prussian Church Union of 1817 was first and foremost the personal decision of the Prussian King Friedrich Wilhelm III.[46] This is certainly true inasmuch as the King followed his own lay-theological ideas about a union. It is also reflected in the fact that this Union was decreed by state authority without the Churches' agreement, even though both Schleiermacher and Sack, the most pronounced supporters of the union, had voiced their opposition against an imposition from outside and above the Church; they envisaged a step-by-step approach complemented by the establishment of a synodal church order. Moreover, Friedrich Wilhelm III himself was Reformed, whereas his wife, Luise of Mecklenburg-Strelitz, was Lutheran. It is easy to see that the King's hope for a union was motivated at least partly by his desire to take communion together with his wife. The actual establishment of the Union was certainly due to the King's initiative. In his political testament of 1808 he had already expressed his conviction that the religious sense of the people had to be revived, that the means by which to achieve a revival of piety was worship, and that, therefore, there was a demand for a renewal of the liturgy.

The King's desire for a union of the two Protestant Churches and his interest in worship changes were closely related from the outset. At the time, the administrative union in which a government department, the Ministry of the Interior, was responsible for the affairs of both Churches was to be expanded to include a union of liturgy and sacraments. Nevertheless, Hans Hillerbrand's assessment that the King "forced the Lutheran and Reformed Churches in Prussia into a merger"[47] is ill-judged. Hillerbrand cites the situation in early nineteenth-century Prussia as an example of the Lutheran sovereign's powerful role in ecclesiastical affairs and their subjects' "inordinate subservience to the ruling authorities";[48] but Friedrich Wilhelm III was, of course, Reformed, not Lutheran. Hillerbrand's analysis, moreover, is an oversimplification of a complex political and theological development.

---

45. Schleiermacher, *Zwei unvorgreifliche Gutachten,* 123.

46. See Stiewe, "Unionen IV," 326.

47. Hillerbrand, "Legacy," 233.

48. Ibid.

On 27 September 1817, the King passed a cabinet order[49] drafted by the court chaplain at Potsdam, Rulemann Friedrich Eylert (1770–1852), in which he decreed that the impending Reformation celebrations be crowned by a church union. The order was not published until 9 October 1817. It did not imply any doctrinal consensus between Lutherans and Reformed, but it definitely expressed the King's desire for a work "that removes the unessential while retaining the main issue of Christianity on which both faiths agree"[50] to be brought about in Prussia. The Reformed would not convert to the Lutheran faith, nor vice versa, but both would become a new, revitalized Protestant Christian Church in the spirit of its holy founder. He claimed that such "a truly religious union of both Protestant Churches, which are only divided by external differences, corresponds to the great purpose of Christianity."[51] Clearly, the King considered the dogmatic subtleties of the two confessional traditions to be irrelevant for the life of the Church. He likewise valued the uniformity of rites much more highly than that of confessions. The cabinet order also stated, however, that he had no intention of imposing the union, and that a church union would be worthwhile only if it were borne out of a unity of hearts according to scriptural principles. It is worth noting that the call for all Protestants to unite would not have been possible if there had not already been a tendency towards a church union. Interestingly, objections to such a union were voiced by non-Prussian theologians. They included Christoph Friedrich Ammon (1766–1850) and Karl Gottlieb Bretschneider (1776–1848) in Saxony,[52] which Clark called the "chief engine-house of Lutheran orthodoxy,"[53] and Claus Harms (1778–1855) in Kiel.[54]

In September 1817, it was decided, incidentally against Schleiermacher's objections, to form a united synod composed of the Protestant clergy of Berlin. The alternative to the one united synod would have been

---

49 A facsimile reproduction and a transcription of the cabinet order are provided in Goeters and Mau, *Geschichte der Evangelischen Kirche der Union*, 88–92.

50. Goeters and Mau, *Geschichte der Evangelischen Kirche der Union*, 91.

51. Ibid.

52. Until 1806 the Electorate of Saxony was part of the Holy Roman Empire. It then became a kingdom and joined the Confederation of the Rhine. After the Congress of Vienna in 1814–15, nearly half of the Saxon Kingdom was annexed by Prussia, but the remaining territory, which included Leipzig and Dresden, remained an independent kingdom. Kiel belonged to Holstein.

53. Clark, *Iron Kingdom*, 120.

54. For more details, see chapter 4 below.

for the four Berlin superintendents to each call a local synod.[55] The Berlin Synod's negotiations started on 1 October 1817, that is before the King's cabinet order was published, and the forty-six assembled clergymen elected Schleiermacher as their president. The majority of these theologians were Lutheran, and their election of Schleiermacher, despite his initial objection against the formation of the Synod, was an expression of their trust in their renowned Reformed fellow clergyman and divinity professor. Before the ministers decided to reconvene on 11 October, one member of the Synod proposed a joint communion celebration on 31 October to mark the tercentenary of the Reformation; the proposal was accepted almost unanimously. The Synod also agreed a standardized form of communion, which it subsequently recommended generally. As president of the Synod, Schleiermacher had to draft and to publish a declaration announcing the joint celebrations, which he presented to the members of the Synod on 24 October 1817. This *Amtliche Erklärung der Berlinischen Synode über die am 30. October von ihr zu haltende Abendmahlsfeier* ("Official Declaration of the Synod of Berlin Concerning the Celebration of Holy Communion Which It Will Hold on 30 October 1817"[56]) clarified that neither a dogmatic consensus nor doctrinal unity would form a precondition for the union. Rather, the new form of communion was to retain all essential elements, and only alter accidental ones. The declaration also emphasized that it was not desirable to form a third church which would be separate from both the Reformed and Lutheran Churches.[57] As Schleiermacher explained in a letter to Ludwig Gottfried Blanc (1781–1866) of 19 August 1818, the declaration first stated the greatest freedom of the congregations and explained that a real union of different congregations could not be conceived of until each had voluntarily adopted the new liturgy for itself.[58] It expressed the hope that the example set by the clergy would be emulated by the congregations. In the end, the joint communion service of the Protestant clergy of Berlin took place in Nicolai Church on 30 October 1817, on the eve of the tercentenary. Schleiermacher had a large responsibility with regard to the anniversary celebrations as president of the Berlin Synod and also as Dean of the Faculty of Divinity at Berlin. Joint communion was then celebrated on 31 October (Reformation Day), wherever

---

55. See Nowak, *Schleiermacher*, 362.

56. For an English translation, see Schleiermacher, *On Creeds, Confessions and Church Union*, tr. Nicol, 17–28.

57. See Stiewe, *Unionsverständnis*, 30.

58. See Dilthey, *Aus Schleiermachers Leben in Briefen* III, 237.

Lutheran and Reformed congregations coexisted. King Friedrich Wilhelm III and the Royal family attended the service in Nicolai Church without taking communion there. They reserved this public act for the service in the by then united Potsdam Court congregation. With this joint communion celebration in Potsdam taking place according to a uniform rite, the King considered the union between the Reformed Court Church and the Lutheran Garrison Church to be consummated. He hoped to set an example with this symbolic act, but his hopes were already thwarted the following Sunday when many congregations returned to their usual form of worship. Lutheran congregations in particular were concerned about the possible financial loss of fees and communion charges: since communion was the sole measurement of people fulfilling their duties as parishioners, every Lutheran who celebrated communion outside a Lutheran church meant a loss of income. Because the standardized formula for communion suggested by the Berlin Synod did not apply to congregations outside the capital, there were considerable local differences in the communion celebrations. As a result, congregations became insecure and reverted to the old trusted formula. In provinces such as Silesia, where the Reformed minority was disproportionally small, this minority was reluctant to accept a union that they perceived as an absorption by the Lutheran majority.[59] In his sermon of 31 March 1822, on the occasion of the unification of the Lutheran and Reformed congregations of Trinity Church in Berlin, at which he had held the office of Reformed pastor since 1809, Schleiermacher looked back on the 1817 Church Union: "only the general desire of all well-intentioned Evangelical Christians was realized in the directive that in our territory the festival of the Reformation of the Church[60] should be a common festival for both branches of the Evangelical Church."[61] The Protestant clergy also declared that they regarded the differences between the two faiths as insufficient to divide them. Therefore, he and his Lutheran counterpart also desired to belong equally to all members of the congregation. There would be a complete unity of property, and both congregations would share everything pertaining to Christian worship and duties.[62]

The claim that King Friedrich Wilhelm III wanted to unite his fragmented territory in order to be able to better rule it centrally has been

---

59. See Gaß, *Briefwechsel*, LXXIII.

60. As in this instance, Schleiermacher frequently used the term "Church improvement" to denote the Protestant Reformation.

61. Schleiermacher, *On Creeds, Confessions and Church Union*, tr. Nicol, 205.

62. See Schleiermacher, "Vorrede," 260–61.

made repeatedly, but this claim cannot be substantiated from the source texts.[63] Indeed, the Union was not primarily seen as a potential conflict between politics and the church, but as a theological problem. Certainly the King's interest in the standardization of his large, diverse territory and in strengthening the loyalty ties between his ruling house, the estates, and his subjects cannot be overlooked. At the same time, there had been numerous expressions in favor of a church union in Prussia from 1770 onwards, such as factual joint communion services, united Lutheran and Reformed schools and hospital chaplaincies, as well as administrative bodies. Gerhard Besier has argued that the Prussian Church Union was "a child of the *Zeitgeist*,"[64] echoing Gaß's claim that in the idea of a union the Royal will would meet the demand of the ecclesiastical majority.[65]

The promulgation of the Prussian Church Union on the tercentenary of the Reformation initially met with approval in all Prussian provinces, and sometimes with enthusiastic assent. The celebration of liberation from the papacy through Martin Luther's actions, and of liberation from Napoleon through the Prussians' own actions were considered to be a manifestation of a German-Protestant sense of community.[66] Where protests arose they were usually directed against the bureaucratization of church administration, which was seen to be a threat to personal piety. The fact that a single Protestant Church would basically cease to be confessional did not appear to enter public consciousness. The question whether or not the united Church would need its own expressly stated doctrinal basis arose only later. However, as Schleiermacher conceded in his 1822 sermon, "we cannot deny nor may we overlook the fact that there are more than enough examples of those who, in order to bring shame on the Evangelical church, again forsake the bosom of the church."[67] In the course of the ensuing restructuring of the Prussian Protestant Church, any close relationship between constitutional reform, reform of worship, and union between Lutherans and Reformed, which Schleiermacher had urged as early as 1808, was dissolved. The church union and worship reform were being handled separately, and a new, synodal constitution was rejected altogether.

---

63. See Mehlhausen, "Theologie," 17.

64. Besier, "Luthertum," 135.

65. See Gaß, *Briefwechsel*, LX.

66. See Wappler, "' Reformationsjubiläum,'" 101.

67. Schleiermacher, *On Creeds, Confessions and Church Union*, tr. Nicol, 209.

THE PROTESTANT CHURCH IN PRUSSIA
AFTER THE UNION

Not surprisingly, problems soon emerged. The King in his role as Prussian sovereign had the *ius in sacra*, the right of law in sacred matters. This right had allowed him, as *summus episcopus* or supreme bishop, to take charge of the Union. However, he was also claiming the *ius liturgicum* for himself in a cabinet order issued in 1822, in which he declared that "the Protestant sovereign has the undisputed right to determine liturgical forms according to his own discretion."[68] On Christmas Day 1821 he had published a "Liturgy for the Main Diet of Worship on Sundays and Feast Days and for Communion," which he had drafted himself. This new liturgy, commonly regarded as high church, was imposed in 1822 on the Reformed Cathedral congregation in Berlin and the Lutheran Petri congregation that also used the Cathedral. There was broad-based resistance to what Rohls called "the compulsory introduction of his Romantic and restorationist agenda of union,"[69] which imposed a cultic or liturgical union to supplement the existing administrative one. Since joining the Union was thus made to imply acceptance of the liturgy drafted by the King, the old opposition between Lutherans and Reformed became virulent again. The new liturgy was based on the Lutheran model of worship. As a consequence, even Reformed congregations that would normally have been in favor of the Prussian Church Union then rejected it. For the Lutherans, conversely, the new liturgy was not sufficiently Lutheran in character. Its forced introduction would eventually lead to the separation of confessionalist Lutherans.

Many, including Schleiermacher, questioned whether the King's *ius liturgicum* did in fact extend to the imposition of a liturgy on congregations against their resistance. A pamphlet war broke out with Schleiermacher as one of the spokesmen against its royal, and thus secular, imposition and against several liturgical decisions, and therewith against the content of the liturgy itself. He fervently advocated freedom of conscience and of doctrine, entering the fray directly in 1824 with the tract *Ueber das liturgische Recht evangelischer Landesfürsten. Ein theologisches Bedenken* ("Concerning the Liturgical Right of Protestant Princes. A Theological Consideration"), which he published under the pseudonym Pacificus Sincerus. Casting doubt on the supreme bishop's very competence in worship matters, he argued that the liturgical right rested with the congregations

68. Niebergall, "Agende," 56.
69. Rohls, *Reformed Confessions*, tr. Hoffmeyer, 291.

themselves; as a consequence, a shared liturgy could emerge only in a church with a synodal constitution. Gaß also aptly noted that the "purely Reformed nature of Schleiermacher was hostile to all Episcopalianism."[70] The increased role of the choir and the extended activity of the liturgist were a particular bone of contention for the Reformed. As a result, only six percent of the Protestant clergy in Prussia were able to accept the new liturgy.[71] From 1827, a book of liturgy with separate editions for the different Prussian provinces was published, taking into account local and regional liturgical traditions. At that point, the majority of the clergy did find themselves in a position to accept it.

Finally, the Prussian General Synod of 1846 agreed that the Protestant Church had been founded on the concurrent doctrinal contents of the entire Protestant Reformation and its symbolic books. The resolutions of this Synod reflected efforts to give a clear doctrinal basis to the united Prussian Church even without a confession of its own. However, these resolutions were never confirmed by the sovereign, now King Friedrich Wilhelm IV (r. 1840–1861). At that same General Synod, the Lutheran Karl Immanuel Nitzsch (1787–1868) tried to introduce a very conciliatory union confession aimed at a consensus union, but his efforts were vetoed by the King. Different confessions continued to be valid in different provinces and congregations. The 1846 General Synod thus ultimately failed either to produce a unitary confession or to form a unitary ecclesiastical constitution for the Protestant Church in Prussia. The failure of the 1848 Revolution also signaled the end of the debate over a separation of church and state[72] in Prussia. In the end, the King retained his *ius in sacra*.

Unlike other territorial churches such as Nassau, the Palatinate, and Baden, the Prussian Church would never have a consensus union. Indeed, in the nineteenth century the confession of faith regained its function as setting the law for doctrine. In a decisive move against those union

70. Gaß, *Briefwechsel*, LXXXIII.

71. See Niebergall, "Agende," 57.

72. A separation of church and state, which entails that the ruler ceases to act as supreme bishop, could be achieved in different ways. The Reformed supported a presbyterian-synodal system of church administration or governance. Schleiermacher emerged as the champion of this collegialism. In large parts, Neo-Lutherans, although they agreed in principle with a separation of church and state, favored a system that would entrust the secular authorities with the responsibility for caring for the church. According to this institutional rather than collegiate understanding, church governance would be assigned to official ministers as the apostles' successors. In this way the Neo-Lutherans arrived at the episcopal system. See Rohls, *Reformed Confessions*, tr. Hoffmeyer, 291–92.

advocates who, like Schleiermacher, pointed to the spirit rather than the exact letter of the confession, the entire confession, not merely its spirit or principle, was declared to be the binding norm for both doctrine and faith by large parts of the restorative Neo-Lutherans. Continuing the tradition of the Enlightenment, on the other hand, union supporters replaced the status of confessions as doctrinal laws with an obligation only to their spirit, for to them the symbolic books' status of doctrinal law meant a transgression against the Protestant principle of Scripture. The reawakening of confessional Lutheranism, not only as an academic pursuit but also as a church phenomenon even on the local level, set in after the wars of liberation, and it took hold firmly from the 1830s.[73]

Neo-confessionalism in the late eighteenth and early nineteenth centuries had developed against the backdrop of the French Revolution and its state terrorism, the new formation of the German states in the wake of Napoleon's invasions in Europe, the German national movement, and the increasing de-Christianization that accompanied many of these events. In this sense, neo-confessionalism was related to the question of the cultural importance of Christianity within the existing confessional identities. The crucial points that Schleiermacher made in opposition to Lutheran neo-confessionalism were already present in his 1819 publication *Über den eigenthümlichen Werth und das bleibende Ansehen symbolischer Bücher* ("On the Proper Value and Binding Authority of Symbolic Books").[74]

For Schleiermacher the spirit of the confession took precedence over its letter. He argued that in case of a liturgical commitment to the confession, the relationship between theology and general academic education would be lost: "the best and most characteristic element in our theology is the more excellent form that dogmatics has acquired through the Reformation together with the lively impulse to engage in study of Scripture and about Scripture."[75] He maintained that the dangers for the Protestant Church that arose from the revival of Lutheran confessionalism and the strengthening of the Catholic Church in the first third of the nineteenth century would not be avoided by the re-establishment of a literal commitment to the text of any confession. Those dangers could be warded off, he insisted, only by reflection on that spirit of the Reformation that expresses itself within those symbolic books.

---

73. See Besier, "Luthertum," 137.

74. See Stiewe, *Unionsverständnis*, 30. For an English translation, see Schleiermacher, *On Creeds, Confessions and Church Union*, tr. Nicol, 161–90.

75. Schleiermacher, *On Creeds, Confessions and Church Union*, tr. Nicol, 177.

On an individual level, Schleiermacher voiced his concern that a confessional commitment would make the situation for many clergy, especially the most courageous ones, difficult if not unbearable. It would do so by interfering with the frank uninhibitedness of their research and communication. Only those parts in which all Protestant confessions perfectly agreed were essential to Protestantism as opposed to Catholicism. At the same time, Schleiermacher rejected the contention that confessions of faith should not have any proper value or characteristic merit, or should be ranked among the deliberations of minor religious disputations and individual dogmatic publications. As a corollary, he explicitly objected to the abolition of the separate Reformed and Lutheran confessions in favor of the sole validity of Scripture, since Scripture could only demonstrate the Christian character of a doctrinal statement, not that it was Protestant: "the symbolic books are the first in which the Protestant spirit was expressed in a public and permanent way, just as in Scripture the Christian spirit was first expressed in a public and permanent way."[76]

76. Ibid., 184. Incidentally, Elector Johann Sigismund of Brandenburg was one of the first to voice the view that the differences in doctrines are of subordinate importance in relation to the acknowledgement by both Protestant faiths of the Scripture principle. See Wappler, "Reformationsjubiläum," 103.

4

Correspondence and Publications
Pro and Contra Church Union

THE MAIN PLAYERS

FROM 1817 ONWARDS, A bitter controversy raged over the Prussian Church Union that King Friedrich Wilhelm III imposed that year, with Schleier-macher on one side of the debate and Lutheran theologians on the other. Lutheran confessionalism was very much on the rise at the time of the Prussian Church Union debates. The strict Lutherans' fear of what Brian Gerrish aptly termed "possible infection from the Reformed"[1] probably accounted for some of the uncompromising attitudes voiced in the debate. Whereas confessionalists strictly opposed any union, more moderate Lu-therans supported a union under the condition that a doctrinal consensus underpin the cultic union.

One of the most prominent anti-Unionists was Christoph Friedrich von Ammon (1766–1850). Born in Bayreuth, he studied at the University of Erlangen, and at the age of 23 he became Professor *extraordinarius* for philosophy there. Three years later, in 1792, he was admitted to the rank of Professor *ordinarius* of divinity, still at Erlangen. He then accepted a call to the University of Göttingen (1794–1804), which included the office of university chaplain. Having rejected further calls to Gießen, Greifswald, and Kiel, he returned to Erlangen in 1804. In 1808 Ammon also took on the office of superintendent in Erlangen. In 1809 a position as Bavarian church councilor followed, and in 1813 he was appointed chief court

1. Gerrish, "Schleiermacher and the Reformation," 190.

chaplain of Saxony at Dresden. This last position as Lutheran chaplain at the Catholic Royal Court of Saxony included the office of councilor in the Lutheran consistory of Dresden. Ammon remained court chaplain until 1849 and died in May 1850.

It is worth noting that, although the Saxon Royal Court under Friedrich August I (r. 1805–1827) was Catholic, the majority of the inhabitants of Saxony were in fact Lutheran. By 1817, Ammon had established himself as one of the most influential Lutheran church leaders in Saxony and beyond. He also enjoyed a reputation as a popular preacher for the educated elite, and as an influential church politician and prolific theological writer. However, he was notorious for a certain inconsistency of argument and conviction. Franz Wilhelm Dibelius noted that his "admirable flexibility of mind" combined with a certain flexibility of character.[2] He added that in particular during his later career, "a superficial verbosity had taken the place of his former impressive thoughts."[3] Ammon had started his career as a fierce defender of rationalist theology, but from 1813 onwards, he showed a marked tendency toward the supranaturalist side—only to return to rationalism in his old age, when that theological era was well and truly past.

Ammon and Schleiermacher, born within two years of each other, never met in person,[4] but they did occasionally correspond. In a letter of 1805, Ammon announced his interest in a scholarly exchange with Schleiermacher, who was then a junior professor at the University of Halle. In 1810, Schleiermacher, in his office as dean of the newly-founded University of Berlin, offered Ammon the chair of dogmatic theology. Ammon declined, despite the offer of a top salary. Schleiermacher and Ammon also corresponded about the issue of the Church Union, and, in the course of this correspondence, Ammon declared his support for that Union. Much to Schleiermacher's annoyance, in 1818 Ammon did a volte-face and published his book *Ueber die Hofnung einer freien Vereinigung beider protestantischer Kirchen: ein Glückwunschschreiben an den Herrn Antistes*[5] *Dr. Heß in Zürich* ("On the Hope of a Free Unification of Both Protestant

2. Dibelius, "von Ammon," 453.

3. Ibid.

4. In his publication *An Herrn Oberhofprediger D. Ammon* ("To Court Chaplain D. Ammon") Schleiermacher mentions explicitly that he does not "have the honor of being known to [Ammon] personally." Schleiermacher, *On Creeds, Confessions and Church Union*, tr. Nicol, 104.

5. *Antistes* was the title for the presiding officer of the synod in Reformed Swiss Churches.

Churches: A Congratulatory Epistle to Antistes Dr Hess in Zürich").
In this epistle, Ammon proceeded to outline his objections against the
Church Union.

Another opponent of Schleiermacher was the pro-unionist Karl
Gottlieb Bretschneider (1776–1848), also a Lutheran theologian and academic. He was born in Gersdorf, Saxony and spent all his working life in
Saxony. He started his career as a lecturer at the philosophy faculty at the
University of Wittenberg from 1804 to 1806. When the French army under Napoleon advanced into Saxony, he abandoned his university career
and started work as a pastor, and later as a superintendent. Bretschneider
eventually returned to academia, and in 1812 he was awarded a doctor-
ate. In 1816 he became the Lutheran chief superintendent in Gotha, Saxony, and the president of the Lutheran Synod. He even published a small
number of religious novels. Bretschneider made his name as an important
representative of rationalism with the publication in 1814 of his *Handbuch
der christlichen Dogmatik*. His published output was considerable, and his
writings are particularly notable for their balanced and unpolemical style.

Bretschneider was very much in favor of the Prussian Church
Union because in his view, the doctrinal differences between Lutherans
and Reformed had basically been overcome. But he vehemently rejected
Schleiermacher's argument that doctrinal disputes between the two Protestant confessions should be ignored with respect to achieving this union.
Instead, he insisted on debating any remaining differences in point of doctrine, if necessary in public. The issue whether doctrinal disagreements
were to be exposed and resolved, or whether they were to be ignored for
practical Christianity, was not simply a matter of opinion. Rather, this very
issue represented one of the deep fissions between Lutherans and Schleiermacher. Lutherans genuinely feared that serious negative consequences
would arise for practical Christianity from the doctrine of absolute predestination. Schleiermacher, for his part, did not share these concerns—quite
the opposite, in fact. He was convinced that doctrinal discussions had no
direct bearing on daily Christian life and should therefore be confined to
the area of scholarship. In a similar vein, Schleiermacher argued that communion celebrants did not need to have exactly the same understanding
of the precise meaning of communion and its elements.

CHRONOLOGY OF THE CONTROVERSY

Schleiermacher's 1819 essay "Ueber die Lehre von der Erwählung, besonders in Beziehung auf Herrn Dr. Bretschneiders *Aphorismen*"[6] ("On the Doctrine of Election, with Special Reference to the *Aphorisms* of Dr Bretschneider") is a direct response to Bretschneider's *Aphorismen über die Union der beiden evangelischen Kirchen in Deutschland* ("Aphorisms about the Union of the Two Protestant Churches in Germany") of the same year. However, Bretschneider's *Aphorismen* also marked the end of a series of both private and published letters about the Prussian Church Union, which Schleiermacher had exchanged with Ammon. A chronological listing of these texts will help illuminate the background of their exchange. Subsequently, a more detailed discussion of the published letters will be attempted.

28 October 1817: Ammon asks Schleiermacher in a private, unpublished letter for a statement clarifying his position toward the Prussian Church Union, which was announced in the cabinet order of King Friedrich Wilhelm III of 27 September 1817.[7] Ammon claims that, as editor of *Magazin für christliche Prediger* ("Journal for Christian Preachers"), he has received critical comments from readers, and that he is presently withholding these comments.

3 December 1817: Schleiermacher protests against Ammon's decision to suppress the critical comments concerning the Church Union. He urges Ammon, also in a private letter, to clarify his own position with regard to the Union.

12 December 1817: Ammon responds to Schleiermacher, again in a private letter.

Round about the same time, and parallel to this correspondence, Claus Harms (1778–1855), who served as archdeacon at St Nicolai Church in Kiel, published ninety-five theses against rationalism. Harms

6. The essay was originally published in the first issue of *Theologische Zeitschrift* in 1819. It was reprinted in Schleiermacher's *Sämmtliche Werke* ("Complete Works") Section I vol. 2 in 1836. Most recently it was edited for the new critical edition of Schleiermacher's works and published in *Theologisch–dogmatische Abhandlungen und Gelegenheitsschriften* (*Kritische Gesamtausgabe* Section I vol. 10), Berlin, New York, 1990. The first English translation, by Iain G. Nicol and Allen G. Jørgenson, is due to be published in 2012. For a detailed discussion of the text, see chapter 6 below.

7. See chapter 3, p. 43 above.

had become a fervent advocate of rational theology when he was a divinity student at the University of Kiel. Rather ironically, his reading of Schleiermacher's *Speeches*[8] convinced Harms that there had to be other reasons for salvation apart from self-betterment. Harms worked as a private tutor before becoming deacon and pastor of Lunden in 1806. His first two published volumes of sermons were translated into Danish and Swedish. In 1816 he was called to St Nicolai Church in Kiel, where he remained archdeacon until he became the main pastor in 1835. The previous year, he had rejected the offer of the office of chaplain at Trinity Church in Berlin, where Schleiermacher had served as co-pastor with the Lutheran Philipp Konrad Marheinecke (1780–1846) until his death in 1834.

Harms' tract, entitled *Das sind die fünfundneunzig Thesen oder Streitsätze Dr Luthers. Mit anderen fünfundneunzig Sätzen als mit einer Uebersetzung aus Anno 1517 in 1817 begleitet* ("These Are the Ninety-five Theses of Dr Luther. Accompanied by Another Ninety-five Theses and a Translation from the Year 1517 in 1817"), caused a considerable stir. Its publication deliberately coincided with the tercentenary of the publication of Martin Luther's ninety-five theses on the door of the Castle Church at Wittenberg on 31 October 1517. Harms intended his own theses to be regarded as an update of Luther's original text.

Harms' theses were a highly polemical attack against rationalism and a sharp protest against the Prussian Church Union. In theses seventy-five to ninety-five Harms argued vehemently against the Union. Proclaiming his own Lutheran confessionalism, he declared church union as such to be an apostasy. He insisted on the ecclesiastical and cultural identity of Lutheranism, which was to be based on Luther's theology and the Lutheran confessions of faith. To Harms, the historical confessions of all denominations formed an integral part of his understanding of culture. He demanded that the church be free to operate without intervention by state consistories. His attitude was diametrically opposed to Schleiermacher's. As Manfred Jacobs points out, he envisaged a Protestant entity in which citizens actively engage in political and religious affairs.[9]

Harms' theses were published in two German editions in 1818, and there was also a Dutch translation. More importantly, this publication triggered an international pamphlet war. Nearly 200 directly related tracts

---

8. *Über die Religion. Reden an die Gebildeten unter ihren Verächtern* ("On Religion: Speeches to its Cultured Despisers"), first published in 1799.

9. See Jacobs, "Entstehung und Wirkung," 35–36.

were published in the same year as the theses themselves.[10] The rationalists' contributions were particularly vitriolic.

On 17 November 1817, Ammon published an examination of Harms' theses with the rather clumsy title "Bittere Arznei für die Glaubensschwäche der Zeit. Verordnet von Herrn Claus Harms, Archidiaconus an der Nicolaikirche in Kiel, und geprüft von dem Herausgeber des *Magazins für christliche Prediger*" ("Bitter Medicine against the Contemporary Weakness of Faith. Prescribed by Mr Claus Harms, Archdeacon at Nicolai Church in Kiel, and Examined by the Editor of the *Journal for Christian Preachers*"). In this essay, Ammon endorsed Harms' anti-union, anti-rationalist position. However, the agreement with Harms, which was also signaled by the title of Ammon's essay, was merely superficial. Ammon's ultimate intention was to instrumentalize Harms' theses against a church union to launch an attack against the joint communion celebrations held in Berlin on 30 October 1817. His essay represented a thinly veiled criticism of Schleiermacher and his role in the instigation of the communion celebration.

To resume the chronology of the Schleiermacher–Ammon exchange:

7 February 1818: Schleiermacher publishes an open letter in response to Ammon's epistle of 12 December 1817, entitled *An Herrn Oberhofprediger D. Ammon über seine Prüfung der Harmsischen Sätze* ("To Court Chaplain D. Ammon On His Examination of Harms' Theses"). He recognizes Ammon's "Bittere Arznei" ("Bitter Medicine") for what it is, namely an anti-unionist tract. Schleiermacher virtually rips Ammon's arguments to pieces and sends a copy of his response to Ammon personally.

23 February 1818: Ammon, in turn, publishes his *Antwort auf die Zuschrift des Herrn D. Fr. Schleiermacher, ordentlichen oeffentlichen Lehrers der Theologie an der Universität zu Berlin, über die Prüfung der Harmsischen Sätze* ("Response to the Letter of Dr Fr. Schleiermacher, Full Public Professor of Divinity at the University of Berlin, on the Examination of Harms' Theses").

7 March 1818: In a private, unpublished letter, Ammon offers Schleiermacher the hand of peace.

Around 20 March 1818: Schleiermacher publishes his *Zugabe zu meinem Schreiben an Herrn Ammon* ("Supplement to My Letter to Mr Ammon"),

10. See Graf, "Restaurationstheologie," 69.

officially his last word on the matter. In a letter to his brother-in-law Ernst Moritz Arndt of 14 March 1818, Schleiermacher provides an insight into his opinion about both the correspondence and about Ammon: "I have been driven to get entangled in a theological feud because I cannot bear the hollow claims made by the Dresden Pope."[11]

12 April 1818: Ammon publishes his *Nachschrift an die Leser* ("Postscript to the Readers") and adds the text to the revised second edition of his *Antwort* of 23 February 1818.

30 July 1818: Ammon publishes a fourth, revised edition of *Bittere Arznei*.

12 August 1818: Schleiermacher rejects August Twesten's request for a public statement in favor of Harms.

The intention of both of Schleiermacher's publications, *An . . . Ammon* ("To Court Chaplain D. Ammon") and *Zugabe zu meinem Schreiben* ("Supplement to My Letter") is to steer away from polemics toward a serious discussion of the controversial doctrines of election and communion.

DETAILS OF THE CORRESPONDENCE

"Bitter Medicine against the Contemporary Weakness of Faith. Prescribed by Mr Claus Harms, Archdeacon at Nicolai Church in Kiel, and Examined by the Editor of the Journal for Christian Preachers" (17 November 1817)

The publication of this pamphlet signaled the start of Ammon's literary attack against the Prussian Church Union. He accused Schleiermacher of arbitrarily ignoring both Lutheran and Reformed doctrines, and of "enticing the nation to doctrinal indifference"[12] in his quest for that Union. The first part of the text is a polemic against rationalism in the Lutheran Church. Here, Ammon agrees with Harms' contention that godless morality is impossible to attain. Reason alone will never lead to a morally good life. Ammon quotes approvingly and at length from Harms' theses, even though some are simply nonsensical. For instance, Harms makes the cryptic statement, which Ammon cites without questioning: "the antichrist of our time with regard to faith is reason, which takes the moon for the sun."[13]

11. Meisner, *Schleiermacher als Mensch* II, 271–72.
12. Ammon, "Bittere Arznei," 439.
13. Ibid., 432.

Ammon also produces some irrational claims of his own in the course of his polemical tract. A case in point is the following statement: "Just as reason has prevented the Reformed from further developing their church and uniting it, the acceptance of reason into the Lutheran Church [through union with the rationalist Reformed] would only cause confusion and destruction there."[14] To maintain that the Lutheran Church was characterized by the entire absence of reason is as misguided as the claim that rationalism had obstructed a unity of different branches of the Reformed Church.

Ammon's real intention, his criticism of Schleiermacher and the part he played in the preparations for the Prussian Church Union, becomes obvious at the point at which Ammon takes a snipe at the Berlin Synod that planned the joint communion celebration. He infers that the Synod referred to the Moravians as an example for a unified community of Lutherans and Reformed who celebrate communion according to a ritual that satisfies both parties. Then he asks sarcastically: to which church would those congregations that have no particular confession of faith be assigned? His subtext is that those congregations are united by pious feelings, and that they celebrate communion according to mixed rites and with changing interpretations. Of course, Schleiermacher had been brought up in the Moravian community and did not fail to recognize Ammon's personal attack for what it was. In his two impartial reports of 1804 he had already noted that with the Moravians "the church union has long been realized. Lutherans and Reformed take communion jointly without any debate about changing confessions."[15] There, he had added passionately that it was absurd to view communion as a dogmatic expression in the first place. This would imply that only those who celebrate communion at the same time in the same way, and who simultaneously agree exactly about the doctrine of communion, should partake of it together. He concluded that this would mean that "one takes communion in order to bear witness to one's belief about the Eucharist."[16] Ammon ends his essay with the statement that "we freely admit that we ... are not able to believe in a complete union of those hitherto so closely related Churches."[17]

14. Ibid., 437.

15. Schleiermacher, *Zwei unvorgreifliche Gutachten*, 49.

16. Ibid., 51.

17. Ammon, "Bittere Arznei," 443.

"To Court Chaplain D. Ammon on His Examination of Harms' Theses" (7 February 1818)

Schleiermacher had already acquired a measure of fame for his pro-union position. Rulemann Friedrich Eylert, the court chaplain at Potsdam who had drafted the King's cabinet order of 27 September 1817, vividly described him as "hurling flashes of lighting and thunderbolts to the left and right, in front and behind him . . . like a church father that raises his protective hand in blessing over the united church."[18] Ammon's attack presented him with a welcome opportunity to explicate in detail his reasons for his endorsement of the Church Union.

As Martin Stiewe notes, Schleiermacher's response to Ammon's polemical and often irrational tract reflects the stance both of the academic teacher responsible for doctrinal issues, and of the chairman of the Berlin clergy, who was taking the lead on church union.[19] His epistle was quite defensive and certainly not provocative. It was also very elegant and profound in its refutation of most of Ammon's arguments. This observation might at first seem surprising, in particular in light of some comments Schleiermacher made in a letter to his friend Ludwig Gottfried Blanc (1781–1866) of 21 February 1818.[20] There, he confessed that Ammon had struck him as "obviously hypocritical and malicious," and as "dishonest." He also reported that Ammon had originally offered to collaborate in bringing the Union about. However, Schleiermacher added, he had not used this piece of information in his reply to Ammon because Ammon's offer had been made privately. Schleiermacher explains the non-provocative tone of his reply to Ammon in the same letter to Blanc. Here, he admits his intention to prevent Ammon from "some long-winded procedures that would lead nowhere,"[21] but that would inconvenience Schleiermacher himself. He refers here to the fact that he did not want Ammon to enter into a discussion about his dogmatic system and potential contradictions to his own publications such as the *Speeches on Religion*. At that time, Schleiermacher was already contemplating to produce a detailed presentation of his dogmatic system in a textbook.

Thus, in his open letter, Schleiermacher denies Ammon's main point of criticism about the union, that is, the alleged doctrinal indifference.

18. Stiewe, "Unionsverständnis," 32, n. 88.

19. See ibid., 32.

20. For the following, see Dilthey, *Schleiermachers Leben in Briefen* III, 230.

21. Ibid.

Schleiermacher demands that different interpretations of different Churches be retained and indeed emphasized. Despite such doctrinal differences, the Church Union should go ahead. Doctrinal matters are only of academic interest, and they have no relevance for practical Christianity. The only doctrinal differences Schleiermacher is concerned about are those between the Protestant and Catholic Churches.

Concerning the doctrine of predestination, Schleiermacher criticizes Ammon's stealthy maneuver of changing the topic from election to providence. As Schleiermacher points out, there have never been any differences about the doctrine of providence between Lutherans and Reformed. Ammon had quoted Calvin as ostensibly claiming that "the good is not grounded in the highest perfection of God, but in his unconditional arbitrariness."[22] Schleiermacher professes ignorance of the evidence of this quote in Calvin's writing. Ammon's interpretation was, of course, a distortion of Calvin's actual argument that everything was grounded in the unconditional will and decree of God. Schleiermacher proceeds to argue that Ammon's claim, even if correct, will lose its horror altogether once its deepest meaning is examined. He refers to the area of the hidden God, which has never been, nor would ever be, disputed between Lutherans and Reformed.

Joint communion was at the heart of the Prussian Church Union. Schleiermacher fully endorsed such celebrations, because within the Reformed Church allowances for different interpretations of the doctrine of communion had always been made. Such variations had been expressed in different confessions of faith. Nevertheless, Schleiermacher argued, Reformed joint communion celebrations had always taken place. In fact, some Reformed confessions, for instance the *Sigismund Confession* of 1614, inferred that the difference from the Lutheran interpretation had all but vanished. From this perspective, Schleiermacher saw no obstacle to joint Reformed and Lutheran communion celebrations.

Church union is to take place without reconciling dogmatic differences. As Schleiermacher states, "we explicitly acknowledge diversity as to dogma."[23] Therefore, negotiations about the Church Union are not to start with dogmatic issues; rather, dogmatics are to be ignored altogether. Schleiermacher concludes: "For my own part . . . I had no desire for this

---

22. Ammon, "Bittere Arznei," 440.

23 Schleiermacher, *On Creeds, Confessions and Church Union*, tr. Nicol, 130.

Union to take place if anybody had to abandon some aspect of one's religious notions."[24]

"Supplement to My Letter to Mr. Ammon" (around 20 March 1818)

Schleiermacher is curious to see what action Ammon will take once he has "recovered from the blow"[25] that Schleiermacher thinks he has dealt him with his tract "To Court Chaplain D. Ammon." He must be disappointed when Ammon's reply, *Antwort auf die Zuschrift des Herrn D. Fr. Schleiermacher . . . über die Prüfung der Harmsischen Sätze* ("Response to the Letter of Dr. Fr. Schleiermacher . . . about the Examination of Harms' Theses") appears on 23 February 1818. It does not properly engage with Schleiermacher's arguments, but continues with personal attacks and polemics instead. Ammon criticizes Schleiermacher for his alleged admission, that he adhered to the Reformed faith even while speaking as chairman of the Reformed Synod of Berlin. Schleiermacher, who actually became chairman of the Synod only after the joint service had taken place, declares Ammon's argument null and void. He also counters Ammon's concern that the Union might be seen as intending the suppression of the Lutheran Church: the Lutheran Church in Prussia is much too strong to be suppressed in the first place, and the Reformed Church has never had the intention of suppressing it at any rate.

Whereas Ammon wants doctrinal differences to be leveled out before any union negotiations take place, Schleiermacher reiterates his contention that "different opinions exist, but we join together in union because we consider the difference to be insignificant. We want to grant that both schools of thought exist side by side in the one Church and that each person should express his or her opinion when necessary."[26] Ammon's demand for a leveling of doctrinal differences also provokes Schleiermacher to ask how such a leveling could be achieved without first examining these differences in detail? It is possible that this particular question reflects his budding intention to proceed with the explorations of those differences. This intention would soon be turned into action with his own essay on election.

---

24. Ibid., 122.

25. *Aus Schleiermachers Leben in Briefen* III, 230.

26. Schleiermacher, *On Creeds, Confessions and Church Union*, tr. Nicol, 154.

In a letter to Ludwig Georg Blanc of 23 March 1818, Schleiermacher acidly refers to the correspondence with Ammon as "Ammoniana." He expresses the sincere hope that his own *Zugabe* will be the final word in this matter, and that Ammon, "conscious of his [own] lack of thoroughness and his waffle,"[27] will get a fright when he reads it. At any rate, Schleiermacher expects that his own silence as a reaction to Ammon's personal attacks will ensure that henceforth personal matters will not form part of the discussion.[28]

"Aphorisms about the Union of the Two Protestant Churches in Germany, Their Joint Communion Celebration, and the Difference between their Doctrine" (1819)

Karl Gottlieb Bretschneider begins his exposition on doctrinal issues with a summary of the debate, in which he recaps that Harms "threw the first stone at the work of the Union."[29] Then, he recalls, the exchange between Ammon and Schleiermacher ensued, and finally J. A. H. Trittin in Leipzig took up the gauntlet and, like Ammon in his "Reply" of 23 February 1818, asserted that the Union intended to subjugate the Lutheran Church to the Reformed Church.

Bretschneider then presents his own arguments. If the Union were to succeed, both Churches would have to yield. The Lutheran understanding of the oral intake of the substance of the body and blood of Christ during communion and the Reformed doctrine of unconditional election are both at stake. As far as Bretschneider is concerned, mainstream Lutherans have already essentially relinquished their interpretation of communion, and, likewise, the Reformed have abandoned the doctrine of double predestination. Bretschneider did have a point here. As early as 1798, the influential court and cathedral chaplain Friedrich Samuel Gottfried Sack (1738–1817) had stated in his *Promemoria* that the doctrines separating the two Churches had lost their importance: "Through the wise tolerance of the sovereigns, thank goodness, the two Protestant Churches in

---

27. Dilthey, *Aus Schleiermachers Leben in Briefen* III, 233.

28. A contemporary monograph by Gottlob Benjamin Gerlach with the promising title *Ammon und Schleiermacher oder Präliminarien zur Union*, published in 1821, unfortunately yields no information about the issue at hand. Instead, it is a lengthy explication of the author's understanding of human nature and religion between supranaturalists and rationalists.

29. Bretschneider, *Aphorismen*, 444.

the Prussian provinces are already so close and united that the difference between the two ecclesiastical systems has lost its former importance, and does not cause an essential separation among them anymore."[30] Sack's understanding did not represent an isolated position in 1798, and it did not do so twenty years later, either.

Bretschneider gained his understanding partly through publications by Reformed theologians. Rather than betraying any influence from the Calvinist theory of election, he notes, these writings instead included statements that were irreconcilable with that theory. Unfortunately for us, Bretschneider does not identify these sources. His understanding is also informed by the fact that Lutheran theologians had not moved an inch towards the Reformed theory. Thus, he reasons, there is no evidence to expect that Lutherans would ever yield their interpretation of the doctrine of election. Bretschneider therefore assumes that the time has come for both Churches to adapt their interpretation of the two doctrines that have traditionally divided them. That is, the Lutheran doctrine of communion would approach the Reformed interpretation, and the Reformed interpretation of predestination would move close to that of the Lutherans.

Even though the official confessions of each Church are still separate, the Lutheran and Reformed teachers agree in principle on doctrinal content. In this sense, Bretschneider suggests, a union has tentatively taken place already. The official Church Union event would simply be a public proclamation of a *fait accompli*. Under these circumstances, the Prussian Church Union appears to Bretschneider to be entirely desirable, feasible and acceptable.

However, he notes, the declaration of the Synod of Berlin concerning the joint communion on 30 October 1817 explained that a doctrinal union between Lutherans and Reformed was not even intended. Rather, such differences in doctrine as existed were to continue to exist. Moreover, Bretschneider points out, Schleiermacher defended the Calvinist theory of predestination, and he insisted that this theory had not been examined thoroughly enough. Bretschneider takes this to be yet another indication that the doctrinal differences are here to stay, at least for the time being. He concedes that his assumption concerning the inclination of the Reformed to relinquish absolute predestination is not only premature, but it is in fact unfounded.

He then proceeds to outline the differences between the Lutheran and Reformed interpretations of the doctrine. In a very lucid exposition

---

30. Wappler, "Reformationsjubiläum und Kirchenunion," 96.

he highlights both their common ground and their differences. Both hold that, as a result of the fall, humanity has lost its claim to blessedness. They agree that redemption is by grace through Christ only. They also share the experience that not everyone has faith. However, the Lutheran and Reformed arguments then diverge. Whereas the Lutherans hold that a human being's resistance against grace is the reason for their unbelief, the Reformed maintain that unbelief is grounded in God's decree. Bretschneider summarizes their respective positions very neatly: According to the Lutherans, God wants everybody to be saved, but not everybody wants it; according to the Reformed, all could be saved if God wanted it, but they won't because he doesn't.[31]

In the course of his exposition, Bretschneider is not only critical of the Reformed theory. He also claims that the Lutheran doctrine contradicts a central assertion of the Lutheran system of belief. This is the assertion that humanity cannot co-operate in its own salvation, that human beings naturally oppose God's grace, and that God's grace has to overcome this opposition. Bretschneider declares this assertion to be misguided. He reasons that, if it were true, it would entail that in cases where such an opposition has not been overcome, the reason for that person's unbelief would lie in God. Since he considers this to be effectively the Reformed stance, Bretschneider cannot bring himself to accept it. Instead, he comes to a highly unusual conclusion: Lutherans should abandon their traditional but untenable claim that human beings are utterly incapable of cooperating in their conversion.

In his opinion, it is inconsistent to retain the notion of humanity's complete incapacity for good after surrendering the doctrine of unconditional election. Two options present themselves: affirming the indispensability of grace and therewith unconditional predestination, or repudiating election and thus advocating synergism. Bretschneider decides in favor of the latter, and he urges his fellow Lutherans to do the same.

As Brian Gerrish points out: "Unconditional grace cannot be had without unconditional election."[32] For Bretschneider, divine grace and the human will cooperate toward moral improvement and ultimate salvation. Election is reduced to the notion that God foreknows a person's future decisions in favor of the gift of grace, and that God elects those persons to salvation. Bretschneider was thus a typical representative of the *fides praevisa* understanding of election.

31. See Bretschneider, *Aphorismen*, 451.
32. Gerrish, *Tradition*, 113.

Throughout his *Aphorismen*, Bretschneider was at pains to demonstrate how the Reformed theory contradicted moral sentiments and the ethical freedom of human beings. He concluded his essay with the prediction that, if both Lutheran and Reformed doctrines continued to exist simultaneously, their co-existence would put both the continuation and the peace of the Prussian Church Union at risk.[33]

33. See Bretschneider, *Aphorismen*, 463.

PART TWO

Schleiermacher's Exploration and Development of Election

5

Schleiermacher's Source Material

INTRODUCTION

SCHLEIERMACHER MAKES REFERENCE TO an astonishing total of forty-eight different theologians, statements of confession, and individual works in his essay on election and in the paragraphs on the origin, subsistence, and consummation of the church of *Christian Faith* (§§113–163). These individuals and texts obviously illustrate points and arguments in the discussion of different aspects of the doctrine of election, as well as more widely pneumatology, ecclesiology, and eschatology, and do not constitute sources in the sense that they give an insight into the genesis of either the essay or *Christian Faith*. As Martin Stiewe notes, Schleiermacher does not cite the confessions as "eternally valid and invariable systems, but as geographically and historically conditioned testimonies in need of further theological reflection."[1] They have no binding normative authority and, as Walter Wyman puts it aptly, "they do not constitute a Protestant *magisterium*,"[2] and they are "subject to critical assessment."[3] Nevertheless, they constitute important statements of faith of different Protestant perspectives, and as such Schleiermacher does take them seriously.

Collating and examining these sources is an opportune task, not only in order to demonstrate the breadth and depth of Schleiermacher's grasp of historical systematic theology, but in order to get an overview of how his interpretation of the doctrine of election differs from his sources, and

1. Stiewe, *Schleiermachers Unionsverständnis*, 101.
2. Wyman, "Role of Protestant Confessions," 357.
3. Ibid., 384.

to position it within the historical and contemporary context of available interpretations.

In his essay and in §§115–120 (On election) of *Christian Faith* alone, he refers to thirty-four sources. These texts were composed by European theologians of the Early Church, by first and second generation Reformers, by representatives of the age of Protestant Orthodoxy, and by Schleiermacher's own contemporaries. They span the entire spectrum of interpretations of predestination—apart from the theory of universal restoration. As source texts in the sense defined above, they implicitly demonstrate the variety of theories Schleiermacher was prepared to include in his union dogmatics.

There is hardly any relevant statement of confession and indeed any significant contemporary or historical dogmatic work that he does not refer to, either in the essay or somewhere within the wider discussion of the doctrine of the church in *Christian Faith*.[4] Nevertheless, there are some important confessions and dogmatic works he does not refer to either in the essay or in the paragraphs concerning the doctrine of election. These omissions and the reasons behind them will be discussed at the end of the following section, which will focus exclusively on sources cited in the essay on election and in §§115–120 (On election) of *Christian Faith*.

REFERENCES TO EARLY CHURCH FATHERS AND REFORMERS

Schleiermacher refers to four Early Church figures: Origen (185–254) is cited once with a quotation from his *Commentaria in Matthaeum* 11,17; John Chrysostom's (c. 350–407) *In Epistolam ad Hebraeos Homilia* and the Montfaucon edition of his *Opera* are mentioned; as is Gottschalk the Saxon (806/8–866/70); and, of course, Augustine of Hippo (354–430). Chrysostom is not known to have developed a particular understanding of election, whereas Origen is best known for his advocacy of universal restoration. Gottschalk, a German monk against his will, saw his task to be that of "proclaiming double predestination in its strictest form."[5] He argued that perdition was grounded in God's eternal decree as the just punishment for those who deny God.

---

4. A chronological list of all forty-eight sources Schleiermacher refers to, together with an indication of where he makes reference to them, is given in the Appendix.

5. Hägglund, *Geschichte der Theologie*, 117.

Augustine of Hippo is the church father whom Schleiermacher mentions most often. He cites his *De correptione et Gratia*, his *Enchiridion*, and his *De Genesi Contra Manichaeos*. Augustine squarely opposed the interpretation of original sin, grace, and free will as propagated by the representatives of the lay movement subsumed under the name Pelagianism. At the heart of the Pelagian Controversy, which sharpened the interpretation of predestination that Augustine had already developed, was the issue of original sin and its consequences. Augustine asserted that Adam's fall had a legal liability affecting all human beings, perverting free will, and making divine grace and the sacraments a necessity. Pelagianism held that Adam's sin only affected Adam himself, that humanity's free will remained intact, and that therefore grace was unnecessary for salvation. Augustine refined his doctrine of absolute predestination in his late works *De Predestinatione Sanctorum* and *De Dono Preservantiae*, both written in 429 AD. There he maintained that election was decreed from eternity by God's hidden counsel. While all were in Adam, only the elect were in Christ, and they were chosen out of the mass of perdition while the majority of human beings was left in perdition. This understanding is characterized by what James Wetzel calls Augustine's "uncompromising deference to a deity of selective compassion."[6]

Augustine's doctrine of predestination originated in St Paul's message of *sola gratia*, which he turned into a closed system of predestination with a causal chain of argumentation. Curiously, though, the very notion of reprobation is in profound contradiction to Augustine's doctrine of predestination. Election affirms God as a loving God by acknowledging him as the inspiration behind all human love of God. It would be hell for a person to desire God and never have that desire requited because the person is not among the elect. According to Augustine, no one comes to desire God unless God's grace is already at work in that person, and therefore there can be no pain of separation from God that is wholly without his grace. Nevertheless, Augustine maintained that this pain was an indication of reality, and thus of reprobation. Those who felt abandoned by God were in fact abandoned by him. Augustine's notion of reprobation is therefore flawed: it assumes both that human beings are capable of experiencing the pain of being forsaken by God and that the God of love has a motive for inflicting that pain.[7]

6. Wetzel, "Snares of Truth," 124.

7. See ibid., 129.

Of the first generation of Protestant Reformers, Schleiermacher cites Martin Luther and Philipp Melanchthon, whereas Huldrych Zwingli's works are referred to only in the section on ecclesiology proper (§§126–156) of *Christian Faith*, not in the section about election or in his essay. Luther's prefix to his exposition of the Epistle to the Galatians is quoted once, and one quote from Philipp Melanchthon's *Loci Communes* appears in §119.3.

It is instructive to note that, apart from John Calvin (1509–1564), individual Reformed theologians find no mention either in Schleiermacher's essay or in the relevant propositions of *Christian Faith*. Very clearly, this absence of Reformed dogmatics is grounded in the fact that Calvin's *Institutio* presents the most comprehensive and authoritative source for the Calvinist doctrine of predestination. Indeed, Calvin's *Institutio* is the most frequently cited source in Schleiermacher's essay, which has in excess of 40 quotes from that work.

Calvin was born a quarter of a century after Luther and Zwingli, and was thus an heir to the Reformation, or a second generation Reformer. His *Institutio Christianae Religionis* was first published in 1536 and was then revised four times.[8] The last edition of 1559 contains nearly four times as much material as the first. As I. John Hesselink notes, Calvin himself called his work "not a *summa theologiae* but a *summa pietatis*."[9] Initially intended as a guide to Scripture for the French King François I (r. 1515–1547), its purpose was pastoral rather than speculative.

In order to assess the importance of Calvin's doctrine of predestination within the system of his theology, it is crucial to determine the context in which he discusses it. His positioning of the doctrine varies considerably in the three main editions of the *Institutio*. In the first edition (1536), predestination is mentioned only in two places, namely in the explanation of the second article of the Creed and with regard to the definition of the church.[10] In the second edition (1539) it is more closely associated with ecclesiology, and there Calvin devotes an entire chapter to the discussion of providence and predestination, which follows an exposition of the work of salvation. In the last edition (1559) Calvin deals with the doctrine of predestination in Book III, which is concerned with the third article of the

---

8. Whereas the first Latin edition takes the form of a catechism, and subsequent ones (1539, 1543, and 1550) have loosely linked themes, the last one (1559) has a framework based on the Apostles' Creed. For this last edition, Calvin undertook a completely new organisation of his material in four books.

9. Hesselink, "Calvin's Theology," 77.

10. See Wendel, "Justification and Predestination," 161.

Apostles' Creed, or "the mode of obtaining the grace of Christ, the benefits it confers, and the effects resulting from it."[11] Now it appears in a pneumatological context. Book III discusses the doctrines of faith (chapter 2), penitence, confession, and atonement (chapters 3–5), the Christian life (chapters 6–10), justification and good works (chapters 11–18), Christian liberty (chapter 19), and prayer (chapter 20) before presenting the doctrine of predestination (chapters 21–24), which, in turn, is followed by resurrection (chapter 25). According to Charles Partree, with the 1559 edition predestination has become "formally and materially part of the understanding of salvation."[12] This positioning also signals the fact that the doctrine of predestination is not at the centre of the *Institutio*. More importantly, it is not at the centre of Calvin's theology.[13] For Calvin, predestination indicated a point of arrival, not a point of departure. Predestination was the last consequence of faith and trust in God's grace, rather than a conclusion of reason based on God's sovereignty. In this sense, it was actually a confession of faith. As Calvin himself stated: "Without the doctrine of gratuitous election, the faithful cannot adequately apprehend how great is the goodness of God by which they are effectively called to salvation."[14]

CONFESSIONAL STATEMENTS

Schleiermacher quotes from four Lutheran and eight Reformed confessions of faith. They all ultimately discriminate between the elect and the non-elect. The particular rather than universal success of salvation constitutes the very essence of their interpretation of predestination—not surprisingly, since universal restoration has never been accepted as orthodox. There are other similarities between individual confessions, but they also differ in a number of aspects.

One distinguishing factor is the construction of the doctrine either as *a posteriori* or as *a priori*. In the first case, that is according to the infralapsarian interpretation, the object of predestination is the fallen human race. Here, the doctrine is embedded within the framework of soteriology,

11. Calvin, *Institutes*, tr. Beveridge, 33.

12. Partee, "Calvin," 82.

13. Calvin's followers, beginning with his immediate successor in Geneva, Theodor Beza (1519–1605), repositioned predestination within the doctrine of God and thus awarded it a place and significance it did not have in Calvin's system.

14. Calvin, *Concerning Eternal Predestination*, tr. Reid, 58.

and a person's justification is understood as resulting from election. As Jan Rohls indicates: "The contingent act of justification of the sinner occurs because from eternity God has elected the sinner."[15] In other words, election is the condition for justification, and it can be discerned only *a posteriori*. Predestination to perdition becomes effective only after the fall.

In an *a priori* construction of the doctrine of predestination, God's pre-temporal decree rather than his soteriological action becomes the point of departure. Predestination in this case is integrated generally within the doctrine of God, and, more precisely, within the doctrine of divine decrees. Taken to its logical conclusion, this supralapsarian understanding implies that Adam's fall forms an integral part of the divine decree. In this case, both the fall and ultimate reprobation are decreed before the creation of the world, and the object of the decree is not fallen humanity, but the unfallen human race before creation.

None of the confessions Schleiermacher refers to are explicitly infralapsarian or supralapsarian. As Philip Schaff observes, of those confessions that deal specifically with predestination, all Lutheran and the majority of Reformed confessions "keep within the limits of infralapsarianism"[16] or at least affirm nothing that is inconsistent with infralapsarianism. In fact, only the *Hungarian Confession* (1557) and the *Consensus Genevensis* (1552),[17] neither of which Schleiermacher mentions, are explicitly supralapsarian confessions.[18]

Another way of distinguishing different approaches to the doctrine of predestination is by the quality of the underlying divine decree. The distinction is then between a single and a double decree, or a conditional and an unconditional decree. In this context it is vital to emphasize that the distinction is not between double and single predestination as such. None of the confessions that constitute Schleiermacher's sources teach double predestination in the sense that perdition is understood as a positive act of God's will. Such an interpretation would ultimately have to concede that God is the author of sin. Rather, predestination is always conterminous with eternal election to salvation. As Rohls observes: "Election and rejection are never subsumed under predestination as two species of the same."[19] The common concept encompassing both election and reproba-

15. Rohls, *Reformed Confessions*, tr. Hoffmeyer, 150.

16. Schaff, *Creeds* III, 635.

17. This confessional statement was penned by Calvin but signed by the ministers of Geneva.

18. See Rohls, *Reformed Confessions*, tr. Hoffmeyer, 152.

19. Ibid.

tion is that of the double decree, not of two separate divine acts. Even though it has not always been realized, there is also a soteriological aspect to the double decree: only this version offers the utmost guarantee for redemption by grace alone.

Single predestination, on the other hand, entails unconditional divine election to salvation combined with divine permission to leave the unelected to damnation because of their sin, their unbelief, or their rejection of the means of salvation. In this case, sin and unbelief, and therefore human demerit, are the precondition for damnation, whereas the reason for election to salvation is God's mercy. Nevertheless, both theories, unconditional and conditional predestination, entail that election to blessedness is entirely non-meritorious.

For our discussion of the different confessional statements cited by Schleiermacher, the distinction between an absolute double decree and a conditional decree will be more productive than that between infra- and supralapsarian tendencies of different confessions. It will reveal that, curiously, just about all[20] confessions adhering to a single decree of foreordination to salvation, with reprobation being caused by sin, were produced in German-speaking territories.[21] This particularity does not have a national or linguistic root. The Holy Roman Empire of the German Nation consisted of several hundred territories and did not constitute a nation in the modern sense, and German-speaking territories also included parts of Switzerland. Instead, this particularity emerged out of unionist tendencies of the Philippists and the German Calvinists, which resulted in the moderate interpretation of predestination that was characteristic of the German Reformed Church. The Reformed confessions produced in German-speaking territories, which affirmed either that predestination was not absolute, or which largely omitted any mention of reprobation, include the Upper German *Confessio Tetrapolitana* (1530), the Swiss *Confessio Helvetica Prior* (1536), the *Heidelberg Catechism* (1563), the Swiss *Confessio Helvetica Posterior* (1566), and the *Brandenburg Confessions* (1614–1645).

20. The *Thirty-nine Articles* of the Anglican Church are the only case of a non-German confession to maintain that there is a single decree of election to salvation. Interestingly enough, part of the intention for producing the *Thirty-nine Articles* was the mitigation of the Calvinist influence on the *Forty-two Articles* on which the *Thirty-nine Articles* were based.

21. The obverse case does not apply, however: Not all confessional statements produced in German speaking territories adhere to the single decree interpretation. Huldrych Zwingli's *Fidei Ratio* and the *Bremen Confession* or *Consensus Ministerii Bremensis* (1598) both represent a case in point.

Of the eight Reformed confessions Schleiermacher cited in his essay and in §§115–120 of *Christian Faith*, the *Canons of Dort* (1619), the *Confessio Gallicana* (1559) and the *Confessio Belgica* (1561) adhere to absolute predestination and the double decree. The *Confessio Helvetica Prior* (1556) and the *Thirty-nine Articles* (1563) do not go into detail about the reasons for reprobation, whereas the *Brandenburg Confessions*[22] state explicitly that the divine decree is not absolute, and that the reason for perdition is to be found outside God.

Lutheran statements of confession do not adhere to a double decree of election and reprobation but to a single decree of election only, with varying interpretations of the reason for perdition. The Lutheran symbolic books referred to by Schleiermacher comprise the *Confessio Augustana* (1530) with Melanchthon's *Apologia* (1531), the *Saxon Confession* (1551), and the *Formula of Concord* (1577).

Confessions Adhering to an Unconditional Double Decree

Without doubt, the *Canons of Dort* offer the strictest version of absolute predestination. "Of Divine Predestination" represents the first head of doctrine, a fact which in itself indicates the importance the doctrine assumed for the Reformed Church in the Low Countries. It states right at the outset that, since all human beings have sinned in Adam and lie under the same curse, God would have done no injustice by delivering all over to condemnation (1). Some receive the gift of faith and others do not; herein is displayed the decree of election and reprobation (6). The elect are by nature neither better nor more deserving than the others, and they are included with them in the same misery; their election has been decreed in order to demonstrate God's mercy (7). God's good-pleasure is the sole cause of their election (10). The others are those whom God in his free, just, irreprehensible, and immutable good pleasure has decided to leave in the common misery into which they have willfully plunged themselves. God condemns and eternally punishes them for their unbelief and for all other sins in order to demonstrate God's justice. This is the decree of reprobation, which declares God to be an awful, irreprehensible, and righteous judge and avenger (15).

It cannot be overstated that the *Canons of Dort*, like all other Reformed confessional statements, proceed from the assumption that as a

22. They consist of the *Sigismund Confession* (1614), the *Relation* produced at the Leipzig Colloquy (1631), and the *Declaration of Thorn* (1645).

result of the fall the entire human race has become utterly corrupt and sinful, and that its condemnation is therefore just. At the same time, and again like most other confessions, the *Canons of Dort* are careful to point out that the cause of sin, and hence of reprobation, does not lie in God, [23] but in the human race. The point of departure for the interpretation of the doctrine of predestination is the very existence of this *massa perditionis* and its just punishment, that is, eternal perdition. The common misery brought on by original sin and, in its wake, by actual sin is the *status quo*. However, God in his mercy has elected a certain number of persons to redemption. They are plucked out of the mass of those who are inevitably going to their just damnation. The rest are simply left to what would be everybody's inevitable punishment if it were not for God's mercy. There is therefore no active will of God to condemn the reprobate; they have caused their own misery and are punished for their sin according to God's justice. God's active will concerns only the elect. As a corollary, of course, God does not want to save everybody. God's eternal decree has two aspects, election and reprobation, and both serve to demonstrate God's glory and majesty.

In his essay on election, Schleiermacher states that he "deliberately refrained from drawing any quotations and justifications from the Synod of Dordrecht" on account of its "really harsh statements that, rather than clarifying the matter only obscure it, and that arose only on account of the fact that people there engaged with vacuous skill for disputation questions that were not derived from a clear perception of the matter."[24] His explanation for this programmatic omission is rather curious and does not convince. The Synod was called to settle the dispute between Calvinism and Arminianism and decided in favor of the former. The dogmatic discussions resulted in the formulation of the logical and systematic consequences from Calvin's interpretation of the doctrine. While the characterization of God as an awful avenger might be harsh, it adequately reflects the *Canons'* strict interpretation of the double decree. Ultimately, Schleiermacher disagreed with this interpretation and its particularism rather than with the "harsh expressions" used to formulate it. However, he did cite the *Canons of Dort* in *Christian Faith* (§120) to underpin his statement that foreseen faith was not the reason for election but God's good-pleasure.

---

23. Zwingli appears to have been the only Reformed theologian to draw "the logical conclusion from the deterministic approach and ultimately declaring God to be the author of sin as well." Rohls, *Reformed Confessions*, tr. Hoffmeyer, 152.

24. Schleiermacher, On the Doctrine of Election, tr. Nicol and Jørgenson, 97.

In both the *Confessio Gallica* (1559) and the *Confessio Belgica* (1561), the article on predestination appears in exactly the same context. It is positioned between anthropology and christology,[25] and thus in a soteriological context. Unlike the *Canons of Dort*, these two confessions do not refer to God as a terrible avenger. The *Belgic Confession* emphasizes that God manifests himself in election "such as he is: merciful . . . [and] just."[26] The *Confessio Gallica*, too, adheres explicitly to the *praedestinatio bipartita*, according to which predestination is a manifestation of both divine mercy and justice. The elect are elected "to display to them the riches of his mercy," while the non-elect are left in their condemnation "to show them his justice."[27] The *Confessio Gallica* also stresses the utter inability of human nature to "have a single good feeling, affection, or thought, except God has first put it into our hearts."[28] Otherwise, these two confessions are materially identical to the *Canons of Dort*. They assert the perdition of some, into which Adam's sin has cast the human race, and God's merciful election of others out of mere goodness according to his immutable decree.

Confessions Adhering to a Conditional Decree of Reprobation

The Reformed *Brandenburg Confessions*, which consist of the *Confession of Sigismund* (1614), the *Relation* of the Colloquy at Leipzig (1631), and the *Declaration of Thorn* (1645) reject the double decree. It is worth dwelling on the *Sigismund Confession* in particular, since this was the confession to which Schleiermacher subscribed at his ordination into the ministry of the Reformed Church.[29]

The *Sigismund Confession* is similar to Heinrich Bullinger's *Confessio Helvetica Posterior* (1566) in that it is a private statement of faith. Unlike Bullinger, however, Elector Johann Sigismund did intend his confession for publication and circulation from the outset. It signifies the culmination of a series of decisions and events that resulted in the Hohenzollern, the Brandenburg ruling house, becoming Reformed, whereas the vast

25. In the *Confessio Gallica* Article twelve, which deals with election, appears after the discussion of original sin (Articles ten and eleven) and precedes that of redemption by Jesus Christ (Article thirteen). In the *Confessio Belgica* Article sixteen (of election) follows the doctrine of original sin and precedes the doctrine of the recovery of fallen humanity.

26. Schaff, *Creeds* III, 401.

27. Ibid., 366.

28. Rohls, *Reformed Confessions*, tr. Hoffmeyer, 155.

29. See Gerrish, *Tradition*, 19.

majority of the population of Brandenburg remained Lutheran. Johann Sigismund produced his *Confession* in the wake of the reprint of the 1562 *Confession of the Reformed Churches of Germany*, and contended himself therefore with a discussion of the four articles of faith which he regarded as contentious between the Reformed and the Lutherans.

Johann Sigismund prefaced the doctrinal discussion with a brief introduction, in which he states his adherence to Scripture and to the word of God, to the Early Church symbols, and to "the *Augsburg Confession*, which in 1530 was presented to Emperor Karl V by the Protestant princes and estates and was subsequently necessarily revised and improved in several points."[30] This is a very clear reference to Melanchthon's 1540 *Variata*, in which the Philippist version of the doctrine of the real presence of Christ in communion approached very closely to the Calvinist one, and which was therefore acceptable to the Reformed. It can be conjectured that Elector Johann Sigismund's particular formulation, which explicitly mentions the *Augsburg Confession* and the year 1530, but not the name *Variata* or the date 1540, represents an effort to pacify his Lutheran subjects.

Having discussed the doctrines of the person of Christ, of baptism, and of communion, Elector Johann Sigismund then explicated his interpretation of the doctrine of predestination. Identifying eternal gracious election with God's predestination to eternal life, he acknowledged that this doctrine was "one of the most comforting of all"[31] because our blessedness was founded on the fact that out of pure grace and mercy and without regard to human merits God had foreordained and elected all who consistently believed in Christ to eternal life. According to God's strict justice, God had overlooked those who did not believe in Christ and had "prepared the everlasting hell fire for them."[32] However, having cited scriptural proof of this assertion, Johann Sigismund immediately qualifies it by emphasizing that God is not a cause for the destruction or perdition of human beings. Indeed, Johann Sigismund explicitly rejected the Reformed interpretation that God's will to salvation was particular: "not that he did not want all to be saved."[33] Instead, the cause of sin and perdition was to be found in Satan and the godless, who, on account of their unbelief and disobedience, had been repudiated by God to damnation. It is clear from this

30. Heppe, *Bekenntnisschriften*, 286.

31. Ibid., 292.

32. Ibid. Warfield's translation, "prepared *them for* the everlasting fire of hell" is inaccurate. Warfield, "Predestination," 82.

33. Heppe, *Bekenntnisschriften*, 292.

statement that Johann Sigismund understood predestination to be a single decree to salvation, and that for him perdition was conditioned by the shortcomings of human beings. Nevertheless, he reiterated and clarified his position between the Lutheran and the strict Calvinist interpretations in the following paragraph. He rejected the Lutheran understanding that God had elected some *propter fidem praevisam*, i.e. on account of foreseen faith,[34] as well as the strict Calvinist version that God begrudged the best part of the human race salvation, and that he condemned absolutely, without any cause, and not on account of sin either. Johann Sigismund then explicitly stated that "God according to his strict righteousness has overlooked from eternity all those who do not believe in Christ,"[35] and that the "righteous God has not decreed anybody to damnation except because of sin, and therefore the decree of reprobation to damnation is not to be regarded as an *absolutum decretum*, a free, independent decree."[36]

The *Sigismund Confession* together with the *Heidelberg Catechism* of 1563 came to be regarded as the ultimate statement of confession of the German Reformed Church. Its moderate treatment of the doctrine of predestination demonstrates in an exemplary way how "Calvinism and Philippism fuse to found a specifically German Reformed confessional tradition."[37] This tradition is characterized by its moderate interpretation of the doctrine of predestination as an unconditional decree to salvation, while perdition is understood as conditioned by human sin, not as part of the divine decree. Obviously, Elector Johann Sigismund was not the first German Reformed to adhere to this interpretation. He founded his Confession on the *Confession of the Heidelberg Divines* of 1562. In its earliest surviving form of 1607, that Confession discusses predestination (Articles 27 to 29) only in terms of eternal gracious election: "For it is certain and infallible that all those who believe in Christ and, without hypocrisy, repent, have been elected to eternal life."[38] The *Confession of the Heidelberg Divines* does not even mention those outside Christ, nor does it hint at reprobation or perdition in the relevant articles. Johann Sigismund's statement of faith fills in these gaps, but decidedly not according to the strict Calvinist interpretation.

---

34. Sigismund characterized this position as Pelagian.
35. Heppe, *Bekenntnisschriften*, 292.
36. Ibid., 293.
37. Rohls, *Reformed Confessions*, tr. Hoffmeyer, 10.
38. Heppe, *Bekenntnisschriften*, 256.

For the deliberations at the Leipzig Colloquy (1631) the *Augsburg Confession* formed the starting point. The official statement produced by the Reformed divines from Brandenburg and Hesse, and the Lutheran theologians from Electoral Saxony, discussed each article of the *Confessio Augustana*. They formulated the points on which both factions agreed, and produced different statements where they did not. The doctrine of election had not been an issue in the early days of the Protestant Reformation, and so neither the 1530 *Invariata* nor the 1540 *Variata* expressly touched on it. However, a century later it had become very much a bone of contention and the theologians at the Leipzig Colloquy deliberated the doctrine in detail. The result of their discussions was that the Reformed and the Lutheran parties agreed (even down to the very wording of some of the points) on the following: that from eternity God had elected not all, but some human beings to eternal blessedness; that their number and names were known to God alone; that election had no cause in the elect themselves but happened entirely by divine grace; that there was no absolute decree; and that an individual could not be assured of election "*a priori*, out of the hidden decree of God, but only *a posteriori*, out of the revealed word of God."[39] This verbatim agreement between both factions continued with a slight but significant difference. The Lutheran text read ". . . and out of [their] faith in Christ,"[40] whereas the Reformed version had ". . . and out of [their] faith and fruits of faith in Christ"[41]—a characteristically Reformed aspect of the doctrine of predestination that would eventually be expressed in the Protestant work ethics.

The Reformed Brandenburg-Hesse statement, the *Relation*, differed from the Lutheran one of Electorate Saxon in one important aspect: the Reformed insisted that election to salvation was entirely gracious. God had "foreseen no cause, or occasion, or preceding means, or condition of such election in the elect themselves, neither their good works, nor their faith, nor even the first salvific inclination, movement or consent to faith."[42] The Lutherans, on the other hand, asserted that God had "from eternity elected those of whom he saw that they would believe in Christ in time by the power and operation of his word and spirit."[43]

---

39. *Colloquium Lipsiense*, [13] and [14].
40. Ibid. [14].
41. Ibid. [13].
42. Ibid.
43. Ibid. [14].

The essence of these two statements presented a remarkable development. In earlier disputes between Calvinists and Lutherans about predestination, the point of departure had always been the reason for perdition: the Calvinist doctrine had asserted the absolute double decree, whereas the Lutheran version had directed the cause of perdition away from God and had put it firmly on the side of human sinfulness. In other words, the debate had been about the absolute versus a conditional decree. At the Leipzig Colloquy, the Reformed party agreed with the Lutherans that there was no absolute decree, and that perdition was caused by sin, impenitence, and unbelief. There was a trivial difference in that the Lutherans only mentioned the repudiation and damnation of the unbelievers, whereas the Reformed asserted that God had ordained those who persist in their sins and unbelief to everlasting damnation and repudiated them. Nevertheless, the Leipzig Colloquy signaled a paradigm shift: now the reason for election rather than the reason for reprobation became the point of departure. The Reformed insisted on *sola gratia*, one of the most important achievements of the Protestant Reformation, whereas the Lutherans brought foreseen faith into the bargain. This was not in itself a new insight, since the *Formula of Concord* (1577) had already discussed foreseen faith as a precondition of election. What was new was that, despite the conciliatory and moderate new interpretation of predestination by the German Reformed, there still was yet no agreement with the Lutheran interpretation.

This *status quo* remained intact well into Schleiermacher's time and, if anything, was entrenched by the insistence of Schleiermacher's Lutheran contemporaries on the human ability to reject actively the means of grace, and hence their refutation of the another crucial insight of the Reformation, the irresistibility of grace.

The Reformed statement of confession produced at the 1645 Colloquy at Thorn, the *Declaratio Thoruniensis* or *Declaration of Thorn*, constitutes the third and last part of the *Brandenburg Confessions*. It consists of the *Generalis Profession* and the *Specialis Declaratio*. The latter deals with agreements with and differences from the Lutheran and Roman Catholic faiths. No separate article was devoted to the doctrine of predestination, but election was discussed under the heading "Of Grace." The *Declaration* reiterates in Article 7 that God "has from eternity elected us in Christ, not of any foreseen faith or merit of works or disposition, but out of mere and undeserved grace,"[44] and in Article 8 that "[t]he rest, who hold back the truth in unrighteousness and contumaciously spurn the offered grace of

---

44. Warfield, "Predestination," 85.

Christ, [are] rejected in righteous judgment."[45] The *Declaration of Thorn* also affirmed the Reformed, and indeed Lutheran, understanding that salvation is particular. That is, although Christ's death and merit are sufficient for all, not all receive the benefit of his death, and the cause of this lies in human beings themselves. The Lutheran view that the elect were chosen because of a foreseen disposition to faith in them was rejected, but the *Declaration* affirmed that in election, faith was foreseen in the elect as a means of salvation foreordained in them rather than a cause for their election. It also rejected the strict Calvinist absolute decree: "in reprobation . . . not only original sin, but also, so far as adults are concerned, unbelief and contumacious impenitence are not, properly speaking, foreordained by God, but foreseen and permitted in the reprobates themselves as the meritorious cause of desertion and damnation, and reprobated by the justest [sic] of judgments."[46] In summary, the *Declaration of Thorn* upheld the principles of *sola gratia*, unconditional election to grace, and conditional reprobation by divine permission, and it rejected foreseen faith as a cause of salvation. In these aspects it was in full agreement with the *Relation* of the Leipzig Colloquy; the only material difference was that the latter retained the irresistibility of grace, whereas the *Declaration of Thorn* appeared to concede the possibility of the rejection of grace.

Confessions without a Doctrine of Reprobation

The *Confessio Helvetica Posterior* (1566), abbreviated 'Expos. Simpl.' by Schleiermacher after its Latin title *Confessio et Expositio Simplex Orthodoxae Fidei, et Dogmatum Catholicorum Syncerae Religionis Christianae*, had a clear infralapsarian bias. The doctrine of election (Article 10) commenced the section on soteriology and preceded christology. As in the confessions discussed above, it appeared immediately after the articles on creation, the fall, and the unfree will, that is after the section on anthropology. There are two crucial differences between this confession and the ones previously discussed: the text was composed in the first rather than the third person, and thus, at least rhetorically, included both the composer and the readers or listeners among the elect: "Therefore, not without means, though not on account of any merit of ours, but in Christ, and on account of Christ, God elected us."[47] The *Confessio Helvetica Posterior* was silent

45. Ibid.
46. Ibid., 87.
47. Ibid., 79.

on the topic of perdition, asserting only that "they are reprobates, who are without Christ."[48] It showed an almost Lutheran slant where it stated that "we must nevertheless hope well of all, and not rashly number any among the reprobates."[49] This phrase obviously had a pastoral element, but it also expressed at least the hope that the divine will to salvation was universal, which decidedly jarred with the Reformed doctrine of the particularity of the divine will to salvation.

It is my contention that the view expressed in the *Confessio Helvetica Posterior* was motivated by the fact that it arose out of a non-public exercise. Penned by Heinrich Bullinger as his private confession, it was not the result of doctrinal disputes, but an explication of Bullinger's own faith written from his and his fellow believers' perspective; hence the first person plural pronoun and the pastoral concern about those who might not be part of the elect. The fact that the confession was widely adopted as one of the most important Reformed symbolic books in Europe is a reflection of its popular reception, not of its initial intention. It was only on account of its moderate stance that Elector Friedrich III of the Palatinate could employ it at all at the 1566 Diet of Augsburg in order to demonstrate the agreement of the Reformed Palatine Church with Protestant Churches abroad. Finally, the *Confessio Helvetica Posterior* numbers among those confessions produced in German-speaking territories that adhere to fore-ordination to salvation without explicit reference to reprobation.

The Anglican *Thirty-nine Articles*, established by a church convocation in 1563, presented a summary of the doctrines of the Anglican Church. Based on the *Forty-two Articles* drafted under the direction of Archbishop Thomas Cranmer in 1553, the *Thirty-nine Articles* were finally accepted by Parliament in 1571. They dealt with the doctrine of predestination in the context of justification. "Of Predestination and Election" (Article 17) appeared after the Article on sin and preceded that on salvation. Predestination to life was defined as the decree hidden from human beings by which God had delivered the elect chosen in Christ "out of mankind"[50] from curse and damnation. Article 17 asserted further that for those who lack the spirit of Christ it was "a most danngerous downefall [sic],"[51] or snare, to have the sentence of predestination constantly before their eyes, and that the devil used it to drive them to desperation. Reprobation was

48. Ibid.
49. Ibid., 80.
50. Schaff, *Creeds* III, 497.
51. Ibid., 497.

not mentioned at all, let alone foreordination to perdition. Incidentally, in his essay on election, Schleiermacher did not mention the *Thirty-nine Articles*. He referred to them only once in the section on election in *Christian Faith*, where he quoted the Latin definition: "Predestination to life is the eternal purpose of God, whereby . . . he has consistently decreed those whom he has chosen in Christ . . . to bring through Christ to eternal salvation."[52]

The Lutheran *Confessio Augustana* did not explicitly deal with predestination, because in 1530 there was no public controversy regarding this doctrine among the divines who composed it. Article II, on original sin, affirmed that after Adam's fall all human beings were born sinful, "that is, without the fear of God,"[53] and that this sin brought eternal death on all who were not born again by baptism and the Holy Spirit. Article XVIII dealt with the free will. It taught that free will had "no power to work the righteousness of God, or a spiritual righteousness, without the Spirit of God."[54] Schleiermacher quoted precisely these two articles in his essay on election. He made no reference to the *Confessio Augustana* in *Christian Faith* §§115–120, only in the ensuing section dealing with ecclesiology proper. Both Articles II and XVIII of the *Confessio Augustana* are at least indirectly relevant to election. Article II insists on the total corruption of the human race and on the eternal death of the unregenerate, and Article XVIII is crucial with regard to the *sola gratia* aspect of righteousness. Article V, about the ministry of the church, encapsulates the concept of the irresistibility of grace. It famously states that the Holy Spirit "worketh faith where and when it pleaseth God, in those that hear the gospel."[55] It is worth mentioning that in his 1540 *Variata* version of the *Augsburg Confession* Melanchthon omitted the phrase "where and when it pleases God."

Melanchthon produced his *Apologia* (1531) as a response to the Roman Catholics' confutation of the *Augsburg Confession*. It did not raise any new points of controversy but dealt with the doctrines disputed at the 1530 Diet of Augsburg. As a result, it did not discuss the doctrine of predestination, either. Neither did the *Saxon Confession* (1552), produced by Melanchthon for the Council of Trent as a reiteration of the *Augsburg Confession*. Schleiermacher referred to the latter at the start of §119 of *Christian Faith*.

---

52. Schleiermacher, *Christian Faith*, tr. MacIntosh and Stewart, §119, 546.
53. Schaff, *Creeds* III, 8.
54. Ibid., 18.
55. Ibid., 10.

Not surprisingly, the *Formula of Concord* (1577) was the Lutheran confession that Schleiermacher mentioned most frequently, both in his essay and in *Christian Faith* in the propositions regarding election. The *Formula of Concord* consists of two parts, the *Epitome Articulorum* and the *Solida Declaratio*. The first is a concise summary of the Lutheran articles of faith. Each article is subdivided into a positive statement, the *affirmativa* or accepted teaching, and the *negativa* or rejected teaching. The lengthy second part, the "Solid Repetition and Declaration," offers an in-depth discussion of each article presented in the *Epitome*, and it augments them with quotations from Scripture, from the Early Church fathers, from older Lutheran symbols, and from private writings of Martin Luther.

Unlike the *Augsburg Confession*, the *Formula of Concord* devotes an entire article to the doctrine of predestination. The affirmative theses make the following points:[56] Divine foreknowledge and predestination must be distinguished (1); foreknowledge extends to both good and evil human beings (3), whereas predestination is identical with eternal election and extends only to a good human being (4). Election is the cause of salvation (4), but foreknowledge is not the cause of perdition; human beings ought to impute perdition to themselves (3). There is no hidden divine decree (5), and the decree of predestination is to be searched for in the revealed word of God (6). The divine will to salvation is universal (7). The ungodly condemn the word of God and "foreclose to the spirit his ordinary way." As a consequence, they have to be seen as the cause of the damnation. Neither God nor his election is to blame if they perish (11). The eternal election of God is to be sought in Christ (12); it is not grounded in any human merit whatsoever (13). The negative theses reject a particular will to salvation, the decree of reprobation, and any position that there is any cause for election to salvation in human beings. The article concerning predestination in the *Formula of Concord* represents the orthodox Lutheran interpretation of the doctrine of election.

Confessions not Mentioned by Schleiermacher

One Reformed statement of confession in particular is not mentioned either in Schleiermacher's essay or in §§115–120 of *Christian Faith*—although he referenced it several times in the section on ecclesiology proper (§§126–156): the *Heidelberg Catechism* of 1563, according to Frauke Thees "the most important Reformed doctrinal and confessional text in

56. For the following see Schaff, *Creeds* III, 165–72.

the German language."[57] This apparent omission is simply a reflection of the fact that the *Heidelberg Catechism* is virtually silent on the doctrine of predestination. Drafted as a unionist document intended to reconcile the conflicting Protestant factions in Electoral Palatinate and Germany more generally, it endorsed only "the positive part of free election of believers, and [was] wisely silent concerning the decree of reprobation, leaving it to theological science and private opinion."[58] As a catechism, it also served a different purpose from a confession of faith, and accordingly it centered on the human perspective. Its three parts deal with the misery of human beings, the redemption of human beings, and their response to the gift of redemption in word and deed.[59] There are allusions to election in several of the 129 questions, and a few to perdition, but indications of an eternal decree of reprobation or of the particularity of salvation are entirely absent. As Bard Thompson points out, the doctrine of election is "made subservient to the controlling idea of comfort,"[60] as the first article, or answer to question 1, demonstrates: "I, . . . both in life and death, am not my own, but belong to my faithful Savior Jesus Christ, who with his precious blood has fully satisfied for all my sins, and redeemed me from all the power of the devil; and so preserves me . . . that all things must work together for my salvation. Wherefore, by his Holy Spirit he also assures me of eternal life . . ."[61] Article 31 affirms that Christ has fully revealed God's hidden decree and will regarding our redemption. Christ has redeemed our body and soul from eternal damnation and has attained for us God's grace, righteousness, and eternal life (37).[62] With reference to the second coming of Christ, article 52 affirms that as a judge Christ "will cast all his enemies, who are therefore my enemies as well, into everlasting damnation; . . . but shall take me with all the elect[63] to him into heavenly joy and glory."[64] Election is most clearly adduced within the context of the doctrine of the church. The answer to question 54, "What do you believe of the holy catholic Christian church?" states that "[t]he son of God has gathered, protects and preserves an elected community to eternal life,

---

57. Thees, "Catechismus," 69.

58. Schaff, *Creeds* I, 454.

59. See Plasger and Freudenberg, *Reformierte Bekenntnisschriften*, 152–53.

60. Thompson, "Palatine Church Order," 347.

61. Warfield, "Predestination," 81.

62. See Plasger and Freudenberg, *Reformierte Bekenntnisschriften*, 160, 162.

63. *Auserwählte*.

64. Plasger and Freudenberg, *Reformierte Bekenntnisschriften*, 165.

. . . and that I too am and shall forever remain a living member of this community."[65]

As these passages demonstrate, the *Heidelberg Catechism* is devoid of a fully developed doctrine of election. It is also another example of Reformed confessions produced in German speaking territories that do not affirm reprobation.

LUTHERAN DOGMATIC WORKS AND THEIR AUTHORS

Apart from Christoph Friedrich von Ammon's *Ueber die Hofnung einer freien Vereinigung beider protestantischer Kirchen: ein Glückwunsch-schreiben an den Herrn Antistes Dr. Heß in Zürich* (1818) and Karl Gottlieb Bretschneider's *Aphorismen über die Union der beiden evangelischen Kirchen in Deutschland*, which, for obvious reasons, Schleiermacher cited frequently in his essay, there are five Lutheran theologians whose explicitly dogmatic works he used as source texts for his discussion of election.[66] Of these, four are by Schleiermacher's contemporaries, two of whom, in turn, were his colleagues. The other one, by Johann Gerhard (1582–1637), belongs to the period known as Protestant Orthodoxy. This period is usually dated from the late sixteenth to the end of the seventeenth century. Its onset is signaled by the publication of the *Book of Concord* in 1580. After the heyday of Protestant Orthodoxy in the early to mid-seventeenth century, it was superseded first by Pietism and eventually by the Enlightenment. The all-pervasive basic tenet of Orthodoxy was the crucial importance of "the true and transparent teaching about God and his revelation for the church as well as for individual believers."[67] Accordingly, theology concentrated on dogmatics and apologetics, and, within this field, particularly on the doctrine of justification by grace alone. Dogmatic textbooks, which had traditionally been structured according to central theological concepts or *loci*, were now organized analytically. The entire dogmatic material was arranged according to one overall topic, the salvation of humanity, as the ultimate aim of God's actions.[68] This type of theology was a response

---

65. Ibid., 166.

66. Three more theologians who find entry into his essay—Johann Gottlieb Töllner, Gustav Friedrich Wiggers, and August Detlev Twesten—are mentioned there because of other, non-dogmatic works. See p. 96 below.

67. Greschat, "Orthodoxie und Pietismus," 10.

68. See ibid., 11.

to the persistent differentiation and resulting conflicts between various Lutheran parties, in which Orthodox Lutherans accused Philippists of watering down Martin Luther's original teaching. The spread and success of Calvinism, as well as mounting pressure from Rome intensified the inner uncertainty Lutherans felt. At the same time, and as a result of the Peace of Augsburg of 1555, the strict delimitation of denominations meant that the confession adopted by a territorial sovereign would have to be adopted by all his subjects. That confession not only characterized the entire life and outlook of such subjects, but it also escalated the existing mistrust, prejudice, and enmity against other denominations. It was in this climate of political and psychological pressure from the counter reformation and the successful advance of Calvinism in Germany that Johann Gerhard, whom Jörg Baur calls the "classic of orthodox theology of the confessional era,"[69] developed his theology of Lutheran Orthodoxy.

Gerhard studied divinity at Jena from 1603 and in 1606 accepted the post of pastor and superintendent in Heldburg in southern Thuringia, and that of general superintendent in Coburg as a protégé of Johann Casimir, Duke of Saxe-Coburg (r. 1596–1633). In 1616, five years after Johann Casimir had refused to allow Gerhard to follow the first call he received as divinity professor to the University of Jena, he was finally introduced there. He taught at Jena until his death in 1637. Apart from his *Loci Theologici* (1610–22), which are discussed below, Johann Gerhard's *Confessio Catholica* (1633–37) is worth mentioning in the context of Lutheran Orthodoxy. Characterized as an "arsenal for confessional disputes in which the title of both Protestant and Catholic is claimed for the teaching of the Lutheran Church,"[70] this work is distinguished by its bitter polemics against the Roman Catholic Church.

Gerhard's nine-volume *Loci Theologici*, first published between 1610 and 1622, represents his major dogmatic work; it is also the text that Schleiermacher refers to[71] in both his essay and in §§115–120 of *Christian Faith*. Begun while he was a minister in Heldburg and finished in Jena, it is a comprehensive framework of dogmatics adhering to the teaching of the *Formula of Concord*. Book II deals with election and reprobation after an exposition of the doctrines of creation and providence. The doctrine of predestination, in turn, is followed by the discussion of the image of God in human beings, original sin, actual sins, and free will. In the section

69. Baur, "Johann Gerhard," 99.

70. Ibid., 115.

71. Schleiermacher quotes from the 1768 Cotta edition of Gerhard's *Loci*.

on predestination (chapter 10) Gerhard asserts the universality of God's mercy (heading IV), Christ's merit (heading VI), and the calling of human beings (heading VII). He insists that reprobation is not absolute (heading X) and defines predestination as "a single act of God, through which, before the foundation of the world had been laid, out of pure grace, men who would believe are effectively decreed to salvation. The reprobate are those whom God foresaw would remain in unbelief and unrepentance; their eternal fate is just because of their sins."[72] This definition represents the essence of the doctrine of predestination according to Lutheran Orthodoxy.

Of the four contemporaries of Schleiermacher whose dogmatic works he mentioned in his essay on election, Gottlob Christian Storr (1746–1805) was the earliest. In 1775 he became Professor *extraordinarius* for philosophy and two years later also for divinity at the University of Tübingen; in 1786 he was appointed to a full professorship. His accession to the divinity faculty at Tübingen marked the beginning of a new epoch there. Storr, according to Dietz Lange a "gruff Württemberg Pietist,"[73] was one of the foremost representatives of conservative supranaturalism. He demanded that there be no concessions to the rationalist zeitgeist in dogmatics, and that all teaching be based exclusively on Scripture.[74] The supranaturalists insisted on the necessity of revelation not only against contemporary rationalists but also against Enlightenment insights and Kantian philosophy. Storr later served as city pastor and in 1797 was appointed chief court chaplain at Stuttgart.

Schleiermacher made repeated reference to Storr's *Doctrinae Christianae Pars Theoretica et Sacris et Literis Repetita*, first published in Latin in 1793. The first German translation by Carl Christian Flatt appeared under the title *Gottlob Christian Storrs . . . Lehrbuch der christlichen Dogmatik* in 1803; by 1836 the second English as well as an American edition based on the first English one had appeared, entitled *Elementary Course of Biblical Theology*. This work represents the last eighteenth-century effort to defend Christian dogmatics in its orthodox interpretation, but methodologically

---

72. Gerhard, *Loci Theologici* I, Book II, col. 169.

73. Lange, "Neugestaltung," 87.

74. It is worth noting that the Translator's Preface to the English edition of 1836 mentions precisely this characteristic where he writes about Storr's "humble and faithful . . . adherence to the doctrines of the Bible," and that he and Flatt "were taught the absolute necessity of building their faith exclusively on the word of God." Storr, *Elementary Course*, 3.

Storr had already turned his back on the scholasticism of the older Lutheran Orthodoxy[75] as represented by Johann Gerhard.

Storr's *Elementary Course* is subdivided into five books, which discuss the divine authority of the Holy Scriptures (I), God (II), created rational beings (III), Jesus Christ the Redeemer of human beings (IV), and reformation of human beings and its relation to their salvation (V). Whereas a whole chapter of book II is dedicated to providence, predestination is not discussed as a doctrine in its own right. Given that Scripture does not expound a fully developed system of predestination, and given that Storr's supranaturalist stance induced him to follow Scripture closely in his dogmatics, this is not surprising. Nevertheless, predestination is mentioned as an example under the heading "God is not in any sense the cause of the ruin of those who are lost"; this section is, in turn, embedded in "The provision made by God for the salvation of man" and is followed by the book on christology.

Franz Volkmar Reinhard (1753–1812) was the only contemporary of Schleiermacher quoted both in the essay and in §§115–120 of *Christian Faith*. Reinhard was a professor of theology at Wittenberg for twelve years from 1780. His fame, such as it was, rested on his preaching as Saxon chief court chaplain in Dresden from 1792. Theologically, like Storr, Reinhard was an outspoken representative of supranaturalism. He opposed rationalism because, as Nicol and Jørgenson argue, he "saw reason at its best in relationship to revelation, wherein the latter limited the former."[76] Reinhard's *Vorlesungen über die Dogmatik* ("Lectures on Dogmatics"), first published in 1801, went through several editions, some of them posthumously. The fourth edition of 1818 was edited "with literary additions" by Johann Gottfried Emmanuel Berger and "amended with new literary additions" by Heinrich August Schott, a professor of theology at the University of Jena. A year after their first publication the lectures were republished as *Grundriß der Reinhardischen Dogmatik, zunächst für Gymnasien und Schulen, in einem gedrängten Auszuge aus dem größeren Werke* ("Outline of Reinhard's Dogmatics, Primarily for Secondary Schools and Grammar Schools, in a Synopsis from the Larger Work"). The revised fourth edition mentioned above discusses predestination in thesis 8, which deals with the divine decrees, namely predestination, grace, and justification. This thesis is positioned between christology (*De Christo, Generis Humani Sotere*)

75. See Schott, "Storr," 457.

76. Schleiermacher, On the Doctrine of Election, tr. Nicol and Jørgenson, 12, footnote 18.

and the doctrine of the order of salvation (*De Ordine Salutis*). Reinhard maintains that God has from eternity foreknown all things and governs the world according to a plan. His decree concerning eternal salvation is part of that general plan. While it is God's will that all human beings be saved, this is no contradiction to Scriptural passages stating that many will be lost forever. Reinhard acknowledges this apparent paradox, conceding that the concepts of eternal salvation and eternal perdition "are still much too dark and vague."[77] Despite his anti-rationalist conviction, Reinhard argues that it is logically impossible that God has decreed that everybody will receive the blessedness Christ has earned, because those who lived before Christ's birth and those whom the gospel did not reach could obviously not have been included.

Reinhard distinguishes two divine wills, a preceding one that wants universal redemption, and a subsequent one that corresponds to the decree of election; only the latter is realized. Election depends on an individual's belief in Christ, therefore the decree is conditional. Scriptural passages relating to God's decree refer only to those who have heard the gospel, but Scripture makes no judgment on those who have not encountered it. Reinhard rejects the notion of irresistible grace because it led Augustine and in his wake Calvin and other Reformed theologians to the conclusion that God's decree was absolute.

Philipp Konrad Marheinecke (1780–1846), a close associate of Schleiermacher, studied philosophy and theology at the University of Göttingen, where he was particularly influenced by Christoph Friedrich von Ammon, Schleiermacher's old adversary. He started lecturing at Göttingen in 1804 before being called to Erlangen as Professor *extraordinarius* and university chaplain. In 1809 he went to Heidelberg, where he first met his future colleague Wilhelm Martin Leberecht de Wette (1780–1849), and where he was admitted to the rank of Professor o*rdinarius*. In 1811 he received a call to the chair of dogmatics at the University of Berlin, where he subsequently taught for 35 years. Marheinecke represented the branch of speculative theology. He directed his dogmatics against both supranaturalism and rationalism: against the former because of its strict adherence to divine revelation, which did not agree with reason; and against the latter because its doctrine of reason was wholly ignorant of divine revelation. He favored theology as a speculative science, avoiding both "the authoritative belief of the supranaturalists as well as the emancipated but subjective

77. Reinhard, *Vorlesungen*, 438.

rationalism of the Enlightenment."[78] In 1819, Marheinecke took over the position as Lutheran pastor of Trinity Church in Berlin as Schleiermacher's colleague; Schleiermacher had held the Reformed pastor's position there since 1809. Marheinecke and Schleiermacher thus formed the Lutheran and Reformed counterparts in both teaching and preaching at Berlin.

Marheinecke's main dogmatic work, *Die Grundlehren der christlichen Dogmatik*, ("Basic Doctrines of Christian Dogmatics") was first published in 1819, and even though Schleiermacher's essay on election appeared earlier in the same year, he did take Marheinecke's work on board and referred to it in his essay. In his *Grundlehren*, Marheinecke deals with the different dogmatic *topoi* in the order of the Apostolic Creed. The doctrine of predestination is discussed as part of christology. Chapter II, entitled "Of God, the Son," consists of three sections: i) Of the eternal existence of the Son from the Father, ii) Of the incarnation of the Son of God, and iii) Of the merits of the Godman. Section ii, in turn, is subdivided into 1) Of divine providence, 2) Of divine redemption and predestination, and 3) Of the person of the Godman. Marheinecke followed very much the contemporary Lutheran interpretation. He took God's decree not to be conditioned by any necessity outside God, since being, action, and will in God were identical. For Marheinecke, the divine decree was independent both of the created world and of the fall, but the behavior of human beings toward election was determined by that election itself. God's will to salvation was universal, but its success was particular. Like Reinhard and Bretschneider, Marheinecke did not consider grace to be irresistible. Also like Reinhard, Marheinecke maintained that individuals and nations that have not encountered the gospel could not therefore be regarded as reprobate.

Wilhelm Martin Leberecht de Wette (1780–1849), also mentioned in Schleiermacher's essay, is regarded by Rudolf Smend as Schleiermacher's "most important companion."[79] Born in Thuringia as a minister's son, he was influenced at a young age by Johann Gottfried Herder (1744–1803), who was also said to have been instrumental in de Wette's decision to study divinity. At the University of Jena de Wette excelled in Old Testament studies. From 1807 to 1810 he taught Old and New Testament at the University of Heidelberg. He then moved to the newly founded University of Berlin, where he, Schleiermacher, and Marheinecke formed the academic staff of the first faculty of divinity, soon to be joined by August

78. Lange, "Neugestaltung," 89–90.
79. Smend, "Wilhelm Martin Leberecht de Wette," 44.

Neander (1789–1850). Between 1813 and 1815, de Wette's two-volume *Lehrbuch der christlichen Dogmatik in historischer Entwickelung dargestellt* ("Textbook of Christian Dogmatics Represented in Its Historical Development") was published. In 1818, de Wette, along with Schleiermacher and Friedrich Lücke (1791–1855), was one of the three co-founders of the new journal *Theologische Zeitschrift*, the first issue of which carried Schleiermacher's essay on election. A deep friendship developed between the two theologians, and de Wette even stood as godfather to Schleiermacher's only son, Nathanael. In 1819 de Wette was forced to resign from the faculty at Berlin for political reasons, and three years later he accepted a call to the chair of Old Testament at the University of Basel, where he taught until his death.

The second volume of de Wette's *Lehrbuch der christlichen Dogmatik* deals explicitly with Lutheran dogmatics. It consists of a historical-critical introduction, a first or critical part on the sources of religious truth, a second or general part, and a third or particular part. The second part discusses theology and anthropology. The section on theology is subdivided into: I) The idea of God according to his absolute independence, II) The idea of God according to his relation to the world, III) The idea of God according to his relation to nature, and IV) trinity. De Wette positions the doctrine of predestination in the third or particular part, which contains soteriology and eschatology. The first section under the heading soteriology, "God's decrees for the redemption of the world," deals with predestination and is followed by christology. Soteriology is subdivided as follows: A) *Benevolentia Dei universalis,* B) *Benevolentia Dei specialis;* a. *Praedestinatio* and b. *Reprobatio.* De Wette maintained under A) that God had decreed that all human beings are to be saved through Jesus Christ because of God's grace, which was universal but not absolute. This decree corresponded to God's preceding will (*voluntas antecedens*). By dint of that decree, God had decided to effectively save those who believe in Christ. De Wette thus regarded election to correspond to the subsequent will of God (*voluntas consequens*). For him, as for his other Lutheran colleagues, reprobation was not part of the eternal and immutable divine decree. Rather, it was a "simple allusion of reason which refutes the idea of divine love and holiness."[80] Its ultimate reason (*causa meritoria*) lies in human beings, not in God.

To recap: the positioning of the doctrine of predestination in the Lutheran dogmatics used by Schleiermacher varied considerably. In Johann

---

80. De Wette, *Lehrbuch*, 132.

Gerhard's *Loci Theologici* predestination was located between providence and anthropology as part of the work of God's governance. Storr's *Elementary course* discussed it in the narrower context of theodicy and in the wider area of soteriology, albeit not as a doctrine in its own right. In Reinhard's *Vorlesungen über die Dogmatik*, too, predestination was interpreted as an aspect of soteriology. God's decrees, predestination, grace, and justification, were positioned between christology and the order of salvation. In Marheinecke's *Grundlehren* (1819) the doctrine of predestination appeared in the context of christology, and more specifically as part of the incarnation. This part included the discussion of providence, redemption, and predestination, and the person of Christ, emphasizing that predestination is part of the salvific work of Christ. It is worth noting that, although like Gerhard, Marheinecke positioned providence and predestination in close proximity to each other, he understood providence not as part of God's governance but as part of the incarnation. De Wette in his *Lehrbuch der christlichen Dogmatik* (1816) finally separated the doctrines of providence and predestination, locating the former within of the doctrine of God, and the latter within soteriology.

With regard specifically to the Reformed doctrine of predestination, Richard Muller has argued that the modern attention to the placement of the doctrine does not predetermine its meaning.[81] Dealing with predestination before the doctrine of God and creation therefore does not automatically imply a given writer's supralapsarian tendency. The positioning of doctrines indicates doctrinal relationships, but it does not create them. The same point can be made about Lutheran dogmatics. There is definitely no indication in the five Lutheran dogmatics discussed above that the placement of the doctrine of predestination determines its meaning. Nevertheless, Dawn DeVries and Brian Gerrish's contention that "the sense of a doctrine is, at least in part, a function of its location"[82] does apply to the positioning of predestination, for instance, in the context of soteriology as opposed to the doctrine of God.

In particular from the late eighteenth century onwards, predestination has been positioned either within or in the vicinity of christology, and hence in a soteriological context. In contrast, Calvin's *Institutio* discussed predestination after the chapter on prayer and before the last resurrection as part of pneumatology. The salvific aspect of the doctrine—predestination is election to salvation—is more obvious in the Lutheran works than

81. See Muller, "Placement of Predestination," 208.
82. DeVries and Gerrish, "Providence and Grace," 189.

in Calvin, but, conversely, there is no evidence that Calvin's thesis has no salvific aspects.

Finally, Schleiermacher mentioned three Lutheran divines outside the narrower context of dogmatic works. Johann Gottlieb Töllner (1724–1774) was cited in the essay as a Lutheran theologian who nevertheless shared Schleiermacher's conviction that dogmatic differences did not present an impediment for a church union but should be discussed in an academic context. Töllner, a minister's son, studied divinity at Halle University and became first a field preacher in 1748, and then in 1756 Professor *extraordinarius* of theology and philosophy at the University of Frankfurt an der Oder. He was a representative of semi-rationalism, which adhered to the revelatory character of Christianity and Christ's divine mission but gradually relinquished the positive doctrines as being religiously indifferent or simply untenable.[83]

The other two Lutheran theologians mentioned in the context of Schleiermacher's discussion of Augustine and the Pelagian controversy were Gustav Friedrich Wiggers (1777–1860) and August Detlev Christian Twesten (1789–1876). Wiggers, a divinity professor at the University of Rostock, was working on a book about that subject when Schleiermacher was composing his essay. It was eventually published in 1821 under the title *Versuch einer pragmatischen Darstellung des Augustinismus und Pelagianismus von den Anfängen der Pelagianischen Streitigkeiten bis zur dritten oecumenischen Synode* ("Attempt at a Pragmatic Representation of Augustinism and Pelagianism from the Beginning of the Pelagian Controversy to the Third Ecumenical Synod"). The Lutheran Twesten had attended Schleiermacher's early public lectures on hermeneutics in Berlin in 1809/10 and became one of his most industrious pupils. In 1814, he was appointed Professor *extraordinarius* for philosophy and theology at the University of Kiel. A sharp critic of rational deism,[84] Twesten shared Schleiermacher's conviction that differences between the Lutherans and Reformed no longer justified the separation of the two confessions, but that their respective symbolic books should nevertheless be retained. After Schleiermacher's death in 1834, Twesten succeeded him to the New Testament chair at the divinity faculty at the University of Berlin. From 1841 he served in the consistory of Brandenburg, and in 1857 he became a member of the supreme church council there. His provisionally entitled Darstellung des Augustinismus und seiner Zeit ("Representation

83. See Fronmüller and Wagenmann, "Töllner," 816.
84. See Heinrici, "Twesten," 173.

of Augustinism and its Period"), which he mentioned in a letter to Schleiermacher of 29 September 1818, and which Schleiermacher subsequently alluded to in his essay, was never published.

"STRAGGLERS"

In §§126–156 (ecclesiology) and §§157–163 (eschatology) of *Christian Faith*, Schleiermacher made reference to fourteen theologians, confessions, and individual works not mentioned in the previous section (pneumatology) or in the essay on election. For the sake of completion, I briefly list them here:

Irenaeus (AD 140–200) and Eusebius of Caesarea (AD 260–340), as well as Augustine's work *De Fide et Opp.* represent the Early Church in the section on ecclesiology proper (§§126–156), whereas Huldrych Zwingli's *De Vera et Falsa Religione Commentarius* (1525) and his *Christianae Fidei Expositio* (1531) are mentioned for the Reformed side. Martin Luther's *Large Catechism* (1529) and his *Schmalkald Articles* (1537) were the only Lutheran texts referred to here, as well as, rather surprisingly, *Theologiae Vere Christianae Apologia* (1637) by the English Quaker Robert Barclay (1648–1690). The Upper German *Confessio Tetrapolitana* (1530) and the *Heidelberg Catechism* (1563), the Swiss *First Basel Confession* (1534)[85] and the *Confessio Helvetica Prior* (1536), the *Scots Confession* (1560), and the Polish *Catechism of Rakow* (1605)[86] complete the list of Reformed documents mentioned solely in §§126–156 of *Christian Faith*. The *Catechism of the Council of Trent* (1566) is the only Roman Catholic text Schleiermacher made reference to in this section. The *Symbolum Romanum*[87] and the *Nicaean Creed* (325), mentioned in the section on eschatology (§§157–163), are the only two texts not hitherto noted.

---

85. Composed by Johannes Oekolampad's (1482–1531) successor Oswald Myconius (1488–1552), this earliest Swiss confession relies heavily on Zwingli's interpretation of the sacraments and of christology.

86. This was the confession of the antitrintarian movement known as Socianism or Unitarianism, founded by Fausto Sozzini (1539–1604).

87. This creed is older than the eighth-century Apostles' Creed but strikingly similar to it. Some form of it was probably in use as early as the middle of the second century AD.

6

The Essay "On the Doctrine of Election" and Its Reception

BACKGROUND

COMMUNION AND PREDESTINATION ARE two of the central Reformed-Lutheran aporia that have traditionally separated the two confessions. Bretschneider had addressed both doctrines in his *Aphorismen*, but Schleiermacher concentrated entirely on the latter in his essay "Ueber die Lehre von der Erwählung, besonders in Beziehung auf Herrn Dr. Bretschneiders *Aphorismen*" ("On the Doctrine of Election, with Special Reference to the *Aphorisms* of Dr Bretschneider").

This essay was Schleiermacher's first publication on a specific dogmatic topic. In a letter to Ludwig Georg Blanc of 23 March 1818, he wrote that Wilhelm de Wette and Friedrich Lücke had "almost forced"[1] him to promise an article for a new theological journal they intended to launch. He originally contemplated a piece on his position regarding supranaturalism and rationalism. In a letter of 14 March 1819 to August Twesten, Schleiermacher announced: "rationalism has been deferred. Instead I intend to start an essay on election next week, which for the time being is to take the place of [the originally planned article on rationalism]."[2] By 28 April 1819 he reported in another letter to Blanc that he was working on an essay about the doctrine of predestination for the new journal, which he would co-edit with de Wette and Lücke. In the same letter he said that the essay would be "a kind of predecessor"[3] for his dogmatics,

1. Dilthey, *Aus Schleiermacher's Leben* III, 233.
2. Meisner, *Schleiermacher als Mensch*, 295.
3. Dilthey, *Aus Schleiermacher's Leben* III, 246.

which he had started to write down, but which had been left lying while he produced the essay on election. As he explained in the letter to Twesten of 14 March 1819 mentioned above, he had been able to complete his lecture notes only up to the doctrine of election, "and since Bretschneider and Schultheß have now reinstigated the affair itself [i.e., the debate about predestination] with regard to myself and to the union, I want to concentrate on this subject first."[4] The new journal, simply called *Theologische Zeitschrift*, was launched in September 1819, but it went through only three issues and succumbed in 1822. I would conjecture that the collapse was related to de Wette's departure for the University of Basel in 1822. Schleiermacher's essay inaugurated the first issue, taking up pages 1 to 119 of the octavo format publication.

Schleiermacher himself was not entirely confident about the stringency of his essay, not least because he had composed it in a rather haphazard fashion and with numerous interruptions. In a letter to Twesten of 30 September 1819 he wrote: "My essay on election has now been printed. Whether or not it will deserve the reputation of a thorough dogmatic method remains to be seen. As far as I remember, there is much wanting to this end; I had to write it in such a fragmented manner."[5] He voiced more criticism of his essay five weeks later in a letter to Joachim Christian Gaß: "I should have given a brief summary at the end, only, as usual, I was in a hurry. This also prevented me from paying particular attention to [Johann Friedrich] Krause, who regards it as the rationalism of the *Formula of Concord* that it has abandoned the idea of predestination. Implicitly, of course, he has been refuted, only people will not easily notice this."[6] In the event, the potential points of criticism Schleiermacher anticipated in these letters did not represent the particular points that his Lutheran opponents would take issue with.

SUMMARY WITH CRITICAL COMMENTS

Schleiermacher's essay is a penetrating and detailed exploration of different aspects of the doctrine of predestination, carried out through a close examination of Bretschneider's arguments and the juxtaposition of Lutheran and Reformed interpretations. If Theodor Mahlmann's observation that "as a union theologian Schleiermacher did not want to achieve more

4. Heinrici, *D. August Twesten*, 335.

5. Ibid., 353.

6. Dilthey. "Drei Briefe Schleiermachers," 41.

than tracing the roots of the dissent to the . . . original premises"[7] is correct, Schleiermacher certainly achieved his aim. However, in the context of the Prussian Church Union his essay did not have the desired outcome, which he specified as assembling both Lutherans and Calvinists around the strict Augustinian form of the doctrine.

Schleiermacher began his essay with the observations that most Reformed had already relinquished their understanding of predestination and that the debate about the doctrine had all but ceased when recent discussions about the Prussian Church Union brought it back to the fore. In historical terms, first Augustine and later Calvin interpreted the doctrine of predestination as an unconditional decree, both because of the strong scriptural evidence supporting it, and because any deviation from that interpretation would inevitably result in inconsistencies with regard to the "purest rational notions"[8] of the nature of God. Although both Augustine and Calvin were acknowledged exegetical experts and eminently logical thinkers, their strict interpretation of the doctrine of predestination was rejected by the majority of the Christian Church. The main arguments brought forward against it were the perceived contradictions of the doctrine to both some scriptural passages and to sound reason. Expressing his astonishment at the success of those who rejected the unconditional decree for those reasons, Schleiermacher did not accept the further explanation that external factors—in Augustine's case the Pelagian Controversy, in Calvin's case his allegedly unexamined endorsement of Augustine's theory—compelled the two theologians to formulate the strict version of the doctrine, rather than their own theological understanding. Schleiermacher voices his disappointment that nobody has stepped forward to defend the original Calvinist or Augustinian doctrine against the Lutherans. He therefore takes up the gauntlet himself and announces his intention to argue the case for the Augustinian or Calvinist doctrine of unconditional predestination, and thereby to rectify the situation in which various points have either been overlooked or simply neglected in the current debate. At the same time, he is at pains to point out that he does not want to be seen simply as a disciple of Calvin. His contemporaries evidently conferred on him the reputation of "a bold and resolute disciple of Calvin,"[9] but, as he remarks laconically, "I do not know with what justification."[10]

---

7. Mahlmann, "Prädestination," 143.

8. Schleiermacher, On the Doctrine of Election, tr. Nicol and Jørgenson, 1.

9. Ibid., 5.

10. Schleiermacher, "Über die Lehre von der Erwählung" 1836, 399. This is a more

Schleiermacher then proceeds to examine and frequently revisit arguments for and against the Calvinist and the orthodox Lutheran interpretations in what Brian Gerrish describes as a "long, erudite and penetrating essay."[11] No titles or sub headings lend a visual structure to the uninterrupted text in the German original, but Nicol and Jørgenson's magisterial translation introduces thirteen very helpful subdivisions:

Section 1, "Election: From Controversy to Consolation," identifies the relation of the Lutheran and Calvinist election theories to the crucial point of the debate. They relate in different ways to the doctrine of the indispensability of divine grace for sanctification. Schleiermacher argues against the Lutheran doctrine of a person's ability to resist God's grace. To complicate matters, Bretschneider in his *Aphorismen* had proposed to abandon the doctrine of a person's incapability to gain faith through their own initiative altogether as unbiblical. He held that it would inevitably lead to the Calvinist doctrine of election. Bretschneider favored full-blown Pelagianism and thus the abandonment of the orthodox Lutheran position. Schleiermacher's essay is a response both to Bretschneider's position and to the orthodox Lutheran interpretation.

In section 2, "Luther and the Lutherans on Election," Schleiermacher refutes Bretschneider's argument, claiming that if everybody could save themselves, Christ would have come in vain. He reiterates the understanding expressed in the *Augsburg Confession*, that the Spirit works faith by divine discretion. At the same time, he notes the shortcomings of the Lutheran statement that the hearing of the gospel is a decisive element in conversion.

In section 3, "Election and the Nature of Faith," Schleiermacher argues that the human ability to resist grace, which forms one of the main elements of the Lutheran doctrine, is untenable. Either human resistance is then stronger than God's universal will to salvation, or it is part of the divine plan and hence predestined.

Then, section 4, "Calvin on Election and Practical Christianity," tries to refute well-known Lutheran arguments against the Calvinist form of the doctrine concerning the perceived negative consequences that unconditional predestination has for practical Christianity.

In section 5, "Election and the Human Faculties," Schleiermacher shows the issues on which the Lutheran and Calvinist doctrines agree,

---

literal translation than Nicol and Jørgenson's "though for reasons unknown to me." On the Doctrine of Election, tr. Nicol and Jørgenson, 6.

11. Gerrish, *Tradition*, 113.

whereas section 6, "Election and the Breadth of Blessedness," demonstrates how Luther and Melanchthon deviated from Augustine's strict doctrine. Here, Schleiermacher also counters three of Ammon's main arguments.

Then, section 7, "Questions Concerning the So-called Two-fold Will of God," refutes the very notion of a prevenient and a subsequent will in God through logical arguments.

In section 8, "Election and the Fall," Schleiermacher develops his argument that it was only with Christ's entry into the world that the human race attained the ability not to sin, and that Adam and Eve were not created more perfect than the following generations. From this point onwards Schleiermacher positions himself outside the mainstream Protestant tradition.

Section 9, "Election, the *Absolutum Decretum* and Creation," defines Schleiermacher's notion of person. His differentiation of person in a civic and person in a religious sense is based on the concept of the human will. Here, Schleiermacher also puts forward the argument that the dead mass of unregenerated persons is capable of being quickened. This allows him to claim that all who are dead in the religious sense, and who in their totality constitute the mass of perdition, nevertheless have the potential to be regenerated. Although he claims to stand in the Augustinian and Calvinist tradition, he has in fact moved away from the traditional Calvinist doctrine here.

Then section 10, "Creation and Redemption Presume One Divine Decree," develops the argument for a single unconditional divine decree that first conditions everything. It determines the very order in which the dead mass of the condemned is gradually regenerated.

In section 11, "Election, the Authorship of Evil, and the Captivity of Reason," Schleiermacher claims that the single decree encompasses the whole human race, and that there are no decrees for individuals.

This theme is reiterated in section 12, "God in Election Intends the Whole." Again in contrast to the Calvinist tradition, Schleiermacher argues that death is not the final point of a person's spiritual development; rather, it is only a stage that will eventually be overcome, even after death. Here he finally and unequivocally declares his belief in universalism, the ultimate restoration of all human beings.

The final section, 13, "Election and Church Union," brings the discussion back to the beginning. Undoubtedly aware that universalism was unlikely to become the banner under which Lutherans and Calvinists would unite, Schleiermacher urges the Lutherans to adopt the Augustinian doctrine of election as the most consistent one for the sake of the Prussian Church Union.

This brief summary of Schleiermacher's essay on election only notes the main points of the debate in the order in which Schleiermacher deals with them. Nevertheless, this overview clearly demonstrates his procedure. He first states his motives for writing the essay and declares his own Calvinist position before dealing with the Lutheran theory, as well as Bretschneider's where he deviates from the orthodox Lutheran understanding. Schleiermacher discusses their concerns about, and the actual implications of, the Calvinist understanding, and associated doctrines such as creation, the fall, free will and the nature of God. From section 8 onwards, however, Schleiermacher starts to develop arguments in favor of universalism while seeking to appear to remain in the Calvinist camp. The last section, on "Election and Church Union," finally, comes across as something of an afterthought.

In the following, I shall outline the main points of divergence between the Lutheran and Calvinist interpretations of predestination as put forward by Schleiermacher, and by discussing his criticism of each, I shall explore and criticize his solutions to the points raised, and comment on his own interpretation of the doctrine of election.

Election, Grace, and Faith

The Augustinian scholar James Wetzel draws a charming picture of a person receiving the gift of faith. "In the dance of redemption, it would seem that the human partner arrives empty-handed and lacking in grace; not only does the divine partner supply the grace, God does all the dancing."[12] Schleiermacher demonstrates the Lutherans' assent with the doctrine of the indispensability of grace for salvation, quoting from the dogmatic works of his Lutheran contemporaries Franz Volkmar Reinhard, Philipp Marheinecke and Wilhelm de Wette. This is the only aspect of election about which Lutheranism, Calvinism and Schleiermacher himself entirely agree—an agreement that is hardly surprising, given that *sola gratia* is one of the main insights of Protestantism. Whilst Lutherans and Calvinists share the understanding that the Holy Spirit works faith where and when he wills, they are diametrically opposed to each other with regard to the doctrine of the irresistibility of grace. Augustine and, in his wake, Luther and Calvin adhered to that doctrine, but it was abandoned by the

12. Wetzel, "Snares of Truth," 125.

Philippists and subsequently the Lutheran mainstream. The latter claimed a person's natural ability to resist grace. Schleiermacher challenges this claim. Even when a person's will is naturally opposed to God, any development of pious feelings or a consciousness of faith must be assisted by God if faith really does come only through grace. If it is God's help that prevents a person's will from denying the beginning of faith, one cannot escape the logical corollary: any neglect or denial of pious feelings occurs only when God's help is not forthcoming. But this absence of divine assistance must be due to divine ordination rather than to human resistance and God's permission against God's own will to salvation. Human power is finite and cannot resist the omnipotent divine will. Also, as Schleiermacher points out, even if somebody resists today, will he or she always do so? Does one's response to God's call to faith depend entirely on the Holy Spirit, or do one's state and position at the time of God's calling influence one's response? What about those who are never put into a position in which the acceptance of faith becomes an issue because they never hear the gospel proclaimed?

According to Lutheranism, the hearing of the gospel is a precondition for the gift of faith, whereas according to the Reformed understanding the only reason and precondition for a person's faith is God's good-pleasure. Schleiermacher points out aptly that the hearing of the gospel is actually of no consequence. If that hearing is based on a person's own initiative it is irrelevant because exposing oneself to God's word does not of itself lead to faith. Moreover, Schleiermacher observes, the claim that an unregenerated person would take the initiative in this way does not sit well with the Lutheran understanding of sinful humanity's natural disdain of God.

In this context it is worth discussing Matthias Gockel's rendition of Schleiermacher's argumentation. His claim that "Schleiermacher agrees that the assumption of a natural opposition to grace correlates with an unconditional decree"[13] is opaque. Natural opposition to grace, which is in fact a common feature in the theology of both Luther and Calvin, is primarily a result of the fall. It does not *per se* relate to an an unconditional, or, for that matter, an absolute decree. What it does correlate with, however, is the irresistibility of grace. Humanity's natural opposition to grace can only be overcome by irresistible grace. The notion of the irresistibility of grace is diametrically opposed to that of the human ability to resist grace. Any divine decree of election that takes the ability to resist grace into account has to be a conditional decree. The condition for election in that scenario is not to reject the gift of grace.

13. Gockel, "New Perspectives," 304.

Gockel further claims that, according to Schleiermacher, "the view that God foreordained salvation for those in whom God foresaw himself as effecting faith by the power of the Holy Spirit . . . does not differ from Calvin's understanding of the origin of faith."[14] This claim is appropriate as far as it goes. However, Lutheranism insists that God's working of faith is effectively checked by his foreknowledge of a person's resistance to grace. Accordingly, God foreordained salvation for those whom God foresaw accepting the gift of grace, and therefore effecting their faith by the power of the Holy Spirit. This interpretation is not congruent with the Calvinist position. Schleiermacher is, therefore, entirely correct when he states that "even if God would elect only those whose faith God foresees it is nevertheless not on account of that foreseen faith that God would be moved to do so":[15] Lutherans as well as Calvinists believe that election occurs without regard to human merit or demerit. They differ with regard to the reason for un-belief.

Both the *Confessio Augustana* and the *Formula of Concord* concur with Augustine and Calvin that after the fall humanity lacks the will to love God, and that faith is brought about only through the work of the Holy Spirit. Therefore, Gockel's argument that "Schleiermacher criticizes the Lutheran position on election for its failure to avoid the untenable claim that human beings are able to love and trust in God even before they receive the gift of faith"[16] is inaccurate. It is true that the notion that in some cases grace is dispensable for faith is indeed untenable, but this does not represent the Lutheran position on election. Rather, Schleiermacher simply mentions this position as a potential argument in the discussion at hand, and without claiming that it was held by Lutherans. What he actually says is: "Indeed, suppose that a human being possessed in [it]self something that would come to the help of those [stirrings of faith], something that in no respect would itself be involved in the nature of desire! But that would have to be something more than the natural moral feeling . . . [it] would have to be precisely that love for God, which the premise from which we have proceeded has denied to the natural human being and which certainly could of itself bring forth precisely those stirrings of the Spirit within us."[17]

Against Bretschneider, Schleiermacher argues that there is no need to abandon the doctrine of the indispensability of grace in order to avoid

---

14. Ibid., 305

15. Schleiermacher, On the Doctrine of Election, tr. Nicol and Jørgenson, 65.

16. Gockel, "New Perspectives," 305.

17. Schleiermacher, On the Doctrine of Election, tr. Nicol and Jørgenson, 14–15.

the terrible consequences of pre-ordained perdition, because, properly understood, these consequences are simply not terrible at all. The Lutherans' main concern about the double decree lay in what they perceived as negative consequences for practical Christianity. Schleiermacher refuted these as follows: the genuinely elect will never be tempted to sin consciously, and by keeping to Christ's promise they can rest assured of their election. Those who think they can give in to sin until grace comes knocking on their door, and those who refuse to act at all in case they cannot accomplish their action, in fact want to justify their sinning or inactivity. Both attitudes are an indication that such persons have not encountered grace yet. Finally, those who feel unable to comfort themselves must not think of God as hardening their hearts if, at the same time, they feel a strong desire to better themselves. Such a desire is a preliminary sign of election. If persons of faith have any doubts about their election, the doctrine points them to the continuous work of the Spirit in the faithful. For those who are not regenerate, doubts serve the purpose of self-examination and awakening; in those who already have faith, doubts will vanish of their own accord in the course of time. Thus, provided one agrees that God's Spirit alone executes God's decree in the elect, there can be no moral disadvantage from the double decree. Indeed, disadvantages for practical Christianity only arise when the doctrine of human incapacity is abandoned and the doctrine is applied "to a praxis which is not dependent on divine grace and is supposed to arise from human self sufficiency."[18] In other words, the doctrine is harmful only if views that are alien to it are compounded with it.

Bretschneider's contention that a pious life is a means to the end of salvation and that, having attained certain holiness, one would want to return to one's former passions and desires, is just such a view. Schleiermacher therefore advises the Lutherans, against Bretschneider, to retain the doctrine of people's inability to gain faith of themselves. It is more stringent than synergism, and its perceived negative ethical consequences can safely be discarded. With Calvin, but against Lutheranism, he also maintains that a fall from grace is impossible: "we know of no predestination in accordance with which any person of faith can be lost."[19]

Schleiermacher's denial of practical consequences from the doctrine of double predestination in the essay signals a decisive change of position. In the first of his two non-commissioned reports on church union of 1804, he had conceded in a footnote that "the doctrine of election is

18. Schleiermacher, On the Doctrine of Election, tr. Nicol and Jørgenson, 33.
19. Ibid., 75.

indeed an important doctrine with regard to its practical influence: surely, however, the fatalistic idea of it is found very rarely among the German Reformed, and in particular in the Brandenburg Church it has never become a symbol."[20]

Universal and Particular Salvation

Schleiermacher observed that "there is one universal characteristic of redemption which the Calvinist doctrine expounds just as well as does the Lutheran doctrine, namely, that as concerns the indwelling power of the act of redemption through Christ . . . nothing stands in the way of any person's being made holy and blessed through Christ as long as God guides matters in such a way that the word reaches a person."[21] He went on to explain that there was also one universal characteristic of redemption which Lutherans and Calvinist equally reject: the universality of the outcome, namely that everybody would come to be blessed. Both faiths therefore claim the particularity of salvation. However, there are some crucial differences. Lutheranism holds that God calculated salvation for all, and that universal salvation is possible in the sense outlined above. Nevertheless, salvation is contingent, not necessary, because of the human freedom to resist grace. According to Lutheranism, Schleiermacher insists, human freedom and resistance is greater and more stubborn than God's grace, and it annuls divine omnipotence. However, this is not a straightforward argument. As Ernst Sartorius countered, God himself limits his omnipotence in order to allow human beings to exercise their free will. Divine omnipotence is not limited by a factor outside God and his creation.[22] What is relinquished here is the irresistibility of grace rather than divine omnipotence.

The Calvinist doctrine insists on the necessity of particular redemption: salvation is only for some because of the double decree to blessedness and perdition. Even though orthodox Lutherans also claimed that the work of the Holy Spirit was particular, they had always regarded the Calvinist *predestinatio gemini* as problematic because of what they perceived as the arbitrariness of God's decree and because of its corollary that Christ had come only for the elect. Schleiermacher tried to alleviate their concerns by pointing out that human ignorance of God's reasons does not make these motives arbitrary of themselves: "it is indeed only because of

20. Schleiermacher, *Zwei unvorgreifliche Gutachten*, 58.
21. Schleiermacher, On the Doctrine of Election, tr. Nicol and Jørgenson, 49–50.
22. Sartorius, *Die lutherische Lehre*, 163.

the imperfection of our knowledge that for us the oneness of what is universal is different from the totality of what is particular."[23] This argument leads him to claim that "in the divine knowledge what is universal and what is particular must be completely merged."[24] This statement already implies Schleiermacher's central argument that there is a single, universal, all-encompassing decree for the entire human race. He attacks Bretschneider's position based on this perspective. In order to undo the appearance of divine arbitrariness and to preserve human freedom, Bretschneider assumes that God has originally created everybody capable of developing all that is good and beautiful of themselves. For Schleiermacher, this position is "destructive of the whole idea of the world."[25] It transfers the arbitrariness of God to the creature endowed with absolute freedom. While this criticism is accurate from the perspective of Schleiermacher's system, in which a person as God's creature has only relative freedom, it does not go to the heart of the Lutheran position, which allows only for synergism but not for the human ability to initiate faith. Nevertheless, it is a good illustration of Schleiermacher's very perceptive early statement that "if the root of the controversy reaches down to the very depths of that way of thinking on which the original propositions are based . . . this fact must at least be understood so that one knows we cannot agree."[26] The whole controversy about the doctrine of election arose out of the different understanding of theological anthropology between the Calvinist and Lutheran camps, and was not much aided by Schleiermacher's own.

To recap: whereas Lutheran orthodoxy asserts that there is a universal divine will to salvation but only a partial success, and that salvation is contingent because God's will is not the only factor in the equation, the Calvinist doctrine holds that because God's very will to redemption is particular, its success is necessarily particular too. For Schleiermacher on the other hand, both the divine will to salvation and the success of salvation are universal and necessary. He argues that God's universal love cannot be reconciled with perdition unless the state of the reprobate is considered as altogether necessary. That state must be integral to the very notion of human nature. If perdition thus forms a necessary part of God's all-encompassing single decree, there is no need to take recourse to God's arbitrariness or to the incomprehensibility of his motives in order

23. Schleiermacher, On the Doctrine of Election, tr. Nicol and Jørgenson, 56.

24. Ibid., 57.

25. Ibid., 67.

26. Ibid., 20.

to explain perdition. Rather, it then has to be regarded as a stage in the development of the human race rather than the final state.

The notion of a conditional or unconditional decree is closely related to that of God's perceived arbitrariness. Schleiermacher agrees with Calvin and his claim that the decree of predestination is unconditional in the sense that it is not conditioned by anything outside God himself. As a corollary, of course, perdition can only be grounded in God's decree. Since humanity cannot fully fathom this decree, it appears to some to be arbitrary. In contrast, Lutheranism holds that the decree is at least partly conditional, in the sense that the precondition for a person's perdition does not lie within God, but in their own perverted, sinful will. Election to salvation, on the other hand, is unconditional also in the Lutheran understanding: it is not based on any human merits or achievements.

Single and Double Decree

One of the main arguments against the double decree of election and perdition is that it does not conform to some scriptural passages that suggest that redemption is universal. It also seems to be inconceivable that God's will to regenerate sinners might be aimed only at some. Lutheranism therefore favors the understanding of the doctrine as a single decree of election to salvation: God elects those whom he foreknows will become believers; those who will reject faith God permits to be damned.

The Calvinist doctrine does not admit of a difference between divine ordination and permission. Instead, the notions of ordination and permission are entirely congruent. This congruence also applies to predestination and *prescentia*, or foreknowledge. What God foreknows he has foreordained, and as Schleiermacher puts it succinctly, "if God has not foreseen all things, God cannot have foreseen anything."[27]

Unless everything is ordered by God's eternal preordination, there can be no acknowledgement of his omnipotence. As a corollary, believers can have a joyful consciousness of the good they possess only if they perceive it as a gift from God. Therefore, both blessedness and perdition must be pre-ordained. God elects and condemns according to his good-pleasure. Schleiermacher argues further that "divine arbitrariness in election and non-election appears to be in no respect different or greater than that in creation."[28] Moreover, a particular detail such as why one person

27. Ibid., 100.
28. Ibid., 73.

is blessed and another one is not, cannot be viewed in isolation. Instead, such a detail "is destined along with the general interconnection to be both what and how God has ordained—but not in and of itself nor in reference to any particularity whatsoever."[29] This argument, however, goes beyond the Calvinist understanding of a double decree, according to which the human race after Adam's fall deserves damnation, and the vast majority of human beings are predestined to perdition. The minority, those elected to blessedness, are the exception to the rule. Schleiermacher here interpolates his own interpretation of the doctrine as universal restoration, emphasizing the general interconnectedness of all things. However, this aspect simply does not feature in the Calvinist interpretation. Indeed, Schleiermacher proceeds to claim that "one cannot speak, in particular, of a divine decree concerning each individual person"[30] and that "it was indeed God's good pleasure from the beginning not to create individual being and life but to create a world, and this is also the way in which the Spirit of God is active, as a world-forming power, and through the Spirit of God there arises not the disorder of individual spiritual life but the spiritual world."[31] This stands in contrast to both the Calvinist and the Lutheran understanding of the decree of election for individual human beings, not for the human race in its totality. Therefore, Schleiermacher's claim that Calvin's statement "according as it pleases God"[32] is simply less precise than the statement "the divine Spirit is active through the Word as a power of nature"[33] is, in effect, a misappropriation.

That the human race *per se* rather than the individual is the object of God's decree forms the main thrust of Schleiermacher's argument for universal restoration. He even speaks of "the constantly perplexing notion of a particular divine decree with reference to the individual person."[34] The constitution and fate of individuals can be derived only from the universal act of creation.

Schleiermacher makes some confusing claims regarding the expression *absolutum decretum* for the divine decree of election. He asserts that this term "is very misleading, to be sure, but is nonetheless also open to having a very exact interpretation,"[35] that it does not appear in Calvin's

29. Ibid., 85.

30. Ibid., 86.

31. Ibid., 91.

32. Ibid. Calvin's original phrase is *"prout visum est Deo."* *Institutes* 3.24.10.

33. Ibid.

34. Ibid., 38.

35. Ibid., 65.

Institutio but is a result of the controversy about predestination, and that "hence, even the *Confession of Sigismund* rejects this expression."[36] The adjective absolute in this context is conterminous with unconditional. Both terms imply that no factors outside God have any influence whatsoever on his eternal decree. It is therefore not clear in which way Calvin's expression is supposed to be misleading. More importantly, though, its ostensible connotations are certainly not the reason why Elector Johann Sigismund opted for the omission of this expression from his *Sigismund Confession* of 1614. He did not adhere to double predestination nor to universal restoration, and therefore not to an absolute decree. It was not the expression but the very notion that he rejected.

Another aspect of the issue of a single *versus* a double decree is that of human and divine causality and the differentiation between divine foreknowledge and foreordination. Schleiermacher criticizes the Lutheran *fides praevisa* understanding "because it sets divine and human causality over and against each other."[37] According to the Calvinists and indeed to Schleiermacher, there is no reciprocity between God and the world. God's decree is unconditional and thus subordinates human causality to divine causality. Divine foreknowledge and fore-ordination are identical. If God's foreknowledge extends further than his fore-ordination, then his will exceeds his production. But, as Schleiermacher observes, if his production lags behind his will, then, "precisely thereby God becomes like one of us."[38] Thus, the following scenarios are all a result of predestination: individuals hearing the gospel but not coming to faith before they die; evil, already present in humanity, erupting into something terrible; and evil accumulating more strongly in some than in others. However, all those scenarios represent instances of "a continual preparation for redemption."[39] For Schleiermacher, the spread of the gospel through human beings during the course of history happens according to God's calculation with the ultimate goal of eschatological universal restoration. Everything that happens plays its part in the unfolding over time of the one divine decree of creation and redemption for the human race.

According to Schleiermacher, in order for the world to be complete, the human race exists necessarily. In other words, humanity is not a contingent but an integral part of creation. Since the human race is composed

36. Ibid.
37. Ibid., 99.
38. Ibid., 58.
39. Ibid., 60.

of individuals in different states of grace and more or less receptive to faith both at present and historically, God has to be active in relation to both the elect and the reprobate. Original sin, too, is then an integral part of the all-encompassing divine act of creation. Accordingly, Schleiermacher endorses the supralapsarian view: "And it is precisely for this reason that I cannot see how the *ordinavit*[40] with regard to the fall can be denied, for otherwise, redemption, which is God's greatest work, must merely be based on an act of permission."[41] Adam fell precisely because of the ordination of humankind to both sinfulness and redemption. He, and in his wake the human race, had to sin so that they could be redeemed. Rather than agreeing with the Reformed tradition, which holds that it was in Adam's nature to be able not to sin, and that he fell so easily because he had not been granted the gift of perseverance, Schleiermacher dispenses altogether with the notion of a fall from grace as a historical event. To him, the universal need for redemption presupposes the universal reality of sin without exception.

Another crucial difference between Schleiermacher's interpretation of predestination and that of both Lutherans and Calvinists, and indeed of the mainstream Western Christian tradition, revolves around the state of an individual at the moment of death. For Lutherans and Calvinists, that state is decisive for the person's eternal fate. If a person has faith at the point of death that person will be saved, otherwise he or she will be damned. For Schleiermacher, however, death is only a stage in a person's spiritual development, but decidedly not its end. As a corollary, election and rejection of any individual are the two contrasting, yet correlated, aspects of the one single divine decree, "whereby through divine power, yet in a natural way, the human race is to be transformed into the spiritual body of Christ."[42] This is the decree "concerning that arrangement within which those of the mass who are capable of individual spiritual life are gradually quickened."[43] Schleiermacher envisages an almost organic process in which the spiritual life arises in accordance with the divine decree in the same way as natural life does.

Another instance where Schleiermacher misappropriates the Augustinian and Calvinist doctrine to demonstrate that he stands in their

40. "he ordained."

41. Schleiermacher, On the Doctrine of Election, tr. Nicol and Jørgenson, 104, footnote xliv.

42. Ibid., 90.

43. Ibid., 73.

tradition can be advanced. He claims that persons prior to regeneration and in contrast to the regenerate "are collectively the 'dead,' the mere mass—an expression which therefore appears so frequently in Augustine and Calvin—which dead mass is capable of being quickened."[44] He quotes from Augustine's *Enchiridion* and his *On Rebuke and Grace*, and from Calvin (who in turn quotes Bernard of Clairvaux in this instance),[45] and all three use the term *massa perditionis*, the "mass of perdition." However, neither Augustine nor Calvin interpret perdition as temporal in the sense in which Schleiermacher does; rather, they regard it to be eternal. The mass of perdition in their understanding consists exclusively of the reprobate: those overlooked by grace (Augustine) or predestined to perdition (Calvin), all of whom will be damned either way. Thus, the "mass" Schleiermacher means and the *massa perditionis* are incongruent notions. It is my contention that Schleiermacher's misappropriation of tradition in this instance is deliberate.

Schleiermacher proceeds to argue that "the remainder of the mass—who have not been warmed up to their proper life and who, even though they never cease to be taken up into the common religious life and for this reason also do not, viewed of themselves, forfeit the possibility in and of themselves of also being quickened, to the extent that they are not quickened—comprise the condemned."[46] His optimistic interpretation that the condemned are those not yet regenerated is diametrically opposed to that of Calvin and Augustine. The condemned in their interpretation are objects of God's justice, not of his love, and they have never had the potential to be regenerated.

Dual or Single Will of God

Karl Gottlieb Bretschneider, like other Lutherans, assumed a twofold or dual divine will: a prevenient or preceding will, which wants the salvation of all human beings, and a subsequent will, according to which the elect are *de facto* saved. Wilhelm de Wette, for instance, also took this position. He distinguished *voluntas antecedens*, reflecting God's decision to save all men without exception through Christ, and *voluntas consequens*, according to which God decided to "genuinely bless those who believe in

---

44. Ibid., 71.
45. Ibid., 105–6, n. lxi.
46. Ibid., 72.

Christ."[47] In a sense, Schleiermacher wittily observes, this interpretation assumes half a will: that which extends to the elect only, whereas the reprobate "will be condemned apart from any such divine will."[48]

The Calvinist doctrine rejects any distinction of divine wills, and Schleiermacher passionately endorses this view when he declares that "it is primarily and precisely for this reason that I could never have done otherwise than also to adhere to the Calvinist formula, because I cannot understand such distinctions."[49] The Reformed distinguish between God's will and his commandments, but these are two separate concepts. The unfaithful who commit an evil deed and thus act against God's commandments still accomplish God's will in the wider context of his eternal decree. Otherwise, God's will would only be done imperfectly.

Schleiermacher argues that the will by which the elect are saved must be the same as that by which the reprobate are damned. If there were a divine prevenient or intending will, it would not even save the elect since salvation is effected by the subsequent will. That means that the prevenient will is non-efficacious and superfluous altogether, as Schleiermacher points out: "How God can have an efficacious will and a non-efficacious will with regard to the same matter is precisely something that I, like Calvin, cannot understand."[50] Everything depends uniformly on God and is conditioned by his one identical will. As Michael Root notes: "The divine decree always proceeds and never follows."[51]

Schleiermacher also criticizes the Lutheran distinction between a preceding divine will corresponding to God's mercy, and a following will representing God's justice. This would imply a universal but ineffective will in God, and a particular will that effectively leads to the salvation only of some. Moreover, "because all justice is based on making distinctions, whereas mercy makes none,"[52] to distinguish believers from non-believers would be a matter of God's justice, not of his mercy. In this view, then, the prevenient will, which wants mercy for all, is ineffective; only the subsequent will, which wants blessedness for some and condemnation for all others, is effective. The latter is deemed to be the one and identical will of God, which refers to both the elect and the reprobate.

---

47. de Wette, *Lehrbuch*, 129.

48. Schleiermacher, On the Doctrine of Election, tr. Nicol and Jørgenson, 52.

49. Ibid., 53.

50. Ibid., 55.

51. Root, "Schleiermacher as Innovator," 104.

52. Schleiermacher, On the Doctrine of Election, tr. Nicol and Jørgenson, 55.

The Elect and the Reprobate

According to Lutheranism, God has pre-ordained those to salvation whom he foreknew would have faith, even though his election is not based on their foreseen faith. Schleiermacher notes that the elect are therefore interpreted to be those whom God will give his Spirit, while the others receive their just punishment. But, he counters, it is inappropriate "to take election of individual human persons to be a special decree and the condemnation of others not to be such."[53] Of course, this is only the case from his point of view, which claims one all-encompassing decree for humanity. According to Lutheranism, in contrast, God's decree is a single decree to election, whereas reprobation is based on the perverted evil will of those who resist God's grace. Schleiermacher's further argument that, since all of fallen humanity is sinful, the difference between the elect and the reprobate does not centre around sin but around the gift of faith, which is given to the first but not the last, does not apply to the Lutheran position. In their view, the difference between the elect and the reprobate centers precisely around sin, namely the stubborn sin of the latter that reject God's gift of grace. Of course, Lutherans too adhere to the doctrine of sinful humanity and that of God's grace as a gift; the point of departure for Lutherans and Calvinists is the reason for reprobation, not the reason for salvation. Schleiermacher points out rightly that in the Lutheran understanding human beings can cause their own damnation but cannot of themselves will their salvation, and therefore a dual causality of election and reprobation is implied. This interpretation does not sit well with his own contention that God's single decree is the effective cause of everything.

For Schleiermacher, the elect are those in whom regeneration through God's Spirit results in pious self-development. God's eternal decree determines the arrangement, that is the manner and time, of the act of regeneration. As to the reprobate, in an apparent act of barrel scraping, Schleiermacher produces some contrived reasons why they should not despair. They should take comfort from the very fact of their existence and "consider that God could also not have created [them] at all"[54] or, indeed, could have created them as beasts. Instead, he argues, even the reprobate as human beings are conscious of their reason and their very existence. The force of his argument is exceedingly hard to see.

53. Ibid., 73.
54. Ibid., 92.

In Schleiermacher's interpretation of the doctrine, the reprobate are those who have so far been overlooked and are not yet affected by the Spirit. They do not cease to be incorporated into the shared religious life and remain objects of divine love, and they therefore do not lose the potential of being regenerated at some point in the future—even after death. Reprobation is compatible with God's love precisely because the reprobate fulfill a necessary role within the historical unfolding and development of the human race as an integral part of God's creation. Schleiermacher thus turns both the Lutheran and the Calvinist traditions on their heads: the issue is not whether perdition is ordained, or foreseen and permitted, but whether it is a necessary or a contingent part of God's decree. If it is a necessary part, it has to be consistent with divine love, and the only way to reconcile both notions is by interpreting reprobation as temporal rather than eternal.

What underpins his universalist interpretation of predestination as opposed to the Calvinist double decree is the rhetorical question, "is the difference between the guilt of one who has become a person of faith . . . and the guilt of one who has continued not to be a person of faith so great that the infinite difference between blessedness and damnation for all eternity could be justified thereby?"[55] However, his argument that "they have the same claims as the rest"[56] is misleading in that according to all Protestant teaching nobody at all has a "claim" to grace and blessedness.

Schleiermacher thus quietly rephrased the question why some are chosen while others are not: why are some already and others not yet regenerated? His answer lies in the limits of historical and natural development, the *modus operandi* of nature. But by rephrasing the ancient question, he arrives at a new interpretation. As Gerrish observes: "The defense of Calvin's doctrine thus leads beyond the doctrine defended."[57]

Schleiermacher's universalist interpretation of predestination departs from both Lutheranism and the Reformed tradition, as well as from Augustine, Luther and Calvin, and indeed from Western Christian orthodoxy across the board, including Roman Catholicism. By claiming that perdition is a necessary temporary stage to be overcome by the ultimate universal reconciliation and restoration of all that has been lost, Schleiermacher has solved the conflict between divine justice and divine love. "The difference at the point of death, then, between the person of faith

55. Ibid.
56. Ibid., 91.
57. Gerrish, *Tradition*, 119.

and the person not of faith is simply the difference between being taken up into the reign of Christ earlier and later."[58] Only with the belief in universal restoration can people of faith bear the thought of the mass of perdition, those that have not yet been quickened. Otherwise, the blessedness of the first would be disturbed by the contemplation of those eternally excluded. The only other way the elect could bear the thought of the reprobate would be to lose compassion for the entire human race or for "everything that belongs to their species."[59]

The main weakness of non-universal interpretations of predestination consists in their correlation of divine mercy and divine justice with the separation into two discrete classes of human beings, the elect and the reprobate. Universal restoration, on the other hand, allows human reason to reconcile the diversity of human beings with the dependence of all on divine grace. It resolves the dichotomy between the divine power of redemption and a person's resistance of grace; and it means that the misery of those who have no faith yet can be considered together with the word of grace imprinted in their memory.[60]

Throughout his essay, Schleiermacher is keen to demonstrate the consistency and integrity of the Calvinist interpretation of the doctrine of predestination as opposed to the orthodox Lutheran one with its insistence on the God-defying power of human resistance. Schleiermacher introduces his own interpretation by partly drawing on Augustinian and Calvinist elements of the doctrine, such as the unconditional nature of the divine decree and the subjection of human to divine causality, and indeed the term mass, which, however, he interprets very differently. Finally, he states, "in that I would confess to holding this [universalist] view, I advance it as a sign of my impartiality in not asserting that the Calvinist theory drives us any more strongly to this view than does the Lutheran theory."[61] He is certainly correct when arguing that his position cannot legitimately be derived from either the Calvinist or the Lutheran doctrine.

The following table sets out the different elements of the doctrine in its Lutheran and Calvinist forms and according to Schleiermacher.

58. Schleiermacher, On the Doctrine of Election, tr. Nicol and Jørgenson, 94.

59. Ibid., 95.

60. Ibid.

61. Ibid.

Doctrinal Aspect	Lutherans	Calvinists	Schleiermacher
Indispensability of grace for salvation	Yes	Yes	Yes
Free will to fulfill divine law	From a person's regeneration only	From a person's regeneration only	From a person's regeneration only
Irresistibility of grace	No	Yes	Yes
Universal vs. particular salvation	Universal divine will but particular success	Particular divine will and particular success	Universal divine will and success
Christ's and the Holy Spirit's work	Christ's work is universal, the Holy Spirit's work is particular	Both are particular	Both are universal
Single vs. double decree	Single decree of election of those whose faith God foreknows	Double decree of election and reprobation	Single decree of eventual election of all
Addressees of decree	Individuals	Individuals	Human race
Conditional vs. unconditional decree	Conditional	Unconditional	Unconditional
Single vs. dual will of God	Dual (prevenient and subsequent)	Single	Single and all-encompassing
The elect	Those whose faith God has foreseen	Those preordained to election due to God's good pleasure	All
The reprobate	Those who resist faith	Those preordained to perdition	Temporarily those not yet regenerated, but eternally none
Perdition	Not ordained, eternal; reprobate are objects of divine justice	Ordained, eternal; reprobate are objects of divine justice	Not ordained, temporal; reprobate are objects of divine love

Doctrinal Aspect	Lutherans	Calvinists	Schleiermacher
Reasons for unbelief	Human resistance to grace	Divine decree	Historical stage of development
Adam's fall	Infralapsarian	Supralapsarian	Supralapsarian
Possibility of fall from grace	Yes	No	No
Death	Final cut-off point	Final cut-off point	Stage in development
Human and divine causality	Human causality can overrule divine causality	Human causality is subject to divine causality	Human causality is subsumed under divine causality

CONTEMPORARY AND MODERN RECEPTIONS OF THE ESSAY

Schleiermacher's friends and students mainly received his essay positively. In more general terms, August Twesten praised its purely theological method, and Joachim Christian Gaß welcomed its clarity throughout. Ludwig Gottfried Blanc noted that Schleiermacher had uncovered the inconsequent nature of the Lutheran system and that he had confirmed the profound stringency of the Calvinist one, while managing to put Calvin's *decretum horribile* in a much more positive light. However, Twesten also predicted that Schleiermacher's refutation of the Lutheran concerns against double predestination as morally detrimental would not find many advocates. The reviews of Schleiermacher's essay published over the ensuing decade were to prove Twesten right.

His close friend Joachim Christian Gaß criticized the essay as being insufficient. Even though it had expressly been written with the aim of clarifying Schleiermacher's relationship to the disputing parties, it did not connect the ecclesiastical element with the theological one.[62] According to Gaß, this was also true of Schleiermacher's publication *Über den eigenthümlichen Werth und das bindende Ansehen symbolischer Bücher* ("On the Proper Value and Binding Authority of Symbolic Books"). Gaß was certainly correct in pointing out that Schleiermacher had failed to successfully link the theological issues with the ecclesiastical aspects. He

---

62. See Gaß, *Briefwechsel*, xxxvii.

had penned his essay as a response to Bretschneider's *Aphorismen* and had consequently dealt with the Lutheran, the Calvinist, and his own interpretation of the doctrine. However, as Schleiermacher himself conceded, his universalist understanding was not derived from either the Lutheran or the Calvinist one, and hence it had no legitimate room in the ecclesiastical debate about the Prussian Church Union. His final plea to the Lutherans, to give up their own interpretation in favor of the Augustinian one as the most consistent form of the doctrine, appears almost ludicrous. It certainly failed to impress his opponents, if not also his supporters.

The theological public received the essay with lively interest. On the whole, though, the published reviews were rather negative. This was partly due to the fact that they were written by Lutheran theologians who were unwilling to accept an essentially Reformed interpretation of the doctrine, or by theologians who objected to the Prussian Church Union and hence to Schleiermacher's efforts to present a unitary doctrine of predestination. The Lutherans' suspicion that Schleiermacher intended their conversion to the Reformed doctrine was not wholly unfounded. While early on in the essay he emphasized the common aspects of both faiths, he later admitted that he wished to facilitate the conversion, and thus the "unity among themselves"[63] of those members of the Lutheran Church willing to convert to the Calvinist doctrine.

Reviews by Reformed theologians are conspicuous by their absence. It is my contention that this is borne out by the fact that the German Reformed never did subscribe to the Calvinist theory in the first place and therefore had no need for an apologist, and to the fact that the Reformed were a small minority in Prussia in contrast to the vast majority of Lutherans and lacked any outspoken representatives apart from Schleiermacher. He appears as a rather solitary, if prominent, Reformed theologian and church politician, supported primarily by King Friedrich Wilhelm III.

A first, albeit brief, comment by an anonymous critic appeared in 1819, the same year as the essay, as part of a review of the first issue of *Theologische Zeitschrift*. It is more interesting in terms of what it omits than concerning what it actually says. It characterizes the essay as a defense of the Calvinist doctrine, comments favorably on the author's acumen and less favorably on his exegetical insight, and it concludes that the essay reconsidered the Union of the Protestant Churches. But it does not even mention Schleiermacher's solution of universal salvation. In this, the anonymous reviewer is not an exception, but the first of many.

63. Schleiermacher, On the Doctrine of Election, tr. Nicol and Jørgenson, 97.

Another anonymous review of Schleiermacher's essay was published in *Theologische Quartalschrift* of 1820. It claimed that the essay was not only an important text for dogmatics as such, but that it was remarkable also because of its timing: not so much as a contribution to the Union debate, but as a statement by a Reformed theologian "at a time when a considerable proportion of the most learned and upright theological teachers of the Protestant Church have cleansed their notion of the doctrine for the sake of reason so much from everything positive that almost nothing but naked reason has remained."[64] This claim is a criticism of Schleiermacher's doctrinal approach in the era of rational theology. Inadvertently, the reviewer also gives an interesting insight into the theological climate prevailing in Prussia: the terms Lutheran on the one hand, and Protestant or evangelical on the other, were used interchangeably by the Lutherans themselves, implying that the Reformed represented a group apart from mainstream German Protestants. Lutheranism was, of course, the dominant Protestant confession in the Holy Roman Empire and in Prussia.[65] A case in point is the reviewer's claim that Schleiermacher wanted to prove against the Protestants that the Calvinist doctrine was scriptural.[66] This anonymous Lutheran reviewer is one of the very few who commented on Schleiermacher's solution of universalism; he dismissed it as an "expediens which neither Calvin nor Augustine thought about."[67] In Schleiermacher's system, he argued, the idea of eternal punishment was absent, and so in his embarrassment he introduced the notion of universal restoration. The reviewer concluded by stating that, while Schleiermacher had given supporters of the Union sufficient reassurance, he doubted whether they would appreciate the price to be paid, that is, effectively, the acceptance of the Calvinist version of the doctrine with universalism as a stopgap.

Christoph Friedrich Ammon, the Lutheran councilor and court chaplain of Dresden, also responded in 1820, in an article in *Magazin für christliche Prediger*. In one sweeping blow, he condemned the Reformed

---

64. Anon., *Theologische Quartalschrift*, 282.

65. Of the other two states apart from Prussia, which emerged after the dissolution of the Holy Roman Empire, Austria was predominantly Catholic, and the Confederation of the Rhine, consisting of sixteen south and west German states, had a considerable number of Reformed, who subscribed to the *Heidelberg Catechism* of 1563.

66. This point is, in fact, made time and again. In 1826, eight years after its first publication, Schleiermacher's essay was still the object of an anonymous commentary wanting to demonstrate that the Reformed doctrine was irreconcilable with the tenets of reason and Scripture.

67. Anon., *Theologische Quartalschrift*, 288.

doctrine and its underlying world view by quoting Immanuel Kant: "Predestination as the doctrine of perdition presupposes an immoral order of the world and is therefore irrational."[68] Ammon saw no need to propound the untenable, sinister, and unconditional double decree. He agreed with Schleiermacher that the differentiation between divine foreknowledge and predestination should be abandoned, but his argumentation was different. Ammon held that God's one decree contained both the communication of salvation to those who wanted to accept it, and the communication of perdition to those who did not. Like other Lutheran reviewers, he too insisted that Schleiermacher's attempt at amalgamating the two Protestant Churches under the banner of the Augustinian interpretation intended "not so much our union, but our conversion."[69] Ammon made no mention of Schleiermacher's universalist solution at all; he was too concerned with his defense of the Lutheran doctrine even to acknowledge it.

Still in 1820, Karl Gottlieb Bretschneider himself responded in an article published in the journal *Für Christenthum und Gottesgelahrtheit*. Unlike Ammon, he expressed his support for the united Church. Remarkably unpolemical, very detailed and thorough, Bretschneider's review is about the same length as Schleiermacher's essay. Bretschneider, a Saxon, had the impression that not only had there been no approach by Lutherans to the Calvinist interpretation of predestination in Prussia, but that nothing at all had been said about it "in all places where the Church Union was being promoted, Berlin excepted."[70] The Reformed, he observed, only perceived the difference in the doctrine of communion, or thought of it as a matter of academic disputes. Bretschneider emphasized his abhorrence of such a "covering up and pasting over,"[71] and he called for a dogmatic consensus in order to achieve unity in faith. Two Churches which are meant to be united, he argued, cannot retain contradictory confessions. In this respect, as in others, Bretschneider was a true exponent of orthodox Lutheranism.

He then proceeded to re-examine the Calvinist doctrine of predestination as presented by Schleiermacher under five headings: predestination according to Calvin, the relation of the doctrine of predestination to the theological system shared by both faiths, and the relation of the doctrine to rational theology, to morality, and to Scripture. In the first section Bretschneider reiterated both the main tenets of the Calvinist doctrine

68. Ammon, "Abhandlung," 3.

69. Ibid., 47.

70. Bretschneider, "Die Lehre Calvins," 2.

71. Ibid.

and the Lutheran contention that divine grace could be resisted by the human will. Nevertheless, he rejected Schleiermacher's claim that, according to Bretschneider, grace was not needed for salvation. Bretschneider countered that his would be a case of throwing the baby out with the bathwater, since he had only rejected the doctrine of *sola gratia* but not the necessity of grace altogether. At the same time, he distanced himself from the *Formula of Concord*, which taught that a human being before rebirth was "like a stone or block."[72] Neither did he accept Schleiermacher's argument that the two Churches differed "only in the way in which the opposite of this universal characteristic is to be expressed, that some will not be saved because God did not will to grant them faith."[73] As Bretschneider clarifies, the Lutheran Church did not eschew the harshness of the expression, but the underlying belief that God was the reason for a person's non-conversion.[74] This was not merely a difference of expression.

In the context of the relationship between election and rational theology, Bretschneider perceptively explicated Schleiermacher's and his own understanding of divine omnipotence. For Schleiermacher, he argued, "omnipotence would cease to be omnipotence if there was any result, even the crudest crime, which it had not determined in a necessary manner." For Bretschneider, and according to rational theology, omnipotence was "only an ability, a power to work everything: 'omni' in omnipotence only signifies that it is sufficient for each and every result, but not that it generates every effect."[75] This has consequences for the understanding of the human will and its ability to limit God's omnipotence. For Bretschneider, the human free will exists only by the power of God's will, and whether a person's and God's will concur is irrelevant, because through his infinite wisdom God will achieve his goal by subjecting the results of human willing to his intentions. Accordingly, if God does not prevent some evil, it is because the results serve his will, but not because he approves of and intends this evil to happen. Bretschneider noted on some occasions that a more subtle interpretation than Schleiermacher allowed was possible, for instance regarding Schleiermacher's juxtaposition of the human will as determined entirely by divine grace and as entirely determining itself. This should be supplemented by a third position, wherein both the divine will and the human will work together towards blessedness. This synergistic position

72. Ibid., 19.
73. Schleiermacher, On the Doctrne of election, tr. Nicol and Jørgenson, 50.
74. Bretschneider, "Die Lehre Calvins," 26.
75. Ibid., 32.

was indeed different from the purely Pelagian one which Schleiermacher had almost imposed on Bretschneider.

Bretschneider evoked a typically rational notion of justice that entailed treating "moral beings according to how their willing and acting relates to the moral law."[76] One cannot expect human beings to consider something relating to God as just, if it appears to be an injustice according to the unchangeable principles of human reason. In a similar vein, he claimed that "we may demand that the end and goal of everything must not contradict our reasonable ideas of wisdom and justice."[77] It is in this context that Bretschneider referred to Schleiermacher's solution of perdition as a temporal rather than an eternal state. The question why God has condemned some human beings, who are no worse than others, to perdition, leads to the end of reason, and since Schleiermacher must have felt the same, Bretschneider concludes, he regarded perdition as temporary and in its intention equal to any other finite or temporal punishment. Bretschneider's criticism of this position exhausted itself in the observation that in this case the doctrine of election would lose much of its importance. Moreover, he concluded wrongly, blessedness and perdition were a temporal state, whereas in Schleiermacher's interpretation blessedness is eternal. This passage is the only occasion where Bretschneider touched on the most explicit characteristic of universalism, but he did so without even mentioning the notion. Quite clearly, he did not consider this solution valid or even worth exploring.

Regarding the relation between predestination and morality, Bretschneider promoted the Lutheran cause by arguing that the divine fatalism of the Calvinist position honored God's omnipotence by destroying the free moral world; "everything great, splendid and divine in human nature will succumb as soon as its moral independence is shattered."[78] He concluded that Schleiermacher's defense of the Calvinist doctrine had failed to convince him. Its claims of *sola gratia*, of perseverance only by divine ordination, and of blessedness only for some, could result only in inertia or the entire inability to do anything towards one's betterment.

Finally, Bretschneider contrasted the Calvinist and Lutheran doctrines with regard to Scripture. Whereas the first, he said, maintains that the Biblical authors express themselves in such a way that suggests divine predestination and follows the letter of Scripture, the latter follows its spirit

76. Ibid., 51.
77. Ibid., 64.
78. Ibid., 68.

and argues that Scripture teaches no such dogma because it is detrimental to a person's moral betterment. He also noted that Schleiermacher himself did not cite any Biblical passages to support his contention that through original sin humankind had become a dead mass corrupted in reason and will. He added that election in the Old Testament was not about election to blessedness after death, and least of all through Christ, but about Israel as the elected nation, and that the New Testament only talked of the election of non-Christians to Christianity.

Bretschneider concluded his review by expressing his hope that it would contribute to the union of the two Churches—a union that "will certainly not be achieved until we have examined the differences of our confessions seriously and in detail."[79] In contrast to Schleiermacher and his efforts to convince the Lutherans of the Augustinian position, he had no desire for anybody who believed in double predestination to change their system.

Wilhelm de Wette reviewed Schleiermacher's essay in the second issue of *Theologische Zeitschrift*. Considering the close personal relationship between Schleiermacher and de Wette, it is rather surprising that the latter offered little, if any, support for Schleiermacher. Schleiermacher himself reacted to de Wette's contribution rather skeptically. In a letter to Friedrich Lücke of 20 June 1820, he announced that de Wette was taking the part of his adversary, but that he doubted very much whether this would be of much benefit to the Lutherans and their doctrine of predestination. Schleiermacher was still hoping for what he called "a proper opponent."[80] Half a year later, on 31 December 1820, Schleiermacher admitted in a letter to Ludwig Gottfried Blanc that he had not yet read de Wette's essay about election properly, but that its basis appeared to him not to be very clear.[81]

In his review, de Wette set out to defend the doctrine of the orthodox teachers of the Lutheran Church, and to rescue it "if not completely, then at least with respect to essential issues."[82] However, he used his article as a forum to develop and propagate his own thoughts about original sin, free will, providence, divine and human reason, and the trinity. His ideas essentially concurred with the Lutheran interpretation, for instance where he stated that faith depended on the human word being preached and heard

79. Ibid., 96.
80. Dilthey, *Aus Schleiermachers Leben in Briefen* III, 263.
81. Ibid., 269.
82. De Wette, "Ueber die Lehre von der Erwählung," 83.

before it could be recognized in faith as the eternal word. Nonetheless, he also distanced himself from the Lutherans, calling their argumentation for election to blessedness "unclear and vacillating."[83] They admitted, he claimed, that God did not elect individuals because of their foreseen faith, but they maintained nevertheless that God elected those of whom he foresaw that they would believe in Christ. De Wette claimed this formula to be untenable, and he demanded that the difference between foreknowledge and predestination be relinquished. He concluded that "the decree of election is indeed absolute."[84]

De Wette first mentioned Schleiermacher's name with reference to the latter's contention that for God evil did not exist. While de Wette provided his own interpretation of this statement, he concurred entirely with its central claim. He then proceeded to explain the Lutheran distinction between the divine *voluntas antecedens* and *voluntas consequens*. The first related to the hidden God, the last to the revealed God. Hence, from the human perspective, he took the distinction of two divine wills to be appropriate, even though there was only one identical divine will.

Finally, on the last three pages of his review of Schleiermacher's essay, de Wette declared his concurrence with Schleiermacher on the issue of perdition. His argumentation is rather curious, though. He first declares that "we agree with Schleiermacher on the view according to which election and perdition are only meaningful in terms of history."[85] Here, de Wette appears to have misunderstood Schleiermacher: for the latter, only perdition is a temporal and therefore historical step in the development of individual human beings and the human race as such, whereas election to blessedness is always eternal. De Wette then emphasizes particularly his agreement with Schleiermacher on the rejection of the doctrine of eternal perdition. He argues that "what is condemned eternally would also need to have been created as condemned, since eternity does not have a beginning."[86] Nevertheless, he proposes not to abandon the doctrine of eternal damnation because of its historical importance, which, in turn, consists in the distinction between good and evil. Thus, while eternal perdition has to be retained as a horror vision, it has to be mitigated by the recognition of the wisdom and grace of God "and the most sublime thought of a triumphant kingdom of God, in which everything that exists

83. Ibid., 114.
84. Ibid., 115.
85. Ibid., 120.
86. Ibid.

is entwined in blessedness."[87] In other words, de Wette concurs with Schleiermacher on universal restoration. At the end of his review, therefore, he abandoned the Lutheran ship he had set out to defend, and declared his position to be biblical rather than heretical. It is remarkable that de Wette's endorsement of Schleiermacher's universalist stance was the only one of its kind. Even more intriguing is the fact that it emanated from a Lutheran, who throughout his review maintained that perdition was not based on God's decree or will, but on human sin, and that therefore the doctrine of predestination had to be conditional. Universalism, he argued, was founded on an absolute divine decree. It is hardly surprising that de Wette's inconsistent argumentation did not bring any more Lutheran supporters of universal restoration out of the woodwork. Nevertheless, his review remains important as the only one to take Schleiermacher's solution seriously.

The pro-Union Lutheran Ernst Wilhelm Christian von Sartorius (1797–1859) discussed Schleiermacher's essay in an appendix to his 1821 book on the inability of the human will to gain a higher morality. At the time of its publication, Sartorius was Professor *extraordinarius* at the University of Marburg. He opposed the rationalism championed by Bretschneider and others and insisted on the doctrine of God's free grace as the sole factor in a person's salvation, rejecting any notion of ethical self-determination in relation to the acceptance of divine grace.[88] Defending the Lutheran doctrine of the dependence of faith on hearing the gospel, he distanced himself from the traditional Lutheran assumption of two divine wills.[89] Sartorius was careful also to discuss some finer points of the argument. He noted that the human inability to better oneself referred not to any moral improvement but to the inability "to fill oneself with pure, divine, moral feelings,"[90] that is to an improvement *coram Deo*. This explication undermined some of the more simplistic Lutheran arguments against the Reformed doctrine's perceived practical implications for moral behavior.

Sartorius was the only reviewer apart from de Wette who mentioned Schleiermacher's universalist theory, and he tentatively signaled his

87. Ibid., 122.

88. See Erdmann, "Sartorius," 382.

89. The divine will is not the only issue on which the Lutheran interpretation is not unanimous. Such discrepancies do not appear to have posed a problem, however. As an anonymous reviewer who disagrees with a passage in the *Formula of Concord* insists, "we still believe to be Lutherans." Anon., "Bemerkungen über die Lehre," 188–89.

90. Sartorius, *Lutherische Lehre*, 136.

agreement with it, conceding that, sooner or later, everybody would be received into the kingdom of God. In an unorthodox interpretation of the Lutheran theory, he even maintained that, because of the universalism of grace, Lutherans would ultimately be forced to accept this solution. For the sake of impartiality, however, Schleiermacher should have admitted that the Calvinist theory with its particularity of grace was much less suited to the universalist solution than the Lutheran one. This is an inconclusive argument, of course, since Lutheranism holds that, although the offer of grace is universal, its success is particular.

Sartorius also made a highly interesting psychological observation: he asserted that Schleiermacher's conviction of the ultimate universal reconciliation and acceptance of all into God's kingdom was not informed by his Calvinist understanding, but by "the goodness of his heart"![91] Sartorius certainly has a point, in that Reformed particularism does not constitute a logical premise for universalism. Conversely, of course, the Lutheran understanding of resistible grace in cooperation with a person's free will to decide their ultimate fate does not represent a precondition for universalism, either. Nevertheless, Sartorius' psychological argument strikes a chord, not least since Schleiermacher elaborated the point that the blessed cannot truly be happy in the knowledge that some are eternally damned. Any eschatological separation of human beings from God would have been unacceptable to him. Sartorius, on the other hand, did not regard salvation and perdition as part of an eternal decree. Instead, he understood salvation as reward and perdition as punishment, but refrained from declaring this punishment eternal. Even though this is effectively an agreement with Schleiermacher, neither he nor Sartorius spoke as representatives of their respective Churches.

Finally, Sartorius stated with some relish, "since Dr Schleiermacher, who calls himself a stubborn defender of Calvin, has relinquished the strictness of the Calvinist doctrine of predestination, we can maintain with certainty that at least in the German Reformed Church there is nobody left who decidedly adheres to it."[92] This remark testifies to Schleiermacher's prominence as a Reformed theologian, but more importantly, it highlights his isolated position in the German Reformed Church, which never did adhere to that doctrine.

In 1822, the Lutheran Johann Christian Friedrich Steudel (1779– 1837), identified by Hermann Mulert as "the head of the Swabian

91. Ibid., 156.
92. Ibid., 175.

supranaturalists"[93] published a cumulative review of recent publications on predestination in three consecutive issues of *Neues Archiv für Theologie und ihre neueste Literatur* ("New Archive for Theology and Its Most Recent Literature"). The first installment gave an overview of the doctrine and its inherent difficulties, such as the unfree will and divine omnipotence. Steudel differentiated carefully between the will as such, which can be neither good nor bad in itself, and the use human beings make of their will, which can be morally good or bad. Human freedom, he affirmed, is not absolute. Rather, it is the freedom of a finite being within the confines of a sphere of activity. It can therefore not have an effect on creation independent of God. True divine omnipotence means that God does not fear any disturbance of the world order or any seeming deterrent to the "external success"[94] of his creation. In the second installment of his review, Steudel clarified this claim: "God's omnipotence works in the area of human freedom in the sense that no result of freedom may disturb the order of the world, in which the expressions of freedom have been integrated."[95]

The second installment of the review dealt almost exclusively with Schleiermacher's essay. Here, Steudel started with the typical Lutheran reservations about the Calvinist doctrine, which "bears something that pure, unadulterated human feeling forcefully resents."[96] He accused it of being un-Christian, and he reiterated the conviction that grace "cannot be imposed"[97] and therefore cannot be irresistible. His detailed criticism of Schleiermacher's essay begins with the observation that, if Schleiermacher thinks he can regard the differences between Lutherans and Calvinists as belonging to academia, it can hardly be expected that he will consider them with the necessary seriousness. This line of criticism demonstrates a profound misunderstanding of Schleiermacher: assigning the discussion of the doctrine to scholarly circles does not imply its relegation, but rather ensures its treatment by the most relevant and best equipped players. Against Schleiermacher, Steudel upheld the distinction between divine decree and permission, and maintained that supralapsarianism was not scriptural: how can redemption be necessary if by sinning Adam only corresponded to the destination that God had accorded him?[98] Steudel

93. Mulert, "Aufnahme der Glaubenslehre," 136.

94. Steudel, "Anzeige," 444.

95. Steudel, "Fortsetzung der Anzeige," 704.

96. Ibid., 667.

97. Ibid., 670.

98. The question of how unavoidable Adam's sin is after God has created the

accused Schleiermacher of adhering to a system of predestination in which everybody is only what God wants him to be. In the same vein, he asked how redemption can be necessary if by sinning Adam only fulfilled God's ordination?

In the first installment Steudel briefly referred to universalism, rejecting it altogether because "sin as sin would disappear entirely from the kingdom of God"[99] if universal restoration were the ultimate fate of humankind. In the second installment he warned that Schleiermacher's promotion of universal restoration was "all the more dangerous because it pushes the last soft bolster underneath the carelessness which turns the doctrine of the absolute decree to its advantage."[100] The assurance that all will be saved irrespective of their conduct, he inferred, was an invitation to a lax generation to let themselves go altogether.[101]

Interestingly, in his essay Schleiermacher also mentioned a supporter he had in the Lutheran camp: "the blessed Töllner, one of those theologians who seems to have been too soon forgotten and who without justification is also not cited by Dr Ammon on this matter but who states: 'With regard to the union of the two churches everything depends upon the controversial points being declared too lofty,'[102] and thus views this difference as well as that regarding the Lord's Supper as one that belongs only to the academy and not to life."[103] Johann Gottlieb Töllner did indeed hold a rather liberal view of the symbolic books of the Church; he "virtually regarded them as a necessary evil"[104] and asserted that nobody had the right to eternally fix a doctrine.

An anonymous contributor to the *Allgemeine Kirchenzeitung* of 1824 gives a verbatim rendition of King Friedrich Wilhelm III's cabinet order of 1817 but only a very concise summary of Schleiermacher's essay. He, too, does not mention universalism. Interestingly enough, he agrees with

---

conditions for the possibility of sin is not posed. Without these conditions, sin would not have been possible, and if God is at least indirectly responsible for sin, was sinfulness not ultimately the destination God had ordained for humankind even according to the Lutheran interpretation?

99. Steudel, "Anzeige," 423.

100. Steudel, "Fortsetzung der Anzeige," 729.

101. The third installment of the review passes on to the interpretations of the doctrine produced by de Wette, Marheinecke, and others.

102. Töllner, "Die kirchliche Vereinigung der Protestanten." *Kurze vermischte Aufsätze*, 2. Sammlung, Frankfurt an der Oder 1766, 147–73.

103. Schleiermacher, On the Doctrine of Election, tr. Nicol and Jørgenson, 98.

104. Fronmüller and Wagenmann. "Töllner, Johann Gottlieb," 816.

Schleiermacher that practical Christian life has no part in the theological exposition of the doctrine of predestination. It is unfortunate that the identity of this reviewer, and, more to the point, his denomination cannot be established.

One more anonymous review, published in 1827, is particularly interesting because of its detailed and logical discussion of many of the issues Schleiermacher raised in his essay. A case in point is the rejection of Schleiermacher's argument that what God permits would have to have its ultimate reason outside God. The reviewer counters that there are three possible reasons for divine permission. 1) God cannot hinder something even though he might want to; that would imply a restriction of his omnipotence. 2) God does not want to prevent something even though he could; that would contradict his perfect goodness. 3) God does not want something and he cannot hinder it either; where this something is of a quality that makes trying to prevent it impossible, there is no restriction to God's omnipotence.[105] Therefore, a logical impossibility, such as the coexistence of ethical freedom and the inability to sin, can cause God to permit rather than ordain something.

Again, this review makes no mention of universalism. It is my contention that this omission by the vast majority of commentators is due to their being Lutherans. As such, they were concerned with the perceived negative consequences of double predestination for practical life, with the suspicion that Schleiermacher was trying to convert them, and with the unacceptable Reformed understanding of the unfree will. Hence, they did not even proceed to a discussion of Schleiermacher's solution. If the premises are inaccurate, the solution to the dilemma does not deserve much attention. In this sense, Schleiermacher's theory of universal restoration was not actually considered to be controversial. Where it was discussed at all, it was not regarded as a serious challenge to Lutheranism, but on the whole it was simply ignored.

Three very recent publications also assess Schleiermacher's doctrine of election. Matthias Gockel's 2006 monograph *Barth and Schleiermacher on the Doctrine of Election* analyses both the essay on election and relevant passages in *Christian Faith*, while Eilert Herms' 2009 article "Freiheit Gottes—Freiheit des Menschen" ("God's Freedom—Human Freedom") focuses entirely on the essay. This is also true of the introduction to the first English translation of the essay by Iain C. Nicol and Allen G. Jørgensen.

---

105. See Anon., "Bemerkungen über die Lehre von der Gnadenwahl," 168.

These contributions represent the most detailed discussion of the essay since the reviews of the 1820s.

Gockel points out in a perceptive introduction that Schleiermacher's new approach was motivated by the traditional anthropocentric interpretation of predestination. He notes that Schleiermacher advocates the strict Augustinian and Calvinist version of the doctrine while arguing for one single divine decree to salvation, and explains the "dialectic of election and reprobation"[106] to be part of the historical realization of the kingdom of God. He points out that Schleiermacher propagated the Calvinist version because "it offers a cogent explanation of the indispensability of divine grace for human salvation."[107] One of the most important insights of the Protestant Reformation, this is a doctrine which Schleiermacher is intent on preserving against Bretschneider and others, who focus on synergism or a person's own contribution to their salvation. Gockel's assessment that Schleiermacher "admits that neither the Lutheran nor the Calvinist view has tended to move into [the] direction"[108] of universal restoration is not entirely accurate. Schleiermacher's intention was to demonstrate his impartiality by not advancing a conjecture about Lutheran or Calvinist tendencies towards universalism, since neither of the two faiths "drives us more strongly to this view."[109]

Gockel makes the important observation that Schleiermacher puts a much stronger emphasis on the work of Christ in election than do other interpretations of the doctrine. This is borne out, for instance, by the view that grace is perceived by a believer as God's gift for Christ's sake, not for the believer's sake. It also becomes evident in Schleiermacher's argument that the first human beings were not created in any way better than the following generations, and that humanity was truly realized for the first time through Christ's appearance. Gockel concludes that Schleiermacher's concept of election remains theocentric, since "neither his Christology nor his pneumatology informs the idea of the single divine decree."[110]

Herms argues that the Lutheran and Reformed views on election differ only with regard to semantics but converge in essence. Expressly disregarding the *Canons of Dort*, as Schleiermacher did, Herms perceives a material convergence between the Lutheran understanding of

---

106. Gockel, *Barth and Schleiermacher*, 14.

107. Ibid., 16.

108. Ibid., 34.

109. Schleiermacher, On the Doctrine of Election, tr. Nicol and Jørgenson, 95.

110. Gockel, *Barth and Schleiermacher*, 36.

the doctrine of election and that of Calvin according to the last, 1559, edition of his *Institutio*, despite their semantic discrepancies. In essence, Herms claims that both confessions, when proceeding from redemption, generally agree on a certain (or specific) inability[111] for self-betterment and on a certain (or specific) indispensability of grace. The difference lies in the degree of "certain": Calvinists insist on the absolute indispensability of grace, whereas Lutherans claim a divine will to grace that can be inefficient, either because of humanity's sin or because of the free will. According to Herms, Schleiermacher shows that, in essence, Lutherans might revert to Calvin, provided that their notion of freedom does not imply a natural human ability to free themselves from sin. It is this understanding of freedom, Herms argues correctly, which Bretschneider advocates against the traditional and contemporary Lutheran interpretation. However, there is a third theory between Bretschneider's Pelagianism and Calvin's indispensability of grace: synergism, the orthodox Lutheran understanding of a co-operation between divine grace and human freedom. In this interpretation, grace is a necessary condition of salvation, whereas in Calvin's view, grace is the sufficient condition. In this sense, it is inaccurate to claim that the orthodox Lutheran doctrine would have to revert to the Calvinist version. Moreover, the real bone of contention between Lutherans and Calvinists was not the attainment of faith, but the reason for the absence of faith in some people.

Citing Article V of the *Confessio Augustana*,[112] Herms asserts that for Lutheranism, too, faith is exclusively the work of God, and it conforms to God's predestination, therefore the Lutheran wording results in the Calvinist formulation. Equally, he argues, the fact that some people do not hear the gospel and are therefore not reached by God's word "according to the Lutheran doctrine, too, can have its foundation only in God's predestination."[113]

Against Herms' claim it is important to bear in mind that the *Augsburg Confession* does not mention predestination at all, and that Article V actually deals with the preacher's office. Therefore, at that point it is concerned only with the relation between preaching and hearing the gospel and the attainment of faith, but it is not concerned with the possibility of a person's rejection of faith. This is a different matter altogether from the

---

111. *gewisse Unfähigkeit.* Herms, "Freiheit Gottes," 199.

112. "*Per verbum . . . donator spiritus sanctus, qui fidem efficit ubi et quando visum est Deo in iis qui audiunt evangelium.*"

113. Herms, "Freiheit Gottes," 200.

scenario Herms describes, where the acceptance or rejection of faith is not an issue because of the absence of God's word. The *Formula of Concord*, on the other hand, deals explicitly with predestination. *Epitome Articulorum* XI, *Affirmata* 11 states that the reason for many being called but few being elected is that those who are not elected either do not hear God's word at all, or willfully spurn it and "block the proper path of the Holy Spirit so that he cannot work in them."[114] Clearly, the difference between the Lutheran understanding that a person can resist the working of the Holy Spirit and the Calvinist contention that grace is irresistible is more than merely semantic, and it certainly does not signal a convergence in essence.

Following Schleiermacher, Herms proceeds to argue that, apart from the Lutheran concerns about the implications of double predestination for practical Christianity, the Lutherans' main objection against Calvin's doctrine is its denial of God's universal will to salvation and its claim that God's intentions are calculated only for some, not for all. Herms refutes the latter with the contention that the Christ-event never comprises the whole of the human race at the same time. Its spread is a historical development that, Herms insists in accordance with Lutheran dogmatics, is itself grounded in God's predestination. He argues further that therefore, "one has to claim, with Calvin, that this particular uniform divine predestination is both the reason for the fact that some are not redeemed as well as that of the blessedness of others at the same time."[115] Nevertheless, contrary to Herms' claim, there is no denying the fact that Calvin advocated a double decree of blessedness and of perdition directed at individuals, not a uniform predestination with different temporal or historical results.

Nicol and Jørgenson provide a detailed introduction to their splendid English translation of Schleiermacher's essay on election. Before engaging in a discussion of his theory of predestination, they first outline his reception of Augustine, of Luther and Lutheranism, and of Calvin. The first of these sections deals in particular with Augustine's work *On Rebuke and Grace*, the only work by Augustine that Schleiermacher refers to in his essay. In the second section, Nicol and Jørgenson introduce the varying positions of Martin Luther's *De Servo Arbitrio*, of Philipp Melanchthon, the Philippists, the Gnesio-Lutherans, and the *Book of Concord*. They conclude this section with the perceptive observation that "Luther himself advanced a notion of predestination that more nearly approximates that of Calvin . . . , while roundly rejecting a Calvinian notion of the Eucharist,

114. *Bekenntnisschriften*, 818.
115. Herms, "Freiheit Gottes," 207.

while Melanchthon does the opposite."[116] The section on Calvin emphasizes the christocentric formulation of his doctrine, and the observation that Schleiermacher "takes up and creatively appropriates"[117] Calvin's doctrine.

Their discussion of Schleiermacher's interpretation of election first takes account of Bretschneider and his position, and of the context of the Prussian Church Union. The translators note that Bretschneider came very close to Pelagianism in his assessment of a person's ability to somehow effect his or her own salvation. They also emphasize his contention that a church union can be forged only on the basis of a clear statement of the doctrinal differences between the two Churches.

The role of Scripture and of a consistent doctrine for Schleiermacher is discussed next. Nicol and Jørgenson point out Schleiermacher's opinion that Scripture cannot be read objectively.[118] They discuss his dismissal of the Lutherans' concern for practical Christianity arising from the double decree, and outline Schleiermacher's development of the notion that God's work spreads historically. A section on creation and redemption is followed by a discussion of Schleiermacher's contention that there is a single decree for the human race as such rather than decrees for individuals, and ends with a summary of Schleiermacher's arguments in favor of the strict formulation of the doctrine. Nicol and Jørgenson conclude their introduction with a consideration of the dogmatic utility of the doctrine of predestination.

CONCLUSION

The most striking factor common to all reviews and recent assessments of Schleiermacher's essay is their reaction, or the absence of a reaction, to his interpretation of the doctrine of election as universal restoration. His contemporaries either ignored this solution or they did not take it seriously. Recent publications on the essay either emphasize the theocentric dogmatic bias of his interpretation (Gockel), or they almost nonchalantly refer to Schleiermacher's creative appropriation of Calvin's version (Nicol and Jørgenson), or they try to demonstrate the implicit convergence of the

---

116. Nicol and Jørgenson, Introduction to On the Doctrine of Election, tr. Nicol and Jørgenson, xx. It should be added that in this respect the German Reformed Church concurs entirely with Melanchthon.

117. Nicol and Jørgenson, Introduction to On the Doctrine of Election, tr. Nicol and Jørgenson, xxv.

118. See ibid., xxix.

Calvinist and the Lutheran doctrines (Herms). These reactions are symptomatic of Schleiermacher's failure to convince either his contemporary reviewers or his modern critics.

Before trying to analyze the reasons why the essay did not succeed in reconciling Reformed and Lutherans under the Augustinian form of the doctrine or in promoting universalism, it is as well to ascertain first why Schleiermacher composed the essay in the first place. There were various reasons: he had been urged by his academic Lutheran colleagues to produce an article for inclusion in a new theological journal; he felt compelled to respond to Bretschneider's *Aphorismen* by defending the Calvinist stance, which he claimed had not been properly represented in the debate; he was lecturing on dogmatics and had reached the doctrine of election, but he had not found the time to write up his extremely scanty lecture notes; he hoped to use the essay as a precursor for his yet to be compiled work on dogmatics; and in the absence of a consensus confession of the united Protestant Church in Prussia, he hoped to convince both Lutherans and Reformed that universal restoration could be the solution in the ongoing debate about predestination. If this solution was unacceptable, he at least wanted to get the Lutherans on the Calvinist side and thus procure a doctrinal consensus on a consistent version of the doctrine of election.

It is not difficult to see that Schleiermacher was trying to kill too many birds with the one stone. More importantly, though, his position was ambiguous. He defended a version of the doctrine which was not at stake against a majority of objectors whose own theory he tried to dismiss as inconsistent, and whom he therefore alienated, only in order to introduce his own solution, which, given the prevailing complacency about the doctrinal differences, was not even called for. Schleiermacher answered the question why he styled himself a spokesperson for the Calvinist doctrine himself in the essay: "since my expectation that there would also surely arise a defender of the original Calvinism, or rather Augustinian, doctrine is all but disappointed, I would no longer restrain myself but would take up this opportunity"[119] to clarify this position.

However, the Calvinist version of election was never at stake in the Prussian Church Union debate. The German Reformed Church had never been purely Calvinist, and none of its confessions adhered to an unconditional double decree of election and perdition. The *Sigismund Confession* of 1614 positively expressed the rejection of the understanding that God "begrudged the better part [of humanity] blessedness and condemns them

---

119. Schleiermacher, On the Doctrine of Election, tr. Nicol and Jørgenson, 5.

absolutely, without their own cause, not because of sin either."[120] Curiously, Schleiermacher subscribed to the *Sigismund Confession* at his ordination, and neither with regard to his ancestors nor in relation to his own biography was he a Calvinist in this respect, whatever his contemporaries may have thought.

The question therefore remains: For whom did he actually speak? Certainly not for the German Reformed Church, whose theory of election came relatively close to the Lutheran interpretation at any rate. I would speculate that by defending the Calvinist version, in a sense, he was simply playing devil's advocate, if only for the sake of a satisfying, exhaustive debate. But such a dubious stance was never going to win over the majority Lutheran side, nor was his universalist solution likely to succeed in a situation where no compromise was called for.

120. Heppe, *Bekennnnisschriften*, 293.

7

Election in *Christian Faith*

BACKGROUND

SCHLEIERMACHER'S *MAGNUM OPUS*, *Christian Faith*, arose mainly out of his lectures at the University of Berlin. It was also motivated by the common practice among theologians (not only those in academia) to publish textbooks, manuals, or compendia on Christian doctrine. Moreover, he was at a station in life at which he was taking stock: his fiftieth birthday on 21 November 1818 appeared to be a symbolic landmark for him. As he confessed in a letter to his friend August Twesten of 14 March 1819: "Shortly before my birthday namely, the thought fell heavily upon my heart that if I wanted to celebrate it with pleasure and without secret pain, it would need to find me engaged in a good and proper piece of work. So, inspired by recent activities and various events, I dedicated myself to writing my dogmatics, on which I am lecturing just now."[1] In the summer semester 1819 he lectured at the University of Berlin on the introduction to his dogmatics, and in the following winter semester on Parts I and II of *Christian Faith*. In the letter to Twesten mentioned above, Schleiermacher also described how the written product was taking shape. He was composing the book from three different ends. "I started simultaneously with the first beginning and the beginning of Part I and the beginning of Part II, on which I was lecturing just then. . . . However, I soon had to abandon the threefold way of working and keep to writing up a lecture subsequently to

---

1. Meisner, *Schleiermacher als Mensch*, 295.

delivering it. Even this I could only continue up to the doctrine of election
... and I dearly wish to finish my dogmatics during summer and fall."[2]

The reason for this rather unusual procedure was Schleiermacher's
practice of developing his lectures from scanty notes in the process of
delivery, and writing down full text versions only after the oral presentation. This does not imply that he did not prepare his lectures well—on the
contrary.[3] Ekkehard Mühlenberg describes the process: Schleiermacher
would devise a plan for the complete lecture series over the entire semester down to the level of weekly and individual lectures and write down
the basic ideas, called propositions, on a jotter. He would then use these
propositions, usually four per lecture, to deliver a coherent text explaining
the propositions in free speech in front of his students. In a letter of 9
January 1819 to his friend Ludwig Gottfried Blanc, he stated that the main
issues were actually discussed in the explanatory notes or subsections
rather than in the propositions themselves. It was not unusual for Schleiermacher to become entirely clear about an issue only in the actual process
of lecturing on it; in this case he would write down a summary of his
thoughts after the lecture. He orally reflected on his topic in the course of
delivering his lectures, and he was scathing about academics who simply
kept on reciting the lecture notes they had once drawn up to generations
of students: this kind of procedure reminded him "uncomfortably of those
days when printing did not exist."[4]

Schleiermacher started writing up his lectures on Part I of *Christian
Faith* in November 1819. In the letter to Blanc mentioned above, he explained that he started so late after the beginning of the teaching term "so
that my birthday should find me engaged in this large work."[5] However, he
had already advanced so far with his lectures that he was unable to catch
up with them in writing. He put Part I aside and started writing down
the text of Part II, and at the time of writing the letter, he was still able to
keep pace with his lectures on Part II. At the same time, he also started to
compile the introduction, on which he had lectured in the previous summer semester, but managed to write down only a few propositions with
subsections. In summer 1821, he still complained in a letter to Blanc that

---

2. Ibid., 295–96.

3. For the following, see Mühlenberg, "Universitätslehrer," 43.

4. Schleiermacher, "Gelegentliche Gedanken über Universitäten in deutschem
Sinn." In *Sämmtliche Werke* III / 1, 577.

5. Dilthey, *Aus Schleiermacher's Leben* III, 244.

his written composition lagged very much behind his lectures, and that he had to revise the text of Part II more extensively than expected.[6]

Christian Faith was first published in 1821/22. It could not be pigeonholed into any one Protestant faction. It was, as Kurt Nowak put it, "neither rationalist nor supranaturalist, it was not revivalist, not confessionalist and not speculatively philosophical."[7] Not surprisingly, it attracted both praise and severe criticism.[8] Within five years, Schleiermacher began to seriously contemplate a second, revised edition, which was finally published in 1830 and has since been regarded as the definitive edition. In a letter to his friend Johann Christian Gaß of 21 November 1829, he mentioned that his work on the revised edition had been greatly delayed by the tragedy of the premature death of his son Nathanael at the age of ten. Schleiermacher was hoping then to finish Part I within the following month and noted: "Up until now, no paragraph has been left the way it was; rather, I'm rewriting everything. Nonetheless, in essence everything remains the same."[9]

DESIGN AND INTENTION

In the following I am referring to the second, revised edition of 1830. As Schleiermacher himself had stated while working on the revision, there is no substantial difference between the two editions. This certainly applies to the section on election. The relevant propositions are materially identical, they follow the same order in both editions, and the structure in which election forms part of pneumatology, which in turn is positioned within the wider context of ecclesiology and preceded by christology, is also the same in both editions. As Matthias Gockel observes, the doctrine of election in the first edition is "identical in content with the slightly enhanced version of the second edition."[10]

In Christian Faith Schleiermacher resolutely opposed the theological efforts of his contemporaries who were seeking to substitute the lost

6. Ibid., 274.

7. Nowak, Schleiermacher, 410.

8. The controversies caused by the publication cannot be detailed here, but it is worth noting that towards the end of the first phase of the reception debate he published in 1829 Dr. Schleiermacher über seine Glaubenslehre, an Dr. Lücke (zwei Sendschreiben), ("Dr Schleiermacher on his Christian Faith, Two Letters to Lücke"), a public defence of its objective and methods.

9. Gaß, Briefwechsel, 219–20.

10. Gockel, Barth and Schleiermacher, 36.

indubitable authority of the church with a timeless objective authority. These efforts were not homogenous but can broadly be identified with the supranatural, rational, and speculative branches of theology respectively. The supranaturalists regarded Scripture as the sacrosanct basis of doctrinal authority; although they had abolished the style of argumentation employed by the old Protestant Orthodoxy of the seventeenth century, and although reason had come to play a part in their argumentation, the supernaturalists represented a conservative trend that uncompromisingly defended the biblical message against the rationalist zeitgeist. In contrast, the rationalists regarded human reason as the authority to be obeyed. Only natural revelation was acknowledged, and as a corollary, biblical miracles had to be explained as natural events. All Christian doctrines were to be understood as serving a moral or ethical purpose. Speculative theology, finally, was still in its infancy in the 1820s, but it was on the road to becoming highly fashionable. Basically a philosophical theology, its main tenet was that dogmatics had to be constructed in a speculative manner proceeding from the idea of God. The timeless authorities evoked by these three theological trends can be summarized as a literal interpretation of Scripture for the supranaturalist, an ethical or moral importance of doctrines for the rationalists, and a speculative idea of God for the speculative theologians.

Schleiermacher, maintaining that God cannot be grasped by human reason and that all reflection is historical, sought a completely new approach. As Dietz Lange explains, he based his Protestant dogmatics on four axioms: dogmatics is a positive, historical science; dogmatics has to give an account of the religious experience of Christians; at the core of dogmatics is therefore God's presence in the historical figure of Jesus of Nazareth; in order to understand Jesus Christ and Christian faith, both theological reflection and historical-critical science are necessary.[11]

Christian Faith consists of a more philosophical introduction preceding the material dogmatics, which is subdivided into two parts. The introduction deals with the definition and method of dogmatics, thus taking the place of the traditional *prolegomena*. Part I then explicates the development of religious self-consciousness, whereas Part II discusses religious self-consciousness as determined by the antithesis of sin and grace. Accordingly, Part II is sub-divided into two aspects. Part I (religious self-consciousness) thus forms the logical precondition for Part II section 2 (consciousness of grace), and Part II section 1 (consciousness of sin)

11. See Lange, "Neugestaltung," 91.

forms the temporal precondition for Part II section 2 (consciousness of grace).

One highly innovative feature of Schleiermacher's dogmatics is the discussion of each material part (I, II 1, and II 2) in three different aspects: in relation to human beings, to God, and to the world. *Christian Faith* has no separate doctrine of God, but a running discussion of different divine attributes in Part I, Part II, 1 and Part II, 2. Its key premise is that all dogmatic statements must be referenced to the contents of pious self-consciousness. The common element in all pious states of consciousness is the feeling of absolute dependence. This implies that piety is not constituted by a person's particular concept or notion of God, but that it is what Matthias Gockel calls "part of the ontological structure of human existence."[12] That human constant does not depend on individuals actually becoming conscious of this feeling of absolute dependence. The particular characteristics of Christian piety are redemption accomplished by Christ, and the contrast between the divine reality of redemption and the inability of human beings to save themselves.

The very concept of absolute dependence of human beings and all creation on God entails that there cannot be any reciprocity or indeed any interaction between human beings and the world on the one side, and God on the other.[13] As Gockel puts it succinctly, "we cannot interact with [God], but we could not interact without him."[14] The sphere of interaction for the human race is the coherent system of nature, and the relation between human beings and the world is one of both relative dependence as well as relative freedom.

STRUCTURE

Part I of *Christian Faith* explicates the development of religious self-consciousness or Christian piety. It encompasses the doctrine of cosmology, which, in turn, consists of creation and preservation, divine attributes,

12. Gockel, *Barth and Schleiermacher*, 43.

13. A corollary of the denial of any special relation between God and human beings is Schleiermacher's rejection of the notion that there are differences in the divine determination of individuals that are reflected in their predestination to salvation or perdition. He has to find an explanation which differs from the traditional explanation for the tension between God's redemptive will and its limited historical success.

14. Gockel, *Barth and Schleiermacher*, 53. This does not mean, however, that there can be no relationship between God and human beings at all, otherwise redemption would be impossible.

and the original state of perfection. The doctrine of creation and preservation discusses religious self-consciousness, which expresses the relation between God and the world. Specifically, it deals with creation itself, including angels and the devil, and with preservation. The divine attributes discussed within the doctrine of cosmology include eternity, omnipresence, omnipotence, and omniscience. The section on the original state deals with the original perfection both of the world and of human beings.

Part II contains explications of the facts of religious self-consciousness as they are determined by the antithesis of sin and grace. Part II, 1 deals with the development of the consciousness of sin, or the doctrine of hamartiology. Hamartiology proper is subdivided into a discussion of original sin and actual sin, and (in relation to the world) of evil. Part II, 1 also discusses the divine attributes that relate to the consciousness of sin: holiness, righteousness, and mercy. Part II, 2 deals with the consciousness of grace; structurally, this is the most complex part. It also consists of three sections: the doctrine of grace, which, in turn, is subdivided into christology (regarding the person and work of Christ) and soteriology (regeneration and sanctification). The second section, the doctrine of ecclesiology, consists of the origin of the church, or pneumatology, the essential characteristics of the church in antithesis to the world, or ecclesiology proper, and the consummation of the church, or eschatology. The third section explicates the divine attributes relating to redemption, namely love and wisdom. The very last section of *Christian Faith* deals with the doctrine of the trinity. The structure of *Christian Faith* can be represented as follows:

Introduction: Definition and method of dogmatics

Part I: Development of religious self-consciousness (logical precondition of Part II, 2)
    Section 1: (human) Creation and Preservation)
    Section 2: (God) Divine attributes I   } Cosmology
    Section 3: (world) Original state   )

Part II: Religious self-consciousness as determined by sin and grace

Part II, 1: Consciousness of sin (temporal precondition of Part II, 2)
    Section 1: (human) Original and actual sin)
    Section 2: (world) Evil   } Hamartiology
    Section 3: (God) Divine attributes II   )

Part II, 2: Consciousness of grace
    Section 1: (man)
        Division 1: Christology
        Division 2: Soteriology
    Section 2: (world)
        Division 1: Pneumatology   )
        Division 2: Ecclesiology proper   } Ecclesiology
        Division 3: Eschatology   )
    Section 3: (God) Divine attributes III)

Conclusion: Trinity

The doctrine of predestination as such is located in Part II section 2, division 1. It forms part of the doctrine of pneumatology, which is concerned with the origin of the Christian Church. After an introduction (§§115–116) Schleiermacher deals with election (§§117–120) and the communication of the Holy Spirit (§§121–125). The doctrine of election itself consists of four parts: an introduction (§§117–118), two theorems—predestination (§119) and the grounds of election (§120)—and a postscript on reprobation.

PNEUMATOLOGY

The Doctrine of Election

The introduction to the doctrine of ecclesiology, or in Schleiermacher's words, the condition of the world in relation to redemption (§§113–114), makes a number of key claims. The Christian Church is identified as being coterminous with the kingdom of God and the fellowship of the regenerate. Schleiermacher distinguishes an inner fellowship comprised of those who live in the state of sanctification, and an outer fellowship of those in whom preparatory grace is at work. The calling into the outer circle represents the beginning of an individual's fellowship with Christ, whereas the inner circle is inhabited by those who have a continuous share in the corporate life of grace. However, nobody is born in the inner circle.

Schleiermacher argues that the emergence of the church was a necessary development because Christ could not have done any redemptive work without the formation of such a fellowship. The doctrinal explication regarding the Christian Church has to cover its origin, its development and preservation, and its consummation. These topics constitute the doctrines of pneumatology, ecclesiology proper, and eschatology. The section of *Christian Faith* preceding ecclesiology, which deals with christology and soteriology, is concerned with the operations of the Redeemer in the individual without regard to the life of the community of believers. Under the heading of ecclesiology, Christ's operations and the individual life of the regenerate are discussed as an integral constituent of the church.

The introduction to the doctrine of pneumatology (§§115–116) states that regeneration is the precondition for membership in the Christian Church. It is made effective through Christ's perfectly powerful God-consciousness. Its communication to an individual creates an unceasing impulse toward the actualization of that person's God-consciousness. In Schleiermacher's words, "with regeneration there is always imparted a strong will for the kingdom of God."[15] The susceptibility or receptivity of human beings enables this divine activity to become historical.

During Jesus' earthly life, already existing pre-Christian religious communities gained a relationship to Christ through his historical appearance, and they, in turn, exercised their influence on others; in this way, existing religious fellowships took on a Christian character. Crucially, though, Schleiermacher argues, as long as Christ's personal activity on earth continued, and as long as he exerted an immediate or direct influence on his contemporaries, the church remained unconstituted. The origin of the actual church is explained through the doctrines of election and of the communication of the Holy Spirit. This interpretation has important consequences for Schleiermacher's christology and his understanding of Christ's role in the founding of the Christian Church.[16]

In the introduction to the doctrine of election (§§117–118) Schleiermacher explains that the inequality between individuals who are regenerate and others who are not, as well as between those who are drawn into the outer circle early and others who do not heed the call of preparatory grace, or who are not called at all during their lifetime, is entirely due to divine ordination. This observation is congruent with the basic tenet of Protestant orthodoxy according to which election is non-meritorious. More specifically, it corresponds to the Reformed understanding that the different degrees of Christ's efficacy historically are rooted in the governance which has its ultimate ground in divine good-pleasure.

---

15. Schleiermacher, *Christian Faith*, tr. MacIntosh and Stewart, §115.1, 532.

16. For a discussion of these consequences see chapter 9 below.

According to Schleiermacher, the empirical observation that there appears to be a lack of faith in some persons provides no basis for the conclusion that they are foreordained never to be regenerate. Indeed, if a part of the human race were eternally excluded from the inner circle of the fellowship, an "insoluble discord"[17] or a conflict in the species-consciousness of the regenerate would occur. Moreover, if the inequality between the regenerate and the non-regenerate were real and eternal, Christ would have come only to bring to light an already existing disparity between those included in and those excluded from fellowship with Christ despite their equality in sin. But such a disparity would have to be rooted in an illusion. As Murray Rae explains, either we "regard as illusory the judgment that we were first created equal and are equally bound in sin, or the judgment that the difference between the regenerate and the unregenerate constitutes an inequality."[18] Either way, the particular and arbitrary character of redemption and perdition would remain intact.

Citing the *Huguenot Confession* and the *Belgian Confession* in support of the traditional Reformed explanation regarding salvation as divine mercy and perdition as divine justice, Schleiermacher himself nevertheless insists that "justice and mercy must not exclude one another."[19] His own solution of the ancient dilemma posed by the notion of foreordained perdition is to interpret the difference between the regenerate and the not-yet-regenerate as vanishing over time, or, in Brian Gerrish's words, as "a transient corollary of history."[20] As in his essay on election, Schleiermacher envisages that everybody will be regenerated "when his time is fully come"[21] and that there is no difference between the earliest and the last regenerate in terms of their worth. Reprobation for Schleiermacher expresses the indeterminate status of non-believers as a temporary divine passing-over.

Schleiermacher thus explicitly divorced himself from the Calvinist tradition, which postulates God's eternal good-pleasure as the ultimate reason for the difference between the regenerate and the unregenerate. He concedes that if there is indeed a double decree to salvation and to perdition, "then the reception of one and the exclusion of the other has its ground in such divine arbitrariness, that we must rightly describe the

---

17. Schleiermacher, *Christian Faith*, tr. MacIntosh and Stewart, §118, 539.

18. Rae, "Salvation in Community," 181.

19. Schleiermacher, *Christian Faith*, tr. MacIntosh and Stewart, §118.2, 544.

20. Gerrish, *Tradition*, 118.

21. Schleiermacher, *Christian Faith*, tr. MacIntosh and Stewart, §118.1, 540.

ordinance as sheer caprice."[22] His clear statement against the Calvinist doctrine of *predestinatio gemini* in *Christian Faith* marks an important development with regard to his essay on election. There, he had consistently argued that the Calvinist understanding of predestination was not grounded in arbitrariness; rather, it was the human ignorance of God's reasons that rendered divine motives for election arbitrary. Moreover, in the essay he had explained that even though the divine decree does have specific effects in the lives of particular individuals, the decree is not about individuals, hence it cannot be arbitrary.

At the start of his discussion of the doctrine of predestination (§119), Schleiermacher quotes from two Lutheran and three Reformed confessions[23] to support his interpretation that election of the justified is predestination to salvation. However, some of the passages he quotes also make reference to damnation. In actually rendering the relevant statements of this aspect of predestination, Schleiermacher not only shows himself to be a theologian with integrity, presenting the evidence available in its entirety instead of selectively quoting only the passages that support his argument; he also prepares the ground for his decisive argument that "the formula suggested as a way out of the difficulty would still deviate from the confessions of both divisions of the Protestant Church."[24] He here signals his departure from the Protestant tradition with regard to the doctrine of perdition. Before developing this formula, he reminds his readers that the manner and time of an individual's regeneration is determined by his or her biography, which in turn is embedded in the historical unfolding of the kingdom of God. In other words, a particular person's regeneration, or entering of the inner circle, represents one aspect of the overall divine government as it manifests itself for this individual at a particular place and time. In this sense, i.e. as one aspect of the foreordained system of nature and the historical development of the kingdom of God, this person's regeneration happens necessarily when and where it does. And in this sense also, "nothing happens in the kingdom of grace without divine foreordination."[25] There is no room for contingency in this coherent system of nature.

---

22. Schleiermacher, *Christian Faith*, tr. MacIntosh and Stewart, §118.2, 543.

23. The *Saxon Confession* and the *Formula of Concord* on the one hand, and the *Thirty-nine Articles*, the *Second Helvetic Confession* and the *Sigismund Confession* on the other.

24. Schleiermacher, *Christian Faith*, tr. MacIntosh and Stewart, §119.3, 551.

25. Ibid., §119.2, 547.

This contention raises questions about those who are evidently not regenerate. According to Schleiermacher, the traditional explanation that they have been passed over, which was offered for instance by Augustine, in the *Sigismund Confession*, and in other Reformed confessions, can apply only in a very limited sense. Comparisons can be made between those already regenerate and those not yet in the inner circle, but nothing can be claimed about those outside the fellowship of Christ other than that, in their case, divine foreordination has not yet attained its aim and redemption has not yet been revealed in them. At the moment of comparison, they appear to the regenerate to have been passed over for the time being. Nevertheless, all human beings are objects of the same divine activity that gathers the church together. Schleiermacher formulates his conclusion rather carefully: "Thus we may reasonably persist in holding this single divine foreordination to blessedness, by which the origin of the church is ordered."[26] There is "no contradiction between the end in view in the divine plan of salvation and the result accomplished by the divine government of the world."[27] In other words, there is an efficacious correspondence between God's decree and his power and will to bring it to fruition. Rae is correct in pointing out that Schleiermacher's deliberations in *Christian Faith* were "exploratory" and his conclusions "tentative rather than assertive"[28] and that therefore his tendency toward universalism did not entirely discard the presupposition of particularism.

Schleiermacher concedes that death can intervene before the election to regeneration has fulfilled itself in an individual. However, he immediately indicates his break with the Protestant orthodox tradition when claiming that the state in which a person dies is only an intermediate state; death does not signal the end of God's work of grace. Schleiermacher's new formulation states: "There is a single divine fore-ordination, according to which the totality of the new creation is called into being out of the general mass of the human race."[29] This formulation is entirely congruent with his statement in his essay on election that "only one divine decree can be assumed, one that embraces all, namely, the decree concerning that arrangement within which those of the mass who are capable of individual spiritual life are gradually quickened."[30] In *Christian Faith*, that concept

26. Ibid., §119.2, 548–49.

27. Ibid., §119.3, 549.

28. Rae, "Salvation in Community," 184.

29. Schleiermacher, *Christian Faith*, tr. MacIntosh and Stewart, §119.3, 550.

30. Schleiermacher, On the Doctrine of Election, tr. Nicol and Jørgenson, 73.

of the single divine decree becomes the basic structural element of the whole work. Indeed, at the very end of Part I of *Christian Faith* (§61.4), Schleiermacher explained that "the divine decree ordaining the whole development of the human race by means of redemption . . . was included in the idea of human nature from the beginning."[31] The gradual, historical development of God-consciousness in individuals and in the human race, and the divine ordering of everything toward redemption, is an expression of the unity of the single decree. All human beings are fashioned in readiness to enter the kingdom of God; every human being has the potential to be regenerated, even after death. In this sense, the realization of redemption is a perfect manifestation of divine good-pleasure and omnipotence. Christ's historical appearance does not constitute a second decree; indeed, it does not even contribute specifically to the actual defining character[32] of the single divine decree.

The second theorem (§120) deals with the ground of election, and concludes with a postscript about reprobation. Calling and regeneration neither imply any merit on the human side, nor do they presuppose any "pre-existing soteriological divide"[33] between individuals or between groups of human beings. Referring to the *Canons of Dort* and the *Brandenburg Confessions*, Schleiermacher maintains that the reason for election is divine grace, not foreseen faith as such. It could be argued that a person's election is determined by the foreseen efficaciousness of preaching at a specific moment of time and the resulting occurrence of the maximum power of faith in the person. Ultimately, however, the understanding that election is grounded in the faith of the elect as foreseen by God, and that election is solely determined by God's good-pleasure, are two sides of the same coin. To seek the ground for election in divine good-pleasure is to seek it at the beginning, whereas to seek the reason for election in divine fore-knowledge is to seek it in the final result. God's foreknowledge must guide his decree. As a corollary, Schleiermacher dismisses the view that human beings are rejected by God because of their non-belief. This, as Gockel claims, would imply "an unwarranted distinction between a [person's] natural aversion towards the gospel as the basis for non-election, and a divinely determined aversion as the effect of non-election."[34]

31. Schleiermacher, *Christian Faith*, tr. MacIntosh and Stewart, §61.4, 253.
32. *Bestimmung*
33. Gockel, *Barth and Schleiermacher*, 81.
34. Ibid., 92.

Schleiermacher rejects altogether any "atomistic view"[35] of the work of redemption that considers only the individual. No individuals become anything in consequence of a special decree relating to them. There is only the one unconditional decree for all of creation. The very shape of the kingdom of God and everything appertaining to it, indeed the whole system of nature within which the church evolves and develops is determined by the divine decree at any given time. That single decree subjects everything to the necessity inherent in the conditions it has established in the coherent system of nature. Hence, contrary to the testimony of the Reformed confessions, there is no special decree regarding individuals, even though from the perspective of an individual, faith in Christ means sharing in the divine good-pleasure.

Only in a postscript to the doctrine of election does Schleiermacher consider "the assumption that a section of the human race remains shut out for ever from the sphere of redemption."[36] To him, reprobation does not specifically refer to hell and the torments traditionally associated with that notion, but to the eternal exclusion from the presence of God.

The problems that arise from reprobation can be summarized as follows: the personal and the species-consciousness of the regenerate is adversely affected by the eternal exclusion of part of the human race from the kingdom of God; it suggests wrongly that human nature is not identical in all; and it cannot be reconciled with the understanding that Christ was sent for the whole human race. If, in contrast, all are included in the divine fore-ordination to salvation, then the high-priestly dignity of Christ, who intercedes for all, "comes out in its whole efficacy."[37] The contention that God regards all human beings only in Christ underpins this christological argument.

Schleiermacher concludes the doctrine of election, and thus the first part of the doctrine of pneumatology, by tentatively formulating the result of his deliberations: "If we take the universality of redemption in its whole range, . . . , then we must also take fore-ordination to blessedness quite universally."[38] This is a rather cautious and muted formulation, or, as Morwenna Ludlow observes, "by no means a forceful and absolute defense of universalism"[39] compared with the outright affirmation of universal

---

35. Schleiermacher, *Christian Faith*, tr. MacIntosh and Stewart, §120.2, 554.

36. Ibid., §120 postscript, 558.

37. Ibid., §120 postscript, 560.

38. Ibid.

39. Ludlow, "Universalism in the History of Christianity," 208.

restoration he had declared in his essay on election. Partly because of the insufficient scriptural evidence for both and partly because of his premise about what constitutes a doctrinal proposition, Schleiermacher did not afford a doctrinal status either to universalism or to twofold foreordination.

The Communication of the Holy Spirit

In the introduction to this doctrine (§§121–122) Schleiermacher clarifies his understanding of the Holy Spirit. As before, he identifies the Holy Spirit with the common spirit that moves in and animates the Christian fellowship. But now he demarcates a decisive line between New Testament statements about the Holy Spirit and the position of the Spirit as the third person of the trinity. He warns his readers not to mix up notions that have emerged from that doctrine with New Testament statements that show us the Holy Spirit only in believers. Schleiermacher is constrained to interpret the Holy Spirit only in the latter sense by the premises of his dogmatics. They stipulate that only propositions conveying immediate statements about the Christian pious self-consciousness are admissible in his dogmatics. However, as he explains in §§170–172, the doctrine of trinity, "as ecclesiastically framed, is not an immediate utterance concerning the Christian self-consciousness, but only a combination of several such utterances."[40] Schleiermacher also claims that, from the point of view of the Christian fellowship of the regenerate, the common spirit of the church and the Christians' universal love for all humanity is the same identical Holy Spirit. For Schleiermacher, this implies that the Spirit could be communicated and received completely only after Christ's departure from earth, or from Pentecost onward. During Christ's activity on earth the common life was incomplete: although the disciples had the indispensable susceptibility necessary to receive the Holy Spirit's communication—this receptivity is posited as a human ontological constant, which developed in the disciples in their company with Jesus—they did not yet have the free spontaneous activity that does not need a new special impetus on each and every occasion to constitute the full common life. In the same sense, the common spirit was not complete during the personal presence of Christ.

Schleiermacher's identification of the Holy Spirit with the common spirit or "the vital unity of the Christian fellowship as a moral person"[41]

40. Schleiermacher, *Christian Faith*, tr. MacIntosh and Stewart, §170, 738.
41. Ibid., §116.3, 535.

is an indication that his doctrine of pneumatology is not fully developed. It is only factually but not programmatically part of the doctrine of the church.

In §123 Schleiermacher offers a definition of the Holy Spirit that excludes both the Spirit's position as the third person of the trinity and the Holy Spirit of the Old Testament. According to the testimony of the New Testament, he argues, those who first received the Holy Spirit described him "as a specific divine efficacious working in believers, though not one to be separated from the recognition of the being of God in Christ."[42] All powers at work in the Christian fellowship and already mentioned in the New Testament have always been traced back to the Holy Spirit. However, individuals partake of the Holy Spirit not in an isolated way in their personal self-consciousness, but they have their share in it only in so far as they share the Spirit as a common consciousness.

Schleiermacher continues his exploration of the communication of the Holy Spirit with the proposition (§124) that there is no living fellowship with Christ without the indwelling of the Holy Spirit, and vice versa. This implies that by virtue of being regenerated, human beings partake of the Holy Spirit and, by the same act and at the same time, they are taken up into the common life with Christ. In other words, Christ's life in believers is identical with the communication of the Holy Spirit in them, and in turn with their being children of God. The communication of the Holy Spirit in the individual regenerate is the basis for the continuing interaction and co-operation among the members of the church, which has taken over and continued the communication of Christ's God-consciousness and blessedness to humanity.

Schleiermacher also ponders the question whether the outpouring of the Holy Spirit at Pentecost was an entirely new and original divine revelation, or whether it followed naturally from Christ's appearance on earth. That question is motivated by the quest for the ultimate basis of Christianity: if the communication of the Holy Spirit is a natural consequence of Christ's appearance, then Christ's appearance constitutes the only supernatural basis of Christianity. Otherwise, the outpouring of the Spirit at Pentecost is as much an original miracle as the appearance of Christ, and equally necessary. Behind this quest lurks the post-Enlightenment concern about the validity and interpretation of miracles, and ultimately about the foundation of the church. Schleiermacher observes that, while the Pentecost account shows sufficiently clearly "the mark of the

42. Ibid., §123.2, 572.

miraculous"[43] later accounts regarding the communication of the Spirit through preaching exhibit the same characteristics, and hence the miraculous element is not part of the essence of the matter. He concludes that the miraculous representation of Pentecost in Scripture is characteristic of the era of its occurrence. But in view of its gradual dissemination effected by the living power of the church and of Christ, the outpouring of the Holy Spirit cannot be considered a miracle at all. Nevertheless, if it is regarded as a sudden leap from the fragmentarily affected reciprocity into a coherent common activity it does remain a miracle.

The last theorem discussed as part of the communication of the Holy Spirit (§125) claims that the church is the perfect image of the Redeemer in its purity and integrity, and that each member of the church forms an integral and indispensable part of this fellowship. However, the ultimate accomplishment of the church is only reflected in the entirety of the human race, and only the totality of all forms of spiritual Christian life represents the complete image of Christ. This will be achieved only gradually. The work of the Holy Spirit is the principle that effected both the origin of the church and its further historical development toward the kingdom of God. In this sense, pneumatology, or the doctrine of the origin of the church, is identical with regeneration, and ecclesiology proper, or the doctrine of the development of the church in the world, is identical with sanctification.

ECCLESIOLOGY

The doctrine of ecclesiology proper follows pneumatology and is concluded by eschatology. Ecclesiology proper deals with the subsistence of the church in the world until its consummation. According to Kurt Nowak, "in Schleiermacher's philosophical-theological conception, the Christian Church appears on the one hand as the partial *gestalt* of the humanity-wide[44] church, and on the other as that form of the Christian collective life that precedes it."[45] The fellowship of believers derives its identity from three factors: the particular fashion in which the divine inhabits them, the behavior of the Holy Spirit as the common spirit of the church, and its striving to shape itself according to the image of Christ. Identifying what the church is not leads Schleiermacher to the conclusion that the fellowship

43. Ibid., §124.3, 578.

44. *menschheitlich*

45. Nowak, *Schleiermacher*, 337.

of the regenerate derives its identity in opposition to the world. Human nature forms part of the world to the extent that it is not determined by the Holy Spirit. The world is the aggregate of individual elements that oppose each other and that combine by chance in many different ways; it can thus appear to the believer to be formless. However, the Christian Church as a pious community develops in the world as a growing circle. It is fostered by the way in which communication between human beings takes place until in its consummation all sin will be expunged. As Rae argues, Schleiermacher did not conceive the consummation of the church in terms of the withdrawal of a perfected fellowship from the general mass of the unperfected human race.[46]

The divine decree is realized historically as a natural phenomenon. The resulting unevenness of the development of the kingdom of God is reflected in the various degrees of the receptivity of human beings, communities, and indeed nations, to preaching and other forms of proclamation. Nevertheless, this development is governed by the single divine decree to redeem, hence the order of historical events is not contingent or indeed arbitrary but necessary: it corresponds to the order of regeneration. In this way, people's regeneration depends on two elements, one external and one internal: their particular place in the world in a particular historical situation, and their personal inner life, which determines their receptiveness to the work of the Holy Spirit.

Schleiermacher distinguishes essential and invariable characteristics of the church as such and mutable or variable elements that characterize the church in its existence in the world. The first section of the doctrine of ecclesiology proper (§§127–147) deals with Christ's testimony: with Scripture and the ministry of the word, Christ's ordinance of forming and maintaining the church, that is, baptism and communion, and with the reciprocal influence of the whole on the individual and vice versa, that is, with the power of the keys and with prayer.

In the course of this exposition, Schleiermacher discusses eternal damnation with regard to the unworthy participation in communion (§142). He first points out the difficulty of establishing exactly where the unworthiness that conduces to such a judgment originates, because those who are not regenerate have no access to the sacrament as a sacrament. Schleiermacher is willing to concede that some individuals take part in communion even though a yearning for the sacrament has not been kindled in them, and that in its origin such a partaking is unworthy. But if the

---

46. See Rae, "Salvation in Community," 187.

judgment described as a consequence of unworthiness is to be understood as eternal damnation, "then it seems impossible to establish any connection between the two things."[47] The only way Schleiermacher can see for even an element of damnation to come into play here is through a condition of non-receptivity brought about by an unworthy, thoughtless partaking of the sacrament. Such a meaningless external performance would amount to a degradation of the sacrament, which, in turn, could induce a hardening of the individual that can be regarded as an element of damnation. In this sense only, communion serves as a means of distinguishing between worthy partaking that promotes the fellowship with Christ, and unworthy partaking that makes the strongest means of consolidating the fellowship with Christ more ineffectual.

At this point of the discussion, Schleiermacher returns to the difference between the Lutheran and Calvinist understanding of communion. According to the Lutheran theory, the unworthy partaking of the sacrament is possible because the sacramental partaking of body and blood is linked to the physical elements of bread and wine. According to the Calvinist understanding, participation in the sacrament is inextricably linked to spiritual participation, so that those who are unworthy of communion cannot enjoy any spiritual participation. Hence, strictly speaking, they are not actually taking part in the sacrament anyway. Schleiermacher identifies the difference between the Lutheran and the Calvinist doctrine of communion as being inherent in only unworthy participation, and he optimistically anticipates this difference to vanish entirely over the course of time as the practice of unworthy participation disappears.

The second section of the doctrine of ecclesiology proper (§§148–156) deals with the mutable or variable elements that characterize the church due to its existence in the world. Schleiermacher here distinguishes the visible church from the invisible one. The invisible church as a coherent entity consists of the totality of all effects of the Holy Spirit. Each visible part of the church, on the other hand, is a mixture of the church and the world, and it is therefore divided and subject to error. In the Christian Church on earth, there is always both error and truth. This observation leads Schleiermacher to a reflection on the Reformed attitude to dogma, according to which no definition of a doctrine can be regarded as valid for all times. Indeed, he claims that every individual has the right to take part in the revision of the church's doctrines. Especially pertinent convictions should be set forth in confessional texts, but these documents only record

47. Schleiermacher, *Christian Faith*, tr. MacIntosh and Stewart, §142.2, 656.

the convictions held at a particular time and place, and they must not be used to prevent any future revisions. Schleiermacher himself exercises that right by pointing to certain differences between the Reformed and Lutheran confessions on the one hand and his own contentions on the other. For instance, both faiths assert "the unity of the Old Testament and the New Testament Church"[48] whereas for Schleiermacher church exists only where there is faith in Christ. Similarly, while both Lutheran and Reformed confessions maintain that the church has been in existence from the beginning of the world, Schleiermacher argues that it began only with Christ's personal activity.

ESCHATOLOGY

In connection with the doctrine of election, the section of eschatology that discusses eternal blessedness (§163) is particularly interesting. After dealing with the last judgment, that is the separation of the human race into the good and the bad, Schleiermacher concludes that such a separation remains "both inadequate and superfluous."[49] He then turns his attention back to eternal blessedness. Curiously, his first proposition stresses that "those who have died in fellowship with Christ will find themselves . . . in a state of unchangeable and unclouded blessedness."[50] This proposition concurs entirely with all orthodox Christian teaching that faith is the *sine qua non* for justification, and that persons who attain faith in this life will enjoy eternal blessedness. As such, it has never been the focus of any debate. But this position is somewhat at variance with Schleiermacher's contention that those who die outside the fellowship with Christ still remain objects of God's love, that death represents only an intermediate state, and that "all belonging to the human race are eventually taken up into living fellowship with Christ."[51] It could be conjectured that eternal blessedness can only be claimed for those who become regenerate in this life because only they can actually have a pious self-consciousness. Nevertheless, this proposition remains curiously particularist.

Schleiermacher's acceptance of universalism is thus somewhat more guarded and tentatively couched in *Christian Faith* than in the essay on election. There is certainly no outright espousal of universal salvation, and

48. Ibid., §156.1, 693
49. Ibid., §162.3, 716.
50. Ibid., §163, 717.
51. Ibid., §119.3, 549.

indeed, Schleiermacher concedes only that universalism is at least as justified as the doctrine of double predestination. In Gockel's words, he "arrives at a qualified affirmation of general redemption and universal salvation."[52]

The doctrine of eternal damnation is treated only in an appendix. Here, the nature of damnation or hell is discussed. If it is conceived as involving bodily pain and physical torment, Schleiermacher opines that damnation would not be irremediable misery, partly because of the mitigating power of habit through which a person would get used to the torment, and partly because the damned would develop a consciousness of their ability to bear pain. Schleiermacher is equally dismissive of damnation involving spiritual misery. If the damned develop pains of conscience, they will actually be better persons in their state of damnation than they were in their earthly lives. If, on the other hand, they develop a consciousness of the blessedness they have previously forfeited, they need to be able actually to picture such blessedness, and this ability would, in turn, constitute an enjoyment that would lessen their misery. Moreover, only if the option to partake in blessedness actually existed for the damned would they be tortured by the fact that they had forfeited this state.

Having humored the defenders of the doctrine of damnation by his almost absurd discussion of what hell could be like, Schleiermacher concludes with the still very careful suggestion that "we ought at least to admit the equal rights of the milder view, . . . that through the power of redemption there will one day be a universal restoration of all souls."[53] It is important to bear in mind that the discussion of these doctrines at this stage in his dogmatics is concerned with "thought forms . . . under the title of *prophetic doctrines*."[54] In fact, he considers them "the efforts of an insufficiently equipped faculty of premonition"[55] or presentiment, and warns that in order for these efforts to remain Christian, they need to comply with Scripture.

In conclusion, it is worth revisiting the features of Schleiermacher's theology on which his universalism in its more tentative form in *Christian Faith* is based. First, he identifies the susceptibility, or receptivity, of human beings that is necessary to receive the Holy Spirit and God-consciousness as constants of theological anthropology, or integral

52. Gockel, *Barth and Schleiermacher*, 93.

53. Schleiermacher, *Christian Faith*, tr. MacIntosh and Stewart, §163 Appendix, 722.

54. Ibid., §159.3, 706.

55. Ibid.

constituents of human nature. Every human being, by virtue of being human, is endowed with these two elements essential for universal redemption. Second, Schleiermacher understands redemption as "universally and completely accomplished by Jesus of Nazareth,"[56] thereby, as Rae put it, "effecting the restoration and revitalization of God-consciousness"[57] of the redeemed. Third, he perceives the Christian Church as a continuously though irregularly growing fellowship that will be consummated when the entirety of the human race has been received into the inner circle. Finally, it is Schleiermacher's contention that death does not signal the end of the work of divine grace.

As Gockel notes, Schleiermacher certainly "overcame the traditional particularism and rediscovered the universal dimension of election."[58] His tendency towards universalism is based on the power of Christ's redemptive work. However, in *Christian Faith* he is careful to assert no more, but also no less, than the possibility that all will be included in the fellowship of Christ. As Rae concludes, "there is something profoundly important in his refusal to accept a concept of salvation that is careless of the plight of one's neighbor—and even of one's enemies."[59]

---

56. Ibid., §11.3, 56.

57. Rae, "Salvation in Community," 177.

58. Gockel, *Barth and Schleiermacher*, 198.

59. Rae, "Salvation in Community," 197.

8

Schleiermacher's Sermons

INTRODUCTION

SCHLEIERMACHER PREACHED HIS FIRST sermon on 15 July 1790 as part of his divinity degree exam, and his last one on 2 February 1834, ten days before his death. He was in the church ministry from 1794 until 1834; first as assistant pastor in Landsberg an der Warthe (1794–1796), and subsequently as hospital chaplain at the Charité in Berlin (1796–1800), court chaplain in Stolp (Pomerania) from 1802, and university chaplain in Halle (1806–1807). In 1809, in one of the King Friedrich Wilhelm III's appointments, he became the Reformed pastor at Trinity Church in Berlin, a post which he filled until his death. During his twenty-four year tenure as professor of divinity at the University of Berlin from 1810 to 1834, he thus also served as parish minister of one and the same congregation.

Before considering the publication of his own sermons, Schleiermacher successfully tried his hand at translating sermons by Hugh Blair, Professor of Rhetoric and Belles Lettres at the University of Edinburgh, a moderate Church of Scotland minister and one of the key figures of the Scottish Enlightenment. Blair's sermons were immensely popular at the time, and Schleiermacher's mentor Friedrich Samuel Gottfried Sack was already engaged in a German translation when he got Schleiermacher interested in joining this venture in 1794. He also translated sermons of "the more brilliant"[1] Scottish preacher Joseph Fawcett into German. These translations were published between 1797 and 1802.

The first collection of Schleiermacher's own sermons was published in 1801. He had preached them during his time as hospital chaplain

1. Dilthey, *Leben Schleiermachers*, 78.

between 1795 and 1800 in various congregations, though not in the hospital itself. By 1832, that first collection had been followed by six others. Apart from these seven published collections, which were all authorized by Schleiermacher, a number of transcripts he had hardly managed to edit and revise appeared in print between 1831 and 1833. Together, they constitute the first four volumes of the ten-volume Section II of the posthumous edition of his collected works, *Sämmtliche Werke* (*SW*). The last six volumes contain previously unpublished exegetical sermons on New Testament books, including the 1820 series on Acts that presents the main focus of this chapter. These thematic sermons are also known as homilies. They formed an integral part of the early Sunday service of worship at Trinity Church at 7am, whereas the sermons published in volumes one to four, with the exception of the first collection of 1801, were delivered at the main service at 9am.[2]

From 1792[3] onward, Schleiermacher never produced complete written drafts of his sermons. In the preface to the first published collection of his sermons of 1801 he admitted: "for several years I have refrained from noting down my addresses verbatim, and . . . therefore what I had preached I could, to a large extent, only reconstruct for publication after detailed drafts. But even some [sermons] which I had the opportunity to bring to paper immediately after their delivery have undergone considerable revision."[4] Before delivering a sermon he meditated on the basic thought, form, and structure of the relevant Scripture passage in such a way that he was able to speak freely and fluently to it without recourse to full notes. All published sermons are therefore based on handwritten transcripts produced either by Schleiermacher himself with a view to publication, or by his listeners, mainly his students. Given the considerable length of his published sermons and the fact that they were intended for an educated reading public rather than the average member of his congregation,[5] it is clear that they represent literary revisions of what was actually said. Indeed, Schleiermacher himself pointed out in the preface mentioned above that a printed sermon may not only be a bit longer and more demanding than the oral version, but that the target audience for printed sermons was not so mixed a group of people as that of his listeners in church.[6]

2. See Redeker, *Friedrich Schleiermacher*, 288–89.

3. See Trillhaas, "Berliner Prediger," 11.

4. Schleiermacher, *Predigten* I (1843), 5.

5. See Unger, "Schleiermacher als Prediger," 15.

6. See Schleiermacher, *Predigten* I (1843), 5–6.

It is worth considering the context in which Schleiermacher delivered his sermons as pastor of Trinity Church. Inaugurated in 1739, this edifice was built for a total occupancy of 1,650 persons on the ground floor, 1,125 of whom were seated; the pews were in fact rented by individuals.[7] King Friedrich Wilhelm I of Prussia (r. 1713–1740) had founded Trinity Church as part of the expansion of Berlin as an inter-denominational church with two congregations and two ministers, one Lutheran and one Reformed. The monarch retained the right to call both pastors. As a result of Prussia's war against Napoleon, in 1807 the church's interior was largely demolished, its doors, wall cladding, and pews were used for firewood, and its organ was badly damaged. In 1811, Schleiermacher and a Lutheran member of the vestry board were tasked with overseeing the necessary renovation work.[8]

On Sundays, the noise of more than 1,600 worshippers in the usually fully occupied church, combined with the clatter of coaches rattling over cobble stones and other commotions outside the building can only be imagined. As Catherine Kelsey points out, such noise levels had implications not only for the actual delivery, but for the complexity of any sermon preached there.[9] A preacher could not afford to mention details only once but had to ensure a measure of repetition. This also applied to Schleiermacher's structuring of his sermons. They typically consist of a short introduction stating the context and theme of the chosen Scripture passage and two or three clearly identified sections, the first explaining the importance of the events of the passage for the apostles and their contemporaries, and the rest presenting an application of what this meant for Schleiermacher's own time. This procedure often entailed his distinguishing sharply between the period of the apostles, namely the followers of Christ who had either known him personally or, like Paul, had had direct communication with him on the one hand, and the time of second generation disciples who had to rely entirely on the communication of the Holy Spirit through others.

Schleiermacher moved to Berlin in December 1807. He was preaching there before he actually started his parish ministry at Trinity Church while he was waiting the customary year before he could move his family into the manse. The French occupiers had expelled him from Halle where, according to Wilhelm Dilthey, he "became the first political preacher in a

7. See Nowak, *Schleiermacher*, 212.

8. See ibid., 211.

9. See Kelsey, *Schleiermacher's Preaching*, 20.

big way, whom Christianity had produced in Germany."[10] between 1806 and 1807. In a letter of 24 March 1808 to his former Swedish roommate Karl Gustav von Brinkmann, with whom Schleiermacher had been friends since their time together in the Moravian seminary at Barby, he described his audience as follows: "Astonishingly enough, my sermons find favor here and are also attended by Moravian families. No catch of fish is more colorful than my audience in church: Moravians, Jews—both baptized and non-baptized—young philosophers and philologists, fashionable ladies, and the beautiful image of St Anthony is always in my mind."[11]

Since the focus of this chapter is on sermons that Schleiermacher gave in 1820 and later, his audience at Trinity Church deserves particular attention. No attempt is made here at reconstructing the make-up of his congregation, but Trillhaas' characterization of Schleiermacher's sermons as "society events"[12] is revealing. It was indeed a cross section of Berlin society that assembled in Trinity Church to hear him preach: people from all walks of life, from "laborers in the porcelain manufacture to university professors and civil servants from the nobility."[13] After he took up his post as Professor of New Testament at the newly founded University of Berlin in 1810 the worshippers also included a large number of his students. His listeners consisted to a considerable part of people not attached to the church, but Schleiermacher programmatically ignored this fact in his sermons and treated his listeners as members and as his equals.[14] In the preface to his first collection of sermons, he stated that he "always speaks [i.e., preaches] as if there still were communities of believers and a Christian Church; as if religion still were a bond uniting Christians in a characteristic way. It really does not look as if this is the case, but I do not see how we can avoid presupposing it anyway. . . . Maybe the matter [faith] will actually be brought about again by virtue of its being presupposed."[15] Schleiermacher thus assumed the attitude that his audience had a similar disposition to himself, and he tried to draw them emotionally "into the act of pious reflection."[16] His charismatic and often emotional ex-tempore deliveries certainly account for the fact that during his lifetime he was not

---

10. Dilthey, *Leben Schleiermachers*, 829.

11. Dilthey, *Aus Schleiermachers Leben* IV, 156.

12. Trillhaas, "Berliner Prediger," 13.

13. Nowak, *Schleiermacher*, 400.

14. See Trillhaas, "Berliner Prediger," 15.

15. Schleiermacher, *Predigten* I (1843), 6–7.

16. Nowak, *Schleiermacher*, 393.

only best known as a preacher but widely regarded as one of the greatest preachers of his time in the German tongue. As Christian Albrecht claims, to a large extent, the nineteenth-century homiletic tradition and the development of its motives, methods, and results are regarded to be due to Schleiermacher.[17]

In his sermons Schleiermacher never drew on examples from his own or his contemporaries' lives and experiences; any illustrations he used were taken from Scripture.[18] Of course, he made reference to historical and contemporary events, not least because a considerable number of his sermons were given on special occasions such as the tercentenary of the *Augsburg Confession* in 1830, or were so-called *Amtsreden*, addresses given *ex officio* at funerals, weddings, christenings and confirmations. But he did not illustrate his sermons with examples from his own or from everyday life in early nineteenth-century Prussia; in fact, he used hardly any illustrations and examples at all.[19]

Schleiermacher's sermons have been described as a conversation in which the preacher assumes the part of the speaker only because it is impossible for everybody to talk at the same time. He does do so not on the basis of the theological dignity of his office, but as a religiously moved Christian. Martin Redeker has defined his sermons as "the confession and testimony of the Christian congregation"[20] with the task of developing the presupposed Christian consciousness, but explicitly not with that of initiating this consciousness in the first place: the uncovering, reinforcement, and promotion of the Christian religious consciousness of the listeners is the sole aim of a sermon for Schleiermacher.[21] His preaching has been characterized by Kelsey as "an immediate communication of his faith within the religious community"[22] and by Wilhelm Gräb as "a communicative act of the Christian consciousness about itself representing the presupposed faith of the worshipping congregation."[23] It was characteristic of his homiletic principle that he did not offer any ready dogmatic theses, but instead, as Helmut Thielicke describes it, "assumed his listeners into the very development of his thoughts."[24]

17. See Albrecht, "Predigtlehre," 93.
18. See Kelsey, *Schleiermacher's Preaching*, 28.
19. See Unger, "Schleiermacher als Prediger," 19.
20. Redeker, *Friedrich Schleiermacher*, 297.
21. See Albrecht, "Predigtlehre," 113.
22. Kelsey, *Schleiermacher's Preaching*," 1–2.
23. Gräb, "Predigt als kommunikativer Akt," 643.
24. Thielicke, *Glauben und Denken*, 196.

As mentioned above, the published sermons fall into two categories: those authorized by Schleiermacher for publication, and unauthorized transcripts printed posthumously. There are also a good many posthumously published sermon outlines, which certainly do not reflect an authentic image of Schleiermacher's sermon deliveries.[25] However, for the purpose of discussing his sermons in this study, all of these issues are disregarded. The focus here is exclusively on the published sermons as potential textual evidence for parallels between Schleiermacher's homiletic and doctrinal output, notwithstanding the circumstances of their target audiences, their delivery, or his understanding of the act of preaching. In this sense, Kurt Nowak's observation that Schleiermacher's sermons do not represent "superficial applications of his theology," but that "their impetus lies in the profundity of the pious Christian self-consciousness"[26] is noteworthy.

Of the plethora of sermons which Schleiermacher preached during his long career as a minister, the series on Acts[27] that he gave at Trinity Church in Berlin in 1820 are closest both in time and with regard to content, to the formulation of his doctrine of predestination. To these twelve sermons, preached between the Third Sunday in Trinity (11 June 1820) and the Twenty-fifth Sunday in Trinity (12 November 1820) can be added his sermon at Pentecost 1821 on Acts 2:41–42, which recapitulates the theme for the entire series, and his 1820 Christmas Day sermon on Acts 17:30–31, which serves as a conclusion. The intention of the sermon series on Acts was to demonstrate the beginning of the church, its structures and geographical spread in order to represent individual Christians as members of the church.

Schleiermacher preached on Acts and on various aspects of his doctrine of ecclesiology between 1830 and 1835, too. These sermons are instructive with regard to the second edition of *Christian Faith* rather than the essay on election, reflecting some of the doctrinal insights which informed this doctrine.

---

25. See Nowak, *Schleiermacher*, 400.

26. Ibid., 394.

27. Published in *Sämmtliche Werke* II.10 (1856). No other sermons on Acts from 1820 or 1821 are extant.

THE 1820 SERIES OF SERMONS ON ACTS

Beginning with the Pentecost sermon of 1821 and ending with the 1820 Christmas Day sermon, the series of fourteen sermons on Acts establish the criteria according to which, in Schleiermacher's view, the Christian Church was founded and on which its development, its geographical, demographic, and numerical expansion depended. After elaborating on the inception of the Christian Church, its structure and spread in the first sermons, he proceeded to discuss the individual Christian as a member of the Church.[28] As he pointed out in the penultimate sermon in the Acts series, he was about to "complete the present series of our reflections on those most important principles and behaviors on which the foundation of the Christian Church rested, and on which the happy continuation of the same still rests."[29] The topics of the sermons can be paraphrased as follows:

- (June 10, 1821) Acts 2:41–42:[30] The continuation of the Christian Church ensues in the same manner as its foundation. The events of Pentecost still recur today in order to safeguard the church's existence and expansion.

- (June 11, 1820) Acts 4:5–14:[31] The preservation of God's grace in Christ and in his Spirit rests on the continuing community of Christians.

- (June 25, 1820) Acts 4:13–21:[32] The main principle established by the apostles, which is true for all times, is that one must obey God more than human beings.

- (July 9, 1820) Acts 6:1–6:[33] The characteristics, order, and organization of the first Christian congregation became a template for all ensuing congregations.

- (July 23, 1820) Acts 7:51–59:[34] Christian martyrdom is of great value as an effective means of spreading and fortifying the Christian community.

28. See Nowak, *Schleiermacher*, 397.
29. *SW* II.10, 177.
30. *SW* II.2, 216–30.
31. *SW* II.10, 1–16.
32. *SW* II.4, 133–49.
33. *SW* II.10, 37–51.
34. Ibid., 52–66.

- (July 30, 1820) Acts 8:18–22:[35] The true and faithful servant of Christian faith remains victorious over all falsity meant to intrude upon the Christian Church.

- (August 6, 1820) Acts 9:3–6:[36] Persecutors of the Church are to be converted to faith as an effective means to establish Christ's Church in the world.

- (August 20, 1820) Acts 11:19–21: God has used what has arisen from the general persecution of Christians as an effective means to establish Christ's Church in the world.[37]

- (September 3, 1820) Acts 11:22–26:[38] Christian love must be able to overcome if its purpose is to be fulfilled and its destiny attained.

- (September 17, 1820) Acts 11:27–30:[39] Overall a union of brethren has arisen in the Christian Church for mutual support and relief: aims and objectives and the extent of the Church as an association for mutual support.

- (October 15, 1820) Acts 13:1–3:[40] The expansion of the gospel has generally been related to the natural, self-presenting circumstances of life; the drive to proclaim the gospel independently of external circumstances is natural.

- (October 19, 1820) Acts 15:22–31:[41] The split threatening to occur within the Christian Church has to be avoided; an example of an impending disruption of the Christian Church is given in order to develop the conduct by which rifts of all kinds can be avoided.

- (November 12, 1820) Acts 20:22–25:[42] The successful course of all Christian affairs depends on this: Christians who know themselves to be bound in the Spirit not being scared off by pleas or admonitions from their families from doing that which they feel bound to do in the Spirit.

---

35. Ibid., 67–82.
36. Ibid., 83–97.
37. Ibid., 89–111.
38. Ibid., 112–28.
39. Ibid., 129–44.
40. Ibid., 145–59.
41. Ibid., 160–76.
42. Ibid., 177–92.

- (December 25, 1820) Acts 17:30–31:[43] A transformation has begun from the appearance of the Redeemer on the earth onward: there is a difference between the times before and since the appearance of Christ.

Schleiermacher preached this series of sermons in the second half of 1820, i.e. in the year after the publication of his essay on predestination, while he was working on the first edition of *Christian Faith*. Thematically, these sermons deal with the foundation, preservation, and spread of the Christian Church and therefore with the doctrines of pneumatology, including election, and ecclesiology in the narrower sense. It will thus be instructive to explore the relationship between these sermons on the one hand and his essay and *Christian Faith* on the other, with a view to possible parallels between his homiletic and his doctrinal insights.

Schleiermacher touches upon universal restoration only on one occasion, in the 1821 Pentecost sermon: "The great acts of God relating to the overcoming of evil, the wiping out of sin, the restoration of the human race, . . . , these were the acts of God the apostles preached."[44] Without developing the topic doctrinally, the sermon continues with the effects of proclaiming God's great acts to the immortal soul of mankind, which "nevertheless has sunk low." [45] The godless will be converted through the powerful voice of the divine Spirit.

Throughout the series of sermons on Acts a tendency towards universality is clearly discernible. In the Pentecost sermon Schleiermacher refers to the expectation that Christianity is supposed to belong to all and to change everyone into the one shape of the human being created in the image of God.[46] In the sermon on Acts 7:51–59, Schleiermacher mentions the consummation of the kingdom of God, "which we are all looking forward to, and towards which all work who do not shy away from suffering for the sake of their faith."[47] On another occasion, he speaks explicitly of "the higher life to which we are all called,"[48] and again of the "most holy and steadfast Christian law" to which the Holy Spirit drives "everybody in the most concurrent way."[49] In the context of reflecting on the Jews'

43. *SW* II.2, 314–28.
44. Ibid., 218.
45. Ibid., 219.
46. See ibid, 228.
47. *SW* II.10, 66.
48. Ibid., 85.
49. Ibid., 130.

hope for a savior as a condition for the Church's emergence, he notes that the Old Testament prophets' statements regarding the spread of his light far beyond the boundaries of Israel can be interpreted to mean only that "all generations of human beings will participate in the inner peace and the blessedness [the savior] will bring."[50] Finally, in his sermon on Acts 13:1–3 Schleiermacher returns to the topic of universal blessedness. Talking about the apostles, he claims that "the further the gospel spread, the more certain they felt that it had been decreed[51] to seize the complete human race and to pour out its heavenly blessings over it."[52]

The universalist tendency, if not elaborated as a central theme, is reinforced by the complete absence of any mention of damnation or perdition. That central Calvinist dogma is programmatically ignored in Schleiermacher's sermons. It is worth noting that election to blessedness as predestination does not appear either.

Election in the sense of the selection of some out of a larger group is mentioned in two of the Acts series sermons, but explicitly so with reference to Jesus' electing individuals in this world. In the Pentecost sermon Schleiermacher talks about the Christian youths of his time who turn towards the Redeemer "as to the one who has chosen them rather than they have chosen him,"[53] thus paraphrasing John 15: 16. In his sermon on Acts 9:3–6 he refers to the "chosen and most glorious tools"[54] of God" who "spread the word of life and are bearers of the divine Spirit,"[55] and later again to the many whom God has chosen for himself as tools.[56] The context of election here is clearly the election of individuals to proclaim the gospel in this world. These instances do not directly relate to the doctrine of predestination.

There is one striking difference between Schleiermacher's homiletic and dogmatic texts: whereas in the latter he makes the central claim that there is one single, universal, all-encompassing divine decree for the entire human race,[57] in the former he tends to speak of various divine decrees. In one sermon he refers to "eternal decrees [which] come to fruition in a

---

50. Ibid., 16.

51. *bestimmt.*

52. *SW* II.10, 149.

53. *SW* II.2, 224.

54. *Rüstzeuge.*

55. *SW* II.10, 87.

56. See ibid., 96.

57. See chapter 6 above.

temporal manner,"[58] that is to more than one decree. In the 1820 series
on Acts he mentions the divine decree of the foundation of the Church
of Jesus Christ and its "essential ingredient" that God turns persecutors
into believers;[59] this conversion, he points out, has to be regarded as an
eternal rule and divine arrangement. In his sermon of 6 August 1820 on
Acts 9:3–6, Schleiermacher focuses part of the discussion on verse five
according to the older version concerning Saul's conversion. In the King
James Version the verse reads, "it is hard for thee to kick against the prick."
Schleiermacher explains this rather obscure phrase as follows: "if you continue on the path you are walking now, you will become aware that you
resist in vain a power that has seized you and directs you; you will realize
that with the human and transient power you have your opposition to a
divine decree from above is in vain."[60] The decree referred to here is the
spread of the gospel and its acceptance by those who have fought against
it and against its adherents. Talking about the speed with which the gospel
spread during the time of the apostles, Schleiermacher conjectures in his
sermon on Acts 4:5–14 that this would have happened much faster if the
authorities in their entirety, rather than simply a great number of ordinary
people, had accepted Jesus. However, "the divine counsel[61] had decided
differently."[62] He stresses in this context that we are not to delve too deeply
into this counsel, and that we would not be able to explore it at any rate.
In his Christmas Day sermon of 1821 Schleiermacher again speaks of the
divine decree in the plural: he mentions "the supreme development of the
divine decrees,"[63] which he equates with the appearance of the Redeemer,
and the stark contrast between that which the divine will commands and
that which "the divine decrees wants to eradicate from the world of intel-
ligent beings."[64]

Since the 1820 sermons on Acts focus on the foundation and continuation of the Christian Church, it is not surprising that statements
relating to the doctrine of ecclesiology abound. Schleiermacher puts more
emphasis on discussions concerning the growth and spread of the church
than its first inception, but the latter features for instance in the sermon

58. Schleiermacher, *Predigten* IV (1844), 411.
59. *SW* II.10, 84.
60. Ibid., 92.
61. *Rath* as opposed to *Rat[h]schluß*, decree.
62. *SW* II.10, 4.
63. *SW* II.2, 322.
64. Ibid., 324.

on Acts 15:22–31. Here Schleiermacher reflects on the conditions for the possibility of the emergence of the Christian Church: "It is certain that Christianity could not have been founded as it was through the appearance of our Redeemer unless in the Jewish nation the hope for a savior and restorer had continued to glimmer, sometimes more weakly, sometimes more strongly."[65] In the following sermon in the series, Schleiermacher talks about the loyalty of the apostles to their calling, their "holding fast to being bound in the Spirit" in the face of dangers and in defiance of the warnings of "weak and anxious souls":[66] only through this unwavering loyalty could the Christian Church be founded. In the Pentecost sermon he finally makes the point that "the Christian Church was brought into being through the effectiveness of the divine Spirit."[67]

Without explicitly noting it in each case, Schleiermacher implicitly assumes that the emergence of the Christian Church is entirely due to the work of the Holy Spirit; the examples quoted above illustrate the different ways in which the Spirit accomplished the foundation of the Church. As to the internal structure of the Church, Schleiermacher interprets the division of labor among the apostles and the early adherents of Christ as the "perfect organization of the first Christian congregation, according to which template all the others subsequently structured and formed themselves"[68] in the sermon on Acts 6:1–6.

The growth and development of the Church, a topic that pervades all sermons in the Acts series, is also based on the lasting and constant work of the divine Spirit. On the one hand, the faithful remain unanimous regarding the teaching of the apostles, their community, the breaking of bread, and prayer.[69] On the other hand, the power of the divine Spirit also effected necessary changes. Schleiermacher's sermon on Acts 6:1–6, for instance, deals with the gulf between the apostles who had been in intimate contact with the Redeemer, and the growing number of new adherents who had accepted the gospel without personal acquaintance with him. A decisive change in the relationship between these two groups came about when the apostles elected a small number of the new adherents to take over the office of leading the community in secular matters—an office which had previously been held exclusively by the apostles.

65. *SW* II.10, 169.
66. Ibid., 186.
67. *SW* II.2, 217.
68. *SW* II.10, 39.
69. See *SW* II.2, 226.

Schleiermacher considers this breaking down of barriers by delegating work to selected second-generation Christians as the work of the Holy Spirit, who moved the apostles inwardly to change this relationship. At the same time, the Spirit encountered some among those who had been converted by the apostles' preaching who "through their natural disposition and the enthusiasm with which they had embraced the cause of the gospel were able to discover gifts in themselves which would enable them to be strong assistants of the apostles."[70] From the human perspective, it was the apostles' establishment of the principle to obey God more than human beings that became crucial for the development and spread of the Church. Schleiermacher describes this principle as "a necessary condition of its continuation."[71]

Schleiermacher does not shy away from declaring martyrdom an integral part of the church's development. One of the effects of martyrdom was the "faster and easier spread of the gospel and, secondly, a faster cleansing of the faith of the early Christians of diverse restricting prejudices and opinions."[72] Schleiermacher was careful not to claim that persecution formed part of the order of salvation. Rather, divine wisdom ensured that the blind persecution of Christ's followers by their enemies helped carry the gospel to places far distant from the original cradle of Christianity: "the Lord even used [persecution] in order to show that he is always and in eternity the same who turns into good what human beings in the blindness and perversity of their hearts intend to be evil."[73]

In several Acts sermons, Schleiermacher points out that the times when God spoke directly and therefore in an extraordinary way to human beings in the Christian Church are definitely gone. Since the end of biblical times there can be no expectation of God addressing human beings immediately or directly. Instead, he communicates "solely through the prophetical word of Scripture, which we still have and through the voice of conscience and the power of the faith founded on that word."[74] The voice of the Spirit cannot be heard anymore "in that sharpness and with the immediate certainty with which it communicated in those days."[75]

70. *SW* II.10, 45.
71. *SW* II.4, 139.
72. *SW* II.10, 99.
73. Ibid., 147.
74. *SW* II.4, 137.
75. *SW* II.10, 186.

As Schleiermacher insists in his sermon on Acts 4:5–14, "the divine revelation in Christ and his Spirit do not dwell in any individual person."[76] It dwells in the Church as the totality of all who are related by faith in the Redeemer. Indeed, the preservation of God's grace depends on the continuation of the community among Christians.[77] In this community each individual is tasked with promoting the great cause by "not only receiving and accepting but also giving and communicating"[78] their gifts of the Spirit. In this way, these gifts are always present in the community and are awakened time and again through the impact of one individual on another. For Schleiermacher, the interdependence of the members of the Church and their active and passive communication of the gifts of the spirit among each other represent the essence of the Christian Church.

In the sermon series on Acts Schleiermacher only once refers to the consummation of the Church, which he equates with that of the kingdom of God. At the end of the sermon on Acts 7:51–59 he proclaims that once the martyrdom in the Christian Church is completed and there is no more need to suffer for the sake of faith, the domain of sin will be broken and the kingdom of God will be made complete.[79] Schleiermacher's differentiation in the essay on election and in *Christian Faith* between those who have not yet been regenerated and those who have been regenerated is reflected in his sermon on Acts 13:1–3, where he explains that "the Son has not yet made us all as free as he has promised; . . . because we are not yet all cleansed and entirely directed and led by the power of the divine Spirit itself."[80]

OTHER SERMONS

In a sermon on Phil 3:20–21 preached in 1834, Schleiermacher distinguishes the community of the consummate or the "transfigured body" of Christ the Lord from his "spiritual body [of Christ], the Church, of which we are members."[81] The latter is yet to be cleansed and transfigured in order to be made uniform with the community of the consummate. This version reflects his distinction between the inner and the outer circle of

76. Ibid., 1.
77. See ibid.
78. Ibid., 71.
79. See ibid., 66.
80. Ibid., 158.
81. Schleiermacher, *Predigten*, edited by Urner, 250.

the Christian Church. Schleiermacher also uses the expression that we will be incorporated into the community of the consummate, each at the time which the Lord has determined for them.[82] However, humankind plays a part in this work since the divine consummation is always simultaneously a human one: "only through the service of human beings, only through that which the divine Spirit works in the faithful, can the work of the Lord be brought closer to its completion."[83]

Schleiermacher considers election in greater detail in a sermon preached in 1832 on Acts 10:31. Starting with the contention that "we can never find the reason for such a divine election in individuals,"[84] he explains that if God elects an individual (as in the case of Cornelius), God does it not for the sake of that individual but for the sake of the others. In this way the divine leadership ensures that the proclamation of the gospel will yield the greatest results in the world.[85]

A recurrent topic of Schleiermacher's sermons is the kingdom of God. It appears in several sermons of 1812 and then again in the 1830s. In his Trinity Sunday sermon on John 3:1–8 of 1812 he distinguishes between the kingdom of God in a wider and a narrower sense. The first notion simply comprises everything everywhere, because this world is the sphere of God's omnipotence. The kingdom of God in the narrower sense "is only in those who are driven by a common spirit which proclaims [God's] will in their hearts."[86] In this narrower sense the kingdom of God is not so much a place where believers dwell but it is in fact in the believers themselves: "the kingdom of God in each person is joy over the Holy Spirit, the joy over the community of human beings with God which far surpasses everything worldly."[87] Schleiermacher maintains that those outside the kingdom of God do not establish any firm community: rather, they form only individual and transient relationships in which nothing which one person does can of itself be considered beneficial for somebody else's purpose. In this comparatively early sermon, the only difference is between the great number of persons who "are born from flesh and are only flesh"[88] and those who in whom the peace and joy of the Holy Spirit dwells.

82. See Schleiermacher, *Predigten* II (1843), 586.
83. Ibid., 741.
84. Schleiermacher, *Predigten* III (1843), 373.
85. See ibid., 374.
86. Schleiermacher, *Predigten* I (1843), 481.
87. Ibid., 482.
88. Ibid.

In the same Trinity Sunday sermon of 1812, Schleiermacher also provides a definition of regeneration. It is "the reconstruction[89] of the will, which represents the center of our whole being, the constant indwelling as the Holy Spirit of that which previously moved the soul[90] only from the outside and transiently as the power of the word and of the church."[91] The differentiation between different spheres within the kingdom of God on earth, or an inner and outer circle of the Christian Church, had not yet been fully developed.

In a sermon of 1816 on Acts 17, 24–27, Schleiermacher's perception of the kingdom of God has moved close to his mature understanding. Here he notes that those who believe that the kingdom of God will come have to realize that "it is already here, even if it appears smaller and less perfect."[92] Finally, in his 1823 sermon on John 6:39–40 Schleiermacher explicitly refers to those who "are only accepted into the outer community of the faithful."[93] This is an almost verbatim reflection of his deliberations in both the essay on election and *Christian Faith* about the inner and the outer circle of the Church. The same sermon also offers a striking parallel to his central claim that the work of grace does not end with an individual's death: all who have been placed in the context of God and his work of redemption will not be lost through death, but will be raised from the dead "in order to further promote the work of salvation which has begun in them and to bring it to its blessed consummation, which he calls having eternal life."[94] Even more explicitly, he continues to explain that even those to whom the spring of salvation has not been shut, but who nevertheless have not been blessed with eternal life before they died, will not be lost.

Only in his later sermons does Schleiermacher talk about providence and the promise or decree to blessedness. In his 1826 Pentecost sermon on 1 Cor 2:10–12 he argues that, since God's creational omnipotence equals the extent of God's love, "everything pertaining to the work of creation and the business of providence has to be explained mainly in terms of this love."[95] This argument leads him to conclude that there is an "eternal decree of divine love to salvation and to man's glorification."[96] In a sermon

89. *Umbildung.*

90. *Gemüt.*

91. Schleiermacher, *Predigten* I (1843): 492.

92. Ibid., 159.

93. Schleiermacher, *Predigten* IV (1844): 405.

94. Ibid., 406.

95. Schleiermacher, *Predigten,* edited by Unger, 205.

96. Ibid.

preached on *Totensonntag*[97] 1826 Schleiermacher mentions "the decree of divine grace";[98] in two sermons of 1833 and 1834 he talks about the "eternal salvific decree of our salvation"[99] and in 1832 about "the decree of the grace of God over the human race."[100]

Nowhere in the later sermons about the Holy Spirit or the Christian Church does Schleiermacher mention predestination. As Friso Melzer observes, "he does not talk about divine judgment and punishment and damnation at all."[101] It was not simply the case that, like Calvin before him, he deemed perdition an unsuitable topic for homiletic purposes, but that he plainly did not believe in the doctrine himself. He was convinced that God "cannot make a creature eternally unhappy,"[102] and he explained in a different sermon: "if everything in which order has been muddled and which cannot exist without strife were supposed to show signs of damnation, we would fall into the deepest misery!"[103] This is another clear parallel to his essay on election and his dogmatics. The God of love and grace is incompatible with eternal misery, and God will use evil and disorder and turn it into good. Moreover, the psychological argument already made so shrewdly by Steudel, that the idea of eternal perdition is simply unbearable for Schleiermacher, is also reflected here. It appears again in the Ascension Day sermon of 1833 on Acts 1:6–11, in which he defines the "damnation of the godless" as an entirely world-immanent event, not as an eschatological event: "they lose more and more of what had originally been given to them, of the divine likeness innate to all human beings, the divine spark in them increasingly dies down, and they are cast out of the realm of spiritual freedom under the dominion of the force of nature. Do we want to desire an even worse damnation for them?"[104] Here, too, temporary damnation is bad enough, but eternal perdition appears to be not only undesirable but inconceivable.

Damnation is always related to some kind of preceding judgment. For Schleiermacher, divine judgment "exists only in the state of unbelief."[105]

---

97. The Sunday before Advent on which day the dead are commemorated.
98. Schleiermacher, *Predigten* IV (1844), 231.
99. Ibid., 244 and Schleiermacher, *Predigten* II (1843), 588.
100. Schleiermacher, *Predigten* II (1843), 362.
101. Melzer, "Dogmatischer Gehalt," 388.
102. *SW* II.7, 80.
103. Schleiermacher, *Predigten* I (1843), 238.
104. Schleiermacher, *Predigten* II (1843), 529.
105. Melzer, "Dogmatischer Gehalt," 413.

The consummation of the kingdom of God, i.e., a situation in which each human being will be in a state of faith, is only a matter of time, hence the notion of final judgment is superfluous. Instead, Schleiermacher holds, "now that we have some insight into God's plan regarding eternity, we allow ourselves . . . the sweet hope of a future reunion."[106] The assumption that those who believe in Christ will not be judged presents another reason why preaching about eternal judgment and punishment would have made no sense to Schleiermacher. He consistently addressed his sermons to an audience whose faith he programmatically presupposed.

The notion of divine judgment is also closely linked to the wrath of God—another notion Schleiermacher decidedly did not approve of. In fact, he preached a whole sermon on the topic "[t]hat we have nothing to teach about the wrath of God."[107] There he argues that there is no reason, let alone any command, to consider the wrath of God as an essential part of the Christian faith. Not only is this notion an anthropomorphism, but it implies nothing "to which anything at all in God's nature could correspond."[108] Moreover, "the divine Spirit is not and cannot be a tool of divine wrath"[109] either. In a sermon on John 3:31–36 preached in 1824, Schleiermacher even reinterprets verse 36 as referring to divine punishment for those who disobey Christ. He maintains that this verse can only mean "that God's punishment remains over those who do not believe the son until they too believe."[110] The argument that coming to faith and thus eschewing judgment is only a matter of time becomes explicit where Schleiermacher states: "If the Lord regenerates one person sooner and another later, he has no other season than the greatest possible development of his kingdom on earth."[111]

Finally, a crucial convergence of his homiletic and his dogmatic work is signaled in a sermon on John 11:15–27 of 1825. Here, Schleiermacher acknowledges his insight from the essay that there is one universal decree to eternal blessedness: "everything must coincide in his eternal decree for the salvation of the world, since this is the only one [decree] for the whole infinite kingdom of his power and wisdom."[112]

106. *SW* II.7, 87.
107. See Schleiermacher, *Predigten* II (1843), 725–38, on 2 Cor 5:17–18.
108. Ibid., 731.
109. *SW* II.9, 518.
110. *SW* II.8, 230.
111. Ibid., 345.
112. *SW* II.9, 259.

PART THREE

Schleiermacher's Account
of Election in Context

9

Related Doctrines

THE DOCTRINE OF ELECTION, like all sections of *Christian Faith*, is related to all other doctrines. However, an exhaustive exposition of the implications of the doctrine of election for all other doctrines discussed in *Christian Faith* would be beyond the scope of this study.[1] Therefore, in the following I will examine Schleiermacher's treatment of the four major doctrines that election is most closely related to: providence, hamartiology, soteriology, and eschatology. These four doctrines explicate the theme of reorientation of the Christian self-consciousness in the universe as "the stage of God's creative and redemptive activity."[2]

PROVIDENCE AND ELECTION

There is a close systematic relationship, first of all, between the doctrines of election and creation, and, more particularly, between election and the doctrine of providence or preservation. In *Christian Faith* Schleiermacher considers creation and preservation as the two inextricably linked aspects of the single activity of God the creator. This understanding not only underpins the important position that the doctrine of providence occupies in the Reformed tradition, it also demonstrates that the creative act of God is not limited to the original event of the creation of the world but has to be expanded in time to the present and the future consummation of

1. The relationship of election to the doctrine of God, for instance, would have to take account of the three sets of divine attributes discussed in *Christian Faith*, and also of all statements about God as Father, Son and Holy Spirit; it would also need to explore its relationship to Schleiermacher's problematic doctrine of the trinity.

2. DeVries, "Schleiermacher," 323.

creation. God's continuous activity in the world corresponds to God's continuous activity in the kingdom of grace, and thus, systematically speaking, to the doctrine of election. The single divine decree to creation and redemption subsumes creation under providence and orders it in relation to redemption.

Providence in the Reformed Tradition

Schleiermacher agrees with the Reformed tradition that emphasizes providence and universal divine sovereignty, what Walter Moore terms "the universality of divine control."[3] God's providence is the reason for everything that happens in the world. However, there are major differences between Schleiermacher's own and traditional concepts of providence. Before exploring Schleiermacher's new conception, the interpretation of the doctrine in the Reformed tradition will be summarized.

Calvin's *Institutio* is used to serve as a model of the Reformed interpretation. In the course of the different editions of the *Institutio*, the exposition of the doctrine of providence went through three stages. In the first edition of 1536, it formed part of the doctrine of God; in the 1539 edition it followed the discussion of predestination, which then formed a chapter in its own right; in the final edition of 1559, it was separated from predestination and treated as part of the doctrine of creation. Schleiermacher's positioning of providence within the doctrine of creation in *Christian Faith* thus corresponds to Calvin's.

In the 1559 edition of the *Institutio* the discussion of providence follows that of creation and the original state of perfection. It consists of chapter XVI, on God's governance, and chapter XVII, on the use of the doctrine of providence, and a refutation of three objections in chapter XVIII that concludes Book I, "Of the Knowledge of God the Creator." Calvin clarifies that "the providence we mean is not one by which the Deity, sitting idly in heaven, looks on at what is taking place in the world, but one by which he, as it were, holds the helm, and overrules all events."[4] Providence, then, is the divine will to order, guide and preserve the universe and humankind; it is the active upholding and cherishing of all creation by God. However, Calvin points out, "the order, method, end and necessity

---

3. Moore, "Schleiermacher as a Calvinist," 169.

4. Calvin, *Institutes*, tr. Beveridge, I.16.4, 175.

of events are, for the most part, hidden in the counsel of God, though it is certain that they are produced by the will of God."[5]

Calvin distinguishes general, special, and most special providence; the first refers to the preservation of the world, the second to that of the human species, and the third to that of individuals. Charles Partree identifies them with the universal operation by which God governs all creatures, the special operation by which God helps the elect and punishes the wicked, and the particular operation by which God governs the faithful by his Holy Spirit.[6]

For Calvin, even though all things are directly governed by God's will, they are not immediately or directly affected by God. Instead, God employs secondary causes to achieve his ultimate goal of protecting the elect. Calvin's insistence on secondary causality is mainly related to human responsibility and ethics. He also upholds the traditional view that God is sovereign over nature and natural laws, and that God may govern, as Moore put it, "with, without, or contrary to natural means."[7]

Schleiermacher's New Conception of the Doctrine of Providence

Schleiermacher positioned providence (§§46–49) in the first section of Part I of *Christian Faith*, i.e., within the doctrine of cosmology, or the description of the religious consciousness that expresses the relation between the world and God. It is preceded by the doctrine of creation. Providence, or, as Schleiermacher prefers to call it, preservation, is followed by Divine attributes I, which comprise eternity, omnipresence, omnipotence, and omniscience. The traditional division into creation and providence is preserved in the sense that the topics actually appear as two different doctrines. Schleiermacher, like Calvin in the last edition of his *Institutio*, connects the concepts of the initial divine act of creation and the continuing activity of divine providence or preservation. However, he maintains that the content of the expression that the world exists only in absolute dependence on God "can be evolved out of either of the two doctrines, provided that in both of them, . . . God is regarded as the sole determinant."[8] Therefore, his emphasis is different from Calvin's in that "the doctrine

---

5. Ibid., I.16.9, 180.
6. See Partree, "Calvin on Universal and Particular Providence," 70.
7. Moore, "Schleiermacher as a Calvinist," 170.
8. Schleiermacher, *Christian Faith*, tr. MacIntosh and Stewart, §38, 146.

of creation is completely absorbed into the doctrine of preservation,"[9] as Jaqueline Mariña very aptly puts it. Schleiermacher's central claim that both doctrines express essentially the same thing is based on his understanding of the absolute dependence of all finite beings on God. Religious self-consciousness, or the feeling of absolute dependence, "coincides entirely with the view that all such things are conditioned and determined by the interdependence of nature."[10] As a consequence, within the system of nature and thus the entire realm of finite beings, God's activity is continually sustaining, and no isolated activities can be ascribed to him. He must be equally immediate to all parts of the system of nature, even though ultimate causes may be hidden within universal interrelatedness. As Moore points out: "Universal divine causality does not nullify secondary causes."[11] Schleiermacher distinguishes universal and particular causality and maintains their co-existence. The first is the divine, absolute, unconditional, and non-reciprocal causality that admits of no cause extrinsic to itself. It is, as Dawn DeVries and Brian Gerrish note, "equal in extent, but different in kind"[12] to natural causes. Rather than superseding the causality of finite agents, universal causality subsumes it within the interdependent system of nature. "All of finite reality is taken to exist in absolute dependence on the divine causality."[13]

Precisely because all things are mutually conditioned and interdependent in the system of nature, the feeling of absolute dependence of all finite things on God is aroused. Since in Schleiermacher's view, universal preservation must include everything, he considers the traditional differentiation between general, special, and most special preservation to be unhelpful: "Everything can happen and has happened only as God originally willed and always wills, by means of the powers distributed and preserved in the world."[14] God must remain apart from all means and occasions of time in sustaining and creating.

In his discussion of divine government, Schleiermacher dispenses with the traditional concept of miracles. He argues that no fact can be interpreted in such a way "that its dependence on God absolutely excludes

---

9. Mariña, "Schleiermacher's Christology Revisited," 186.

10. Schleiermacher, *Christian Faith*, tr. MacIntosh and Stewart, §46, 170.

11. Moore, "Schleiermacher as a Calvinist," 169.

12. DeVries and Gerrish, "Schleiermacher on Justification," 194.

13. Van Driel, "Supralapsarian Christology," 253.

14. Schleiermacher, *Christian Faith*, tr. MacIntosh and Stewart, §46.2, 177.

its being conditioned by the system of nature."[15] The world consists of the interaction of the nature mechanism and free agents, therefore free causes are also objects of divine preservation and are maintained in absolute dependence on God. Schleiermacher only holds on to "one great miracle, the mission of Christ,"[16] whose aim is the restoration of what free causes have altered in their own field of activity, but explicitly not in either the system of nature, or in the course of events originally ordained by God. Christ's incarnation itself forms part of providence.

Schleiermacher gives two main reasons for the traditional upholding of miracles: prayer and regeneration. He argues that everything, including prayer and its fulfillment or refusal, are part of God's providence, and that the appearance of Christ is not a supernatural miracle in the traditional sense. The traditional notion of miracles posits divine activity apart from and occasionally contrary to natural causes. In Schleiermacher's system, in contrast, the interests of natural science and religion meet at the point where the idea of the supernatural is abandoned. In a rather prophetical anticipation of the modern debate about science and religion, he saw that with our growing understanding of the laws and causes of nature, the scope of miracles to explain hitherto unexplained events would be diminishing, and at some stage in the future we might be able to explain every natural phenomenon scientifically. However, if the notion of miracle as a supernatural intervention in the system of nature is abandoned, nothing that stimulates the pious self-consciousness will be prejudiced by the possibility that it might be explained scientifically in the future. In other words, ever-increasing scientific knowledge will not at any stage preclude the stimulation of the feeling of absolute dependence on God.

Good and evil as integral parts of divine preservation are discussed in §48. Here, Schleiermacher argues that all excitations of the self-consciousness have the potential to evoke the feeling of absolute dependence on God. They encompass both excitations of sad moments, or repressions of and restraints against life, and serene and joyful moments expressing advancements of life. He defines evil[17] as "conditions which bring a

15. Ibid., §47, 178.

16. Ibid., §47.1, 180.

17. Schleiermacher distinguishes *Übel* (ills), *das Böse* (evil), *natürliche Übel* (natural ills), and *gesellige Übel* (social ills). However, for the sake of consistency and in order to avoid confusion, I will employ the translations given by MacIntosh and Stewart: evil for *Übel*, moral evil for *das Böse*, natural evil for *natürliche Übel*, and social evil for *gesellige Übel*.

persistent and regularly renewed consciousness of life's obstacles,"[18] and he characterizes moral evil as a state rather than an activity. Distinguishing two types or classes of evil, he maintains that natural evil, "in which human existence is partly negated"[19] is different from social evil, which, in turn, is characterized by the influence of moral evil, and he concedes that there is some overlap between natural and social evil. However, from the point of view of absolute dependence on God, there is no difference between the two. Indeed, "evil and good are alike rooted in universal dependence on God."[20] In other words, both repression and advancement of life, or limitation and progress, are equally ordained by God and condition each other. Neither evil nor good ever exist in isolation and therefore, Schleiermacher claims, evil as such and good as such are not ordained by God, "but each thing or event is ordained by God that it should be both."[21] Evil is ordained only as it relates to the good, namely as one condition for this good.

Schleiermacher also rejects the traditional dogmatic distinction between helpful and unhelpful divine cooperation because any such activities would be placed outside the relation of absolute dependence. Rather, "everything real without exception is the result of divine co-operation."[22] In the finite world there is no absolute isolation. Therefore, the notion of providence cannot imply that God wills particular things for their own sake. Neither does God's providential activity manifest itself as distinct decisions about and for individuals: it is directed to the entire world and the human race as a whole.

In the final section on the doctrine of preservation, Schleiermacher discusses the issue of free agents, and particularly of the free will, within the system of nature as ordained by and as absolutely dependent on God. In Robin Parry and Christopher Partridge's words, he argues that human freedom and choice are "compatible with the total divine determination."[23] The perceived opposition between the consciousness of free will and that of absolute dependence is therefore a misunderstanding; as a matter of fact, "we are only capable of the feeling of absolute dependence as freely acting agents."[24] Free causes, free agents, and their free will are all integral

---

18. Schleiermacher, *Christian Faith*, tr. MacIntosh and Stewart, §48.1, 185.

19. Ibid.

20. Ibid.

21. Ibid., §48.2, 187.

22. Ibid., 188.

23. Parry and Partridge, "Introduction," xxii.

24. Schleiermacher, *Christian Faith*, tr. MacIntosh and Stewart, §49.1, 190.

parts of the general system,[25] and their activity as well as the nature system in which it takes place, are equally ordained by God. As Eilert Herms puts it: "With unequalled consistency Schleiermacher represents the transcendental sense of the doctrine of creation as a theory of the conditions for the possibility of finite freedom."[26] There is thus no opposition between freedom and natural necessity in finite beings. Instead, they can choose freely from among all available options in any given situation—but it is God who ordains the range of options. Only as freely acting agents are human beings capable of the feeling of absolute dependence: "we are conscious of our freedom as something which is received and is gradually developed in a universal system."[27] Divine preservation entails that God also upholds free causes. His causality is entirely different from any reciprocal action. Reciprocity only takes place within the system of nature, that is between human beings and the world, a sphere which is characterized by relative freedom and relative dependence.

In Schleiermacher's reconstructed doctrine of providence the understanding that God is a particular cause is abandoned altogether. Instead, God is the absolute and universal cause of everything that happens. Divine and finite causality must be distinguished sharply: God's causality is coextensive with but different in kind from the nature system.[28] There is no reciprocity in the relation between God and finite beings. God does not interact with, nor react to, individuals, and hence the traditional distinction between general, particular, and most particular providence becomes meaningless. Equally, miracles, which would disrupt and therefore annul the system of nature, have no place in Schleiermacher's system. That nature system as a whole rather than any individual human being is the object of divine preservation; as a corollary, individuals relate to God only as constituent parts of the whole system.

There is a price to be paid for the establishment of such a coherent system in which the particular causality and free will of finite beings are distinguished from but ultimately subsumed under God's absolute and universal preservation. As Michael Root points out: "This history in its final entirety is the only possible history."[29] There is no coercion, but if everything that happens happens with necessity, then the emergence of sin

---

25. *Allgemeiner Zusammenhang.*
26. Herms, "Schleiermachers Eschatologie," 127.
27. Schleiermacher, *Christian Faith*, tr. MacIntosh and Stewart, §49.1, 190.
28. See DeVries and Gerrish, "Schleiermacher on Justification," 196.
29. Root, "Schleiermacher as Innovator," 97.

as well as that of the Redeemer become inevitable. Ultimately, of course, this means that there is no need, and indeed no real possibility for reconciliation between God and the world. Schleiermacher's restructuring of the doctrine of providence results in "an impoverishment of the primary language of faith."[30]

The Christian consciousness of redemption is a necessary ingredient in the system of nature, but it focuses on Christ's assumption of human beings into his perfect God-consciousness, not on pacifying God's wrath and thus attaining righteousness. Regeneration, and the ultimate universal restoration of all that has been lost, expressed in the doctrine of election, can be seen as an extension of the doctrine of preservation as God's continuous activity in the future. As Matthias Gockel notes, the "combination of election and redemption is controlled by the concept of divine preservation."[31]

HAMARTIOLOGY

Traditionally, the doctrine of sin accounts for the inexcusability of the human race. Since the fall, human beings have been incapable of attaining salvation by their own will and power. The systematic-theological relation between hamartiology and the doctrine of predestination tends to be expressed in terms of original sin and eternal perdition, disobedience and punishment, freedom versus bondage, and the free versus the unfree will. Calvin's treatment of the main elements of the doctrine of sin in his *Institutio* may again serve as a model of the traditional treatment. In Book II, "Of the Knowledge of God the Redeemer," the first three chapters deal with the following topics:[32] 1) "Through the fall and revolt of Adam the whole human race made accursed and degenerate. Of original sin." 2) "Man now deprived of freedom of will, and miserably enslaved." 3) "Everything proceeding from the corrupt nature of man damnable."

Schleiermacher posits hamartiology at the start of Part II of *Christian Faith*, which deals with the "Explication of the facts of the religious self-consciousness as they are determined by the antithesis of sin and grace."[33] The first aspect of the antithesis is the explication of the consciousness of sin, the second that of the consciousness of grace. In that the doctrine

30. Ibid., 101.

31. Gockel, *Barth and Schleiermacher*, 14.

32. See Calvin, *Institutes*, tr. Beveridge, 32.

33. Schleiermacher, *Christian Faith*, tr. MacIntosh and Stewart, xvi.

of sin precedes the doctrine of grace, Schleiermacher follows tradition. However, no Protestant dogmatics before his *Christian Faith* had assigned such a prominent position to the doctrine of sin, and his explication of the doctrine departs significantly from traditional accounts.

In the first section, he deals with original and actual sin, in the second with the relation between sin and evil, and in the third with the question whether God is the author of sin or not.

Sin and Grace

Schleiermacher first sets his parameters. He posits that God-consciousness occurs only under the general form of self-consciousness as an antithesis between pleasure or joy[34] on the one hand, and lack of enthusiasm or lack of pleasure[35] on the other. Neither is a pure state: pleasure is never entirely without some lack of joy and vice versa. Christian piety is well acquainted with the experience of subjective alienation from God, and human beings are conscious of this experience of alienation "as an action originating in ourselves, which we call sin."[36] However, the alienation from God is not conceived of as an active revolt, as it is in traditional accounts of sin. Rather, it manifests itself as an obstruction to the development of God-consciousness.

Schleiermacher thus introduces a new conception of the doctrine of hamartiology: "sin in general exists only in so far as there is [also] a consciousness of it."[37] Sin *per se* does not properly exist, it occurs only as consciousness of sin. Moreover, any discussion even of the consciousness of sin as such, i.e., without any relation to redemption, would be an entirely abstract consideration. The consciousness of sin can properly be considered only in relation to redemption.

An acknowledgment of the need for redemption emerges only in connection with the consciousness of sin. As Alister McGrath observes, the first consciousness of the actuality of sin is effectively the first presentiment of the possibility of redemption.[38] The consciousness of a disruption

---

34. *Lust.*

35. *Unlust.* The translation "pain" used by MacIntosh and Stewart seems inappropriate to me.

36. Schleiermacher, *Christian Faith,* tr. MacIntosh and Stewart, §63, 262.

37. Ibid., §68.2, 277. The German text has "also," whereas MacIntosh and Stewart's translation does not.

38. See McGrath, *Justitia Dei,* 381.

of nature or an arrestment of the God-consciousness is always caused by a preceding good, which, in turn, is a result of the original perfection of the human race. Sin only manifests itself by means of already existent good, and what it obstructs is in fact future good.

Since there is no reciprocity between human and divine actions, redemption cannot be a divine response to human sin. On the one hand sin is "that which would not be unless redemption was to be," and on the other "that which can disappear only through redemption."[39] As such, sin is a necessary precondition of redemption: human beings have to be sinful in order to be redeemed. Schleiermacher thus turns the traditional account on its head. That sin comes before grace is simply an expression of the human need for redemption reflected in the structure of most dogmatics. It does not imply a temporal sequence. Sin is a means and redemption the goal of divine causality.

For methodological reasons Schleiermacher treats the subjects of sin and of grace separately, although in the Christian consciousness they are never dissociated. It is Schleiermacher's contention that the consciousness of sin occurs when the God-consciousness determines our self-consciousness as lack of enthusiasm or pleasure. In the words of traditional dogmatics, "we conceive of sin as a positive antagonism of the flesh against the spirit."[40] However, this agreement is only superficial, since the antagonism between spirit and flesh is more precisely "an arrestment of the determinative power of the spirit, due to the independence of the sensuous functions."[41] Sin occurs whenever the free development of God-consciousness is arrested.

The independent activity of the flesh precedes the development of the God-consciousness both in the human race as a species and in individuals. It is a fact of human development that sensory[42] self-consciousness develops prior to higher self-consciousness. In this sense, the activity of the flesh is prior to the emergence of the pious self-consciousness. It represents the germ of sin, but not sin in the proper sense, since sin can only be present simultaneously with and in relation to God-consciousness. As soon as God-consciousness awakens in human beings, they also become conscious of sin, but not any earlier.

39. Schleiermacher, *Christian Faith*, tr. MacIntosh and Stewart, §65.2, 270.

40. Ibid., §66, 271.

41. Ibid., §66.2, 273.

42. This appears to me to be a more accurate translation of *sinnlich* than MacIntosh and Stewart's "sensible."

Another aspect of this developmental account of sin is the unequal development of intellect and willpower in human beings. The relation of self-consciousness to intellect and to willpower reflects a disparity in their development. Self-consciousness is more rapidly stimulated upon intellectual discernment than it is able to determine excitations or stirring of the will. This developmental disparity between intellect and willpower lies in human nature itself, not in any bondage of the will to sin. It mirrors the disparity with which the consciousness of sin is given in different individuals at different times. Without this disparity between intellect and willpower no consciousness of sin could arise at all.

Schleiermacher also gives a social account of sin. Sensory consciousness develops before higher self-consciousness not only in individuals but in the human race as a whole. The formation of an individual depends "upon a larger common type"[43] just as the constitution of a later generation depends on that of earlier ones. Therefore, individual human beings are conscious of sin partly as of their own doing and partly as having its source outside them. Each act through which a sensory stimulation arrests the God-consciousness is a sinful act originating in the individual. At the same time, there is a fundamental disposition toward sinfulness that is inherited and passed on socially and historically. This innate sinfulness is, in turn, ratified by each individual through their voluntary actions.

In contrast to the consciousness of sin as a human disposition and action, human beings are conscious of any experience of fellowship with God "as resting upon a communication from the Redeemer, which we call grace."[44] The purpose of redemption must be directed at a transformation of the self-consciousness from God-forgetfulness to dominant God-consciousness. Christ had a perfectly powerful God-consciousness and was therefore the only one capable of performing redeeming activities. Although actual sin is contingent in the sense that it does not happen necessarily, sin is in effect inevitable for everybody apart from Christ. Nevertheless, human nature has the potential to be completely permeated by God-consciousness. The very possibility that God-consciousness could develop progressively from the first human to the purity which it manifests in the Redeemer entails that sin is a disruption of human nature, but not its utter corruption. As a corollary of this contention, Christ is different from all other human beings merely in quantitative terms, but not in qualitative ones.

43. Ibid., §69.1, 279.
44. Ibid., §63, 262.

Original Sin

Having established that sin and the consciousness of sin coincide, and that the sins of individuals are caused both by themselves and by factors outside themselves, Schleiermacher now turns to original sin. He describes it as a universal and inherent disposition within the human race toward sin that exists prior to any individual's own action. Original sin is humanity's total incapacity for good and thus forms an anthropological constant. It has its ground outside the being of individuals, and it can only be removed through redemption. That incapacity for good is identified with the inability to attain a dominant God-consciousness unaided by one's own volition. Notwithstanding this inability to actively influence one's God-consciousness, human beings are fully capable of receiving grace. "The capacity to appropriate the grace offered to us is the indispensable condition of all the operations of . . . grace."[45] There are, of course, different degrees of that receptivity to divine grace in different human beings across time. Lower levels correspond to a weaker God-consciousness, higher levels to a more dominant God-consciousness.

Original sin is both the corporate act and the guilt of the human race, and it is the sufficient ground of all actual sin in the individual. In this sense it is originating original sin: it brings forth and increases the sin in each individual, and it is transmitted to others by the voluntary actions of individuals. Original sin represents the possibility of sin until it becomes reality through a person's own action.

Original sinfulness is timeless, and corporate guilt is identical in all individuals. As Robert Lee Vance puts it: "The fundamental structures of created existence are found to harbor the locus and the origin of sin."[46] Every single person participates in the corporate life of sinfulness by virtue of the fact that nobody is born in isolation from sinful society. DeVries defines original sin according to Schleiermacher as "the sin which every human 'inherits' from [their] participation in structures and social forces that militate against the development of authentic God-consciousness."[47] Schleiermacher thus offers a new conception of the doctrine of original sin. Indeed, as Robert Williams points out, Schleiermacher was the first theologian to formulate the thesis that human beings are constitutionally fallible.[48] While dispensing with the hereditary dimension of original sin,

---

45. Schleiermacher, *Christian Faith*, tr. MacIntosh and Stewart, §70.2, 283.

46. Vance, "Sin and Self-consciousness," 197.

47. DeVries, "Schleiermacher," 323.

48. See Williams, "Theodicy, Tragedy, and Soteriology," 408.

he retained the result of this view, namely the inevitability of sin. He could thus affirm the traditional understanding of the doctrine in two respects: all individuals will inevitably sin, and human beings are held responsible for their sins.

Schleiermacher's analysis of sin in its corporate and structural dimensions implies that the preoccupation with the fate of individuals apart from a new corporate life does little to overcome the reality of sin.[49] This is a parallel to his argument elsewhere that the doctrine of predestination is concerned not with individuals but with the collective body of the human race.

According to what Walter Wyman calls Schleiermacher's "dramatically revisionist"[50] analysis of the doctrine of original sin, sin and redemption can be properly understood only on the basis of their corporate character. The universality of sin is reflected in "a social and historical theory of the interconnectedness of individuals and generations."[51]

Schleiermacher's interpretation of original sin disagrees with others that confine the incapacity to do good to the first table of the Decalogue, while equating the works of the second table with a civil righteousness that can be fulfilled without the aid of God's Spirit. Schleiermacher insists that even the very best elements of civil righteousness and human wisdom can rank only as the righteousness and wisdom of the flesh. He dispenses altogether with the distinction between duties toward God and duties toward one's neighbor.

Actual Sin

In Christian self-consciousness, original sin issues always and in everybody in actual sin. The precise historical manifestation of original sin as actual sin in an individual depends on the contingent choices of that individual. While sinfulness is an innate characteristic of all human beings, there are different degrees and modes of actual sin, or of obstructions of the power of God-consciousness. Nevertheless, because of the universal sinfulness of the human race, there cannot be a single perfectly good action that purely expresses the power of God-consciousness. The same claim applies to thoughts or desires, which are also considered to be

49. See DeVries, "Schleiermacher," 324.
50. Wyman, "Sin and Redemption," 134.
51. Wyman, "Rethinking the Christian Doctrine," 211.

actual sins. Only Christ, who is excluded from the context of sinfulness, is acquitted of actual sin.

Schleiermacher reinterprets the traditional distinctions between outer and inward, intentional and unintentional, and mortal and venial sins. He distinguishes actual sins that are more an expression of desire and actual sins that are more a vitiation of God-consciousness. But ultimately, he maintains, "all activities of the flesh are good when subservient to the Spirit, and all are evil when severed from it."[52] As a corollary, the actual sins of the unregenerate are always originating. Those of the regenerate, in contrast, cannot annul the divine grace of regeneration and are therefore no longer originating.[53]

Also, voluntary or free actions even of the regenerate invariably result in sin because they issue from original sin or universal human sinfulness. At the same time, no actual sin is exclusively an individual's doing, but it is always also a corporate action. Schleiermacher's innovative account of hamartiology integrates original and actual sin.

Divine Causality

While the sinful self-determinations of an individual are that individual's own actions, thoughts, or desires, those determinations do not rule out the possibility of a relation between sin and divine causality, on the contrary. As Schleiermacher argues, "in so far as the consciousness of our sin is a true element of our being, and sin therefore a reality, it is ordained by God as that which makes redemption necessary."[54] Only because and in so far as sin exists do we "feel bound to posit a special divine activity bearing upon it"—but not "upon sin purely by itself."[55]

Because human life exists by divine ordination, there is no escaping the fact that sin, as proceeding inevitably from human nature, is part of this ordination. At the same time, if God in this sense ordains universal sinfulness, God does so only in relation to universal redemption. Schleiermacher formulates his understanding of the origin of sin from the point of view of redemption: "as we have no consciousness of grace

---

52. Schleiermacher, *Christian Faith*, tr. MacIntosh and Stewart, §74.1, 307.

53. As Jürgen Moltmann points out, Schleiermacher thus takes up the traditional doctrine of perseverance and declares that the regenerate cannot commit mortal sins. See Moltmann, *Prädestination und Perseveranz*, 167.

54. Schleiermacher, *Christian Faith*, tr. MacIntosh and Stewart, §81.3, 335.

55. Ibid., §79.3, 325.

without a consciousness of sin, we must also assert that the existence of sin alongside of grace is ordained for us by God."[56] It is God's ordination that sinful human nature is a "blending of the being and not-being of the God-consciousness"[57] and that the "continually imperfect triumph of the Spirit"[58] becomes sin to us.

For Schleiermacher, divine ordination is identical with the single universal decree to salvation. From the outset, indeed from before creation, everything has been ordained in relation to God's activity of redemption in Christ. Schleiermacher's integration of sin and redemption in this prime divine intention entails that the position sin takes in *Christian Faith* is markedly different from that of traditional dogmatic accounts. It becomes the causal precondition of grace. His revisionist account also entails that because sin was not ordained *per se*, it cannot properly be considered for itself either. Sin does not exist in its own right; it only exists as attached to grace. This is a clear parallel to the understanding that human evil, too, exists only as attached to good, not for itself or in its own right.

From the human perspective, eternal and temporal divine causality has as its corollary the feeling of absolute dependence. It is that same divine causality that will annul sin through redemption. Nevertheless, Schleiermacher's clear break with tradition remains intact: inasmuch as redemption is conditioned by sin, God is the author of sin.

Given the divine causality of all things, nothing is more or less arbitrary than anything else. Schleiermacher's claim that divine causality accounts for human sinfulness also includes a rejection of the traditional distinction between causing and permitting causality. The question of the compatibility of the divine authorship of evil with the divine attributes of holiness and justice hardly even arises due to the single universal decree to create and redeem. Schleiermacher's account of the single universal decree of ultimate redemption is a soteriological postulate, claiming both that sin and finitude do not coincide, and that there will be no eternal separation from God.

Schleiermacher then discusses the relation between sin and human freedom. Traditionally, free will or freedom of choice is regarded as the ground for actual sins. Schleiermacher accepts this formulation but again reinterprets its meaning. With regard to other human beings and the world, individuals are free to choose. But, as Edwin van Driel insists,

56. Ibid., §80, 326.
57. Ibid., §81.1, 331.
58. Ibid., §81, 330.

vis-à-vis divine causality, they do not have the freedom to choose or indeed to originate a different action from the one they choose.[59] Human freedom is ultimately ordained by God and is thus itself grounded in divine causality. However, as Robet Lee Vance argues, the issue of divine causality versus human freedom "devolves into the question how human freedom functions while still being under the determinative structure of existence as set out by God."[60] Human beings are free to act as they choose, but their capacity for spontaneous choosing is, in turn, determined by divine causality, and they cannot ultimately contravene God's will for them.

The traditional antithesis between freedom and bondage is also subjected to a reinterpretation by Schleiermacher. While he agrees that freedom can only grow out of a state of bondage as a result of redemption, he rejects the notion that human beings ever have absolute freedom. As a result, freedom even of the regenerate will always exhibit at least traces of bondage. The contrast between freedom and bondage takes a different shape in different human beings and also across time in the same individual, but this is an expression of different relations to redemption. In some individuals, God-consciousness is not, or not yet, as predominant as in others, so that their freedom is relative small in relation to their bondage.

Original Perfection and the Fall

Schleiermacher deals with the original perfection of the world and of human beings at the very end of Part I of *Christian Faith*. His analysis has important consequences for his interpretation of the doctrine of sin. Original perfection does not mean some primordial state of innocence or the ability not to sin. Original perfection is not a one-time state at all, but it is the human capacity to receive grace or, as Dawn DeVries puts it, "the possibility for the actualization of God-consciousness both within the human race as a whole and within humanity."[61] It implies that the innate human tendency toward God-consciousness can never be lost. Original perfection cannot be annulled by the existence of sin. This contention entails that no sin, including the first sin of any supposed first human beings, has the potential to destroy original perfection or, in traditional terms, to totally corrupt human nature.

---

59. See Van Driel, "Schleiermacher's Supralapsarianism," 255.

60. Vance, "Sin and Self-consciousness," 194.

61. DeVries, "Schleiermacher," 320.

It is, of course, impossible to formulate a relevant doctrine regarding the experiences of the first pair of humans since we have no consciousness of the matter. Schleiermacher is not interested in the details of the nature of those first humans at any rate. His point is that there is no need to explain universal sinfulness as a result of a fall from a previously perfect state to assert the subsequent corruption of the nature of all following generations. In his interpretation, there never was an original state of human nature different from the present one. No ontological change in human nature ever took place.

Schleiermacher dispenses with the fall because the presupposition of a preceding perfect state of innocence renders the fall itself incomprehensible.[62] He rejects the traditional account that assigns guilt to an individual for something received externally,[63] and he replaces it with a corporate understanding of original sin. In this way, he abandoned the fall motif but retained its intent, the necessity for redemption. He also conceded that the fall narrative had an illustrative quality in that it demonstrated the universal process of the rise of sin across space and time.

The very notion of an alteration of human nature is unnecessary in Schleiermacher's conception, according to which universal sinfulness is innate. It was an integral part of human nature even before the first actual sin of the first pair or first generation, and it subsequently manifested itself as actual sins as human beings developed naturally and socially. Classical accounts either suppress the evil already present, or they assign it to a different agent, or they interpret it as a result of the fall. Traditional explanations for the first sin include a seduction through Satan, a misuse of the free will, or original disobedience. For Schleiermacher the problem is neither the human will nor the direction of one's love. He argues that, without assuming a foundation for the emergence of the first sin in a prior sinfulness, its emergence would be difficult to explain. Whatever took place as a result of the first sin must have preceded that first sin. Moreover, within Schleiermacher's conception, the nature of a species cannot be changed in an individual while this individual remains the same. Neither can an individual act upon the nature of the species. Therefore, universal sinfulness cannot be derived from the first sin of the first pair. In Schleiermacher's words, it must be seen "as identical with what in them likewise preceded the first sin, so that in committing their first sin they were simply

---

62. See Williams, "Theodicy, Tragedy, and Soteriology," 399.

63. In the Mosaic narrative of the fall, this external factor is symbolized by the serpent and the fruit.

the first-born of sinfulness."[64] What preceded the first sin was the innate sinfulness of the human race, the incapacity for good. It was as native to the first pair as the original perfection of the human race. Schleiermacher dismisses the "fantastic notion"[65] that the nature of the physical world could be changed by the first occurrence of sin.

Sin and Evil

The second section on hamartiology discusses the constitution of the world in relation to sin. Here, Schleiermacher deals with evil and its origin, and the relation between sin and evil, which he identifies with the punishment for sin. He argues that without sin there would be no evil in the world. Indeed, "evil arises only with sin, but, given sin, it arises inevitably."[66] As Robert Williams points out, evil thus belongs to the economy of salvation.[67] The measure in which evil is present corresponds to the measure in which sin is present, and evil is the only consequence of sin. The first sin did not produce a magical effect on the world,[68] just as it did not cause an ontological change of human nature.

Moreover, sin is not punished on an individual level. Evils affecting an individual must never be interpreted as a direct result immediately related to the sins of that individual, nor must the measure of evil befalling individuals be related to their sins. Instead, since sin is an organic whole social evils can be interpreted as directly dependent on sin as it occurs within the complete system of nature. Corporate sin is always the primary or original element, and social evil the secondary or derivative element, but both are corporate actions of the human race. Penal suffering, in contrast, may indeed fall pre-eminently on one person, even if he or she is free from the common guilt. In Schleiermacher's words, "within the common sphere of sin it is possible for one to suffer for the rest." [69] Yet, the notion that evil befalls people proportionate to their sins does not square with such an event. Schleiermacher thus rejects what he considers a misleading assumption that God correlates evil with sin as exemplified in

64. Schleiermacher, *Christian Faith*, tr. MacIntosh and Stewart, §72.4, 299.

65. Ibid., §82.1, 339.

66. Ibid., §75.1, 316.

67. See Williams, "Theodicy, Tragedy, and Soteriology," 411.

68. See Schleiermacher, *Christian Faith*, tr. MacIntosh and Stewart, §75.3, 317.

69. Ibid., §77.2, 322. This conception has important implications for the doctrine of the person of Christ.

human legal punishment. A positive correlation between sin and penalty exists only as a means of generating the consciousness of redemption. Evil is instrumental and presupposes a "cosmic-soteriological constitution of the world."[70] As a consequence, states Hans Walter Schütte, the traditional notion of the wrath of God "appears like the evocation of a form of incomplete God-consciousness."[71]

Some classical versions of the doctrine also tend to retain the notion of eternal punishment for original sin. According to these conceptions, not all evil will ultimately be transformed into good, but, as Williams notes, "God allows some evil to remain evil."[72] In this sense, the Calvinist notion of a double decree to salvation and perdition compromises the principle that evil ultimately serves a good purpose. In contrast, Schleiermacher's conception implies that original sin is ordained in teleological reference to redemption. Just as he does not recognize a correlation between good and reward, he denies a correlation between original sin and the idea of eternal punishment.

Conclusion

Schleiermacher retained a number of aspects of the traditional doctrine of sin, but by reinterpreting others, he arrived at a major revision of the traditional doctrine of hamartiology.

He retained the traditional structure of dogmatics by placing his discussion of sin in front of grace, and he upheld the Augustinian and Reformed understanding that sin is humanity's doing whereas grace is from God alone. He agreed with tradition in his analysis that human freedom is the ground for sin, and evil is its consequence. However, there is no direct or immediate relationship between a particular sin and its punishment, just as there is no direct relation between a good deed and its reward. He also retained the notion that sin is inevitable and that individuals are to be held responsible for the actual sins they commit. Schleiermacher further agreed with the traditional dichotomy between flesh and spirit, and he upheld the intent of the fall motif that redemption is necessary. Finally, his understanding of original sin as the total incapacity for good was also congruent with traditional teaching.

---

70. Williams, "Theodicy, Tragedy, and Soteriology," 410.

71. Schütte, "Ausscheidung," 391.

72. Williams, "Theodicy, Tragedy, and Soteriology," 403.

Schleiermacher's reinterpretation of the doctrine of sin revolves around two issues. He conceptualized sin in terms of consciousness of sin rather than as active revolt, and he located it in human God-forgetfulness, thus making sin a religious rather than a moral issue. He argued further that original sin was corporate rather than hereditary. Superficially observing the classical distinction between original sin and actual sin, he tied both notions closely together. He maintained that original sin was an anthropological constant that had already applied to the first human beings, and he held that this innate disposition to universal sinfulness inevitably issued in the actual sins of individuals. As such, actual sins are the result of a personal choice or application of freedom, but human freedom, in turn, is grounded in divine causality. This causality entails that God is the author of sin, but only in the sense that sin is the necessary precondition for redemption.

By integrating sin and redemption in the single universal divine decree to create and redeem, Schleiermacher prepared the ground for his doctrine of predestination. Universal sinfulness corresponds to universal redemption and thus the ultimate restoration of all to the presence of God. As Matthias Gockel points out, the notion of original and universal sinfulness "radicalizes the Protestant understanding of total depravity . . . as a correlate to the idea of God's gracious, unconditional election."[73] There is no eternal punishment for original sin because original sin is part of the divine causality. There is no actual distinction between divine cause and permission, either.

Schleiermacher also redefined original perfection as the capability to receive grace, and thus as a necessary precondition for redemption. He dispensed with the traditional understanding of original perfection as a state of innocence or original righteousness and argued that human nature from the very start and throughout all generations had remained basically unchanged. According to his conception, a fall from grace that results in an ontological alteration of human nature was unintelligible.

He thus departed from rationalism by breaking with the view that human beings were inherently good and not in need of redemption, and he departed from supernaturalism by offering a naturalistic explanation for original sin instead of the Mosaic account of a fundamental ontological change in human nature.[74]

---

73. Gockel, *Barth and Schleiermacher*, 67.

74. See Wyman, "Sin and Redemption," 137.

Although Schleiermacher's interpretation of the doctrine of sin is entirely coherent, his re-conceptualization leaves some open questions. For him, the only possible relationship between sin and consciousness of sin is that sin is the object of the consciousness of sin. In Schleiermacher's system, sin *per se* is an abstraction. But, as Günter Bader argues, sin is also a subject of the consciousness of sin insofar as sin dominates self-consciousness.[75] For the same reason, psychological effects of sin such as fear, hopelessness, or desperation are considered to be evils not directly related to an individual sinful act, thought, or desire. They become mere abstractions as well. Indeed, what Wyman describes as Schleiermacher's "subjectivistic reduction of the reality of evil to a phenomenon of consciousness"[76] results in the absence of any exploration of the relationship between sin and moral evil. It could be argued that the moral dimension of the human condition is neglected altogether. Schleiermacher's contention that "the Christian consciousness could never give rise to a moment of activity specially directed towards the cessation of suffering as such"[77] can have problematic and troubling implications for Christian praxis.

SOTERIOLOGY

Soteriology, the doctrine of the saving work of Christ, provides the ultimate context for the doctrine of election in *Christian Faith*. Here, in contrast to the Reformed tradition, election is closely related to christology. A brief exposition of the role of Christ in predestination according to the Reformed tradition will precede a discussion of the fundamental issue, Schleiermacher's understanding of the manner in which human beings come to salvation through fellowship with Christ the Redeemer. His reinterpretation of soteriology reflects the christological approach of *Christian Faith* as a whole, which, in turn, is also discernible in the doctrine of election. For this reason, the importance for soteriology of the doctrine of election as part of the universal decree to salvation will also be considered here.

---

75. See Bader, "Sünde," 77.

76. Wyman, "Sin and Redemption," 138.

77. Schleiermacher, *Christian Faith*, tr. MacIntosh and Stewart, §78.2, 324.

The Role of Christ in Election in the Reformed Tradition

Augustine had formulated his doctrine of grace in such a way that a strict doctrine of predestination resulted from it. He argued that prior to any conversion, the prevenient grace of God must release the human will from its bondage to sin before it can freely turn to will what is good *coram Deo*. Whether or not individuals receive the gift of grace depends on whether they are elect or not. In this way, predestination to salvation becomes a precondition of grace. As David Fergusson notes, for the *ordo salutis* of each individual, "divine election now becomes sovereign."[78] The Reformers restated Augustine's radical doctrine of grace and confirmed his view of the decree of predestination as a corollary of the *sola gratia* interpretation of faith. Only if God's good-pleasure alone determines the eschatological fate of each member of the human race can there be certainty that faith is exclusively brought about by God's grace without any human input or merit.

Calvin's doctrine of christology is characterized by its soteriological bias. Christ has a unique function as mediator between God and human beings, and, as Calvin argues, "no knowledge of God without a Mediator was effectual to salvation."[79] The necessity for his incarnation lay in God's determination to redeem. The object of Christ's work of mediation therefore is atonement, the reconciling of God to humanity. In Christ's death, sin and death are abolished, and in his resurrection righteousness is restored.[80] But while salvation is in Christ and can only be obtained in union with him, this union is effected by the Holy Spirit. The Spirit unites the elect with Christ, and their part consists only in assuming the union already established by God in the incarnation.

In Calvin's theology and in the mainstream Reformed tradition, the first cause of salvation is thus God's eternal decree of election, and the efficient cause is God's good-pleasure. Christ is the material cause, and in this sense he is subordinate to the divine decree of election. His function in election consists in acting as the mirror of election and as the source of the assurance concerning election for individuals, giving testimony and conveying the grace by virtue of which election takes place. As John Reid notes, "Christ is accorded the office of exhibiting our election, and

---

78. Fergusson, "Predestination: A Scottish Perspective," 459.

79. Calvin, *Institutes,* tr. Beveridge, II.6.1, 293.

80. For this and the following see Cuncliffe-Jones, *History of Christian Doctrine,* 393–94.

applying it with resulting comfort to the soul."[81] But election itself belongs to God and has its ultimate ground in God's *arcanum concilium*, his hidden counsel. According to Calvin, it is "God's eternal decree, by which he determined with himself whatever he wished to happen with regard to every man."[82] Christ has not been admitted into the inmost recesses of the divine decree. Calvin's statements that "Christ claims the right of electing in common with the Father" and that he "makes himself the author of election"[83] refer to Christ's election of disciples on earth rather than eternal predestination.

If the eternal decree precedes and indeed conditions grace, then God determines the eschatological fate of each human being before the work of grace becomes operative. In this sense, the function of Christ is to carry out a task—implementing the divine decision about election—that has been determined without his active involvement. He plays no part within the decree of election itself since the ground for election is not to be found in Christ's merits but exclusively in God's good-pleasure.

With regard to the other constitutive part of the double decree, reprobation, Christ is not only, as in election, excluded from the decree itself, but now also from his role as executor of the decree. Reid puts it very pointedly: "At no point throughout its course, from its initial conception to its eventual accomplishment, does Christ have any hand or part in it."[84] If anything, he passively suffers the neglect of the reprobate and represents that from which they are alienated. Thus, in the theological tradition that stretches from Augustine via Calvin (and Luther) to the Reformed, Christ plays no operative role in the double decree of predestination. The purpose of his work is to appease the wrath of God, but salvation does not ultimately depend on his death on the cross but on God's good-pleasure.

In Schleiermacher's version of the doctrine of soteriology, in contrast, Christ's work is indispensable for salvation. It is directed at the transformation of human consciousness from God-forgetfulness to God-consciousness. According to Wyman, Schleiermacher reinterpreted sin and redemption "in terms of a conceptuality provided by a philosophical anthropology."[85]

---

81. Reid, "Office of Christ," 15.
82. Calvin, *Institutes*, tr. Beveridge, III.21.5, 206.
83. Ibid., III.22.7, 219.
84. Reid, "Office of Christ," 17.
85. Wyman, "Sin and Redemption," 130.

Schleiermacher's Reinterpretation of the Person and Work of Christ

In *Christian Faith*, the doctrine of the person and work of Christ is discussed at the start of Part II, 2, the consciousness of grace. The person and work of Christ on the hand, and regeneration and sanctification on the other, form the first and second divisions of this aspect. Christology and soteriology together reflect Schleiermacher's interpretation of human beings in the state of grace. The doctrine of soteriology is followed by the doctrine of ecclesiology, or the constitution of the world in relation to redemption. Essentially, as Paul Nimmo states, Schleiermacher thus deals with redemption twice: first with respect to the individual within the community, then with regard to the community comprised of individuals.[86]

In an introduction (§§86–91), Schleiermacher defines the task of demonstrating how the communication of Christ's sinless perfection to other human beings works in relation to his immediate disciples and to later generations. He explains his understanding of redemption as an expression for the complete work of Christ, and his contention that Christ represents the perfection of the creation of human nature. Redemption, Christian consciousness, and the divine decree are related to each other through the claim that, "if we can bring rightly and completely into consciousness what has come into the world through redemption, then we shall thereby have given the content of the divine decrees also."[87] Schleiermacher emphasizes the divine decree to redeem all humankind, which implies his criticism of the Reformed understanding of redemption being decreed on an individual basis.

Before launching into the doctrine of christology proper, Schleiermacher argues that, even though the person and work of Christ are different with regard to the individual propositions discussed, "their total content is the same."[88] Christ's identity is inextricably linked with his function: the person of Christ must be commensurate with and grounded in his work, and vice versa. Hence, the two doctrines cannot be isolated,[89] and they cannot be separated in the consciousness of the believer, either.

---

86. See Nimmo, "Mediation," 195.

87. Schleiermacher, *Christian Faith*, tr. MacIntosh and Stewart, §90.2, 370. The plural "decrees" is noteworthy.

88. Ibid., §92.3, 374.

89. See McGrath, *Modern German Christology*, 43.

In that consciousness, Christ's sinless perfection represents a spontaneous activity whereas the human need for redemption represents receptivity.

In his discussion of christology and of regeneration and sanctification, Schleiermacher first gives an introduction with an exposition of his own understanding. Then he enters into a detailed dialogue with the traditional Protestant—both Reformed and Lutheran—interpretations as recorded in the symbolic books or confessions.

The Person of Christ

The purpose of this doctrine is to explain the historical person of Christ, which introduces something fundamentally new from outside history into history, but this new thing is not given as such in human self-consciousness. Christ appears in history, but he cannot be deduced from it. Schleiermacher tries to reconcile these two aspects by interpreting Christ, in Helmut Thielicke's words, "as the original model of humanity."[90]

He first posits the ideality[91] of the personal dignity of Christ as well as his perfect historicity. The concept of ideality relates only to his God-consciousness, not to his growth and development as a human being. His personality developed as a "continuous transition from the condition of purest innocence to one of purely spiritual fullness of power."[92] Ideality means the fulfillment of the idea of humanity as the most complete subject of God-consciousness. This ideal has appeared in history in a unique, exclusive way through Christ. However, as Edwin Van Driel observes, Christ's appearance cannot be explained "out of the causal nexus of finite reality."[93] In Schleiermacher's words, Christ can only be understood "as an original act of human nature, i.e. as an act of human nature as not affected by sin."[94] He entered into the corporate life of sinfulness, but he cannot have proceeded from it. This entrance of the ideal into the historical sphere must be recognized "as a miraculous fact"[95] in the sense that his peculiar spiritual character can only be explained through "a creative divine act" in which "the conception of man as the subject of the God-consciousness comes to

90. Thielicke, *Glauben und Denken*, 250, my tr.
91. *Urbildlichkeit*.
92. Schleiermacher, *Christian Faith*, tr. MacIntosh and Stewart, §93.4, 383.
93. Van Driel, "Supralapsarian Christology," 260.
94. Schleiermacher, *Christian Faith*, tr. MacIntosh and Stewart, §94.3, 389.
95. Ibid., §93.3, 381.

completion."[96] His human nature is completely identical with that of all other human beings. Human sinfulness does not enter the equation here because "sin is so little an essential part of human nature that it can only be regarded as a disturbance of nature."[97] What differentiates Christ from all others is the constant complete potency of his God-consciousness, which Schleiermacher identifies with his original spirituality,[98] the being of God in Christ,[99] and thus with his divinity. Still, even this being of God in him must have had a development in time. All human beings by virtue of being human have the potential to receive complete God-consciousness too, if only after they have been separated out from the context of universal sinfulness. From this point of view, the difference between Christ and all other human beings is merely quantitative.

Schleiermacher's conception of redemption depends on the following premises: The Redeemer must have the ability to mediate between God and the human race. In order to connect with the historical and conditioned existence of humanity, he must share the common human condition, excepting its need for redemption, and at the same time be able to communicate and impart his perfect God-consciousness. The human race, the object of redemption, must require redemption and have the potential of receiving it through fellowship with the divine being in Christ. Finally, redemption must be offered from outside the universal sinfulness of humanity. Therefore, four christological heresies are to be avoided: Docetism, according to which Christ was not fully human; Ebionitism, which denies his divinity; Pelagianism, which argues that human beings can redeem themselves; and Manichaeism, according to which humans cannot be redeemed.

Schleiermacher reinterpreted the traditional doctrine of the two natures of Christ that defines the existential relationship between Christ's person or dignity, and his work or activity. He agreed with its intention "to describe Christ in such a way that in the new corporate life a vital fellowship between us and Him shall be possible, and, at the same time, that the being of God in Him shall be expressed in the clearest possible way."[100] But he rejected the traditional formulae of nature, persons, and essence as

96. Ibid.
97. Ibid., §94.1, 385.
98. See ibid., §94.3, 389.
99. See ibid., §94.2, 387.
100. Ibid., §96.1, 391.

"scientifically incompetent and ecclesiastically useless."[101] That is, if each person is also a nature, "we come almost inevitably to three divine natures for the three divine Persons in the one Divine Essence."[102] Instead of an ontic being of God in Christ, he posited that God is spiritually present in Christ as his perfect God-consciousness.

Schleiermacher next entered into a critical discussion of the statements regarding the person of Christ in the Protestant confessions. In the course of this discourse, he rejected the doctrine of the *communicatio idiomatum*, the mutual communication of attributes of the two natures of Christ. He also denied the virgin birth, arguing that "the being of God in Christ cannot possibly be explained by the fact that no male activity had any share in its conception."[103] Schleiermacher did retain the doctrine of the essential sinlessness of Christ without which he could not have been the Redeemer, but he related it to "the union of the divine and the human in His person" as the "adequate ground within His personality itself."[104] Since he "could appear only at a particular time and only out of the midst of his people"[105] and was thus conditioned by the historical circumstances which then prevailed, the traditional doctrine of the absolute perfection of Christ has to be restricted to state only his physical healthiness.

In the last proposition concerning the doctrine of the person of Christ, Schleiermacher argues: "The facts of the resurrection and the ascension of Christ, and the prediction of his return to judgment, cannot be laid down as properly constituent parts of the doctrine of his person."[106] He reasons that neither the Spirit, nor Christ's message was mediated through the resurrection or ascension itself, and that his immediate disciples did not have the faintest premonition of these events, but nevertheless they recognized the Son of God in him.[107] Christ's redeeming efficacy

---

101. Wyman, "Role of Protestant Confessions," 373.

102. Schleiermacher, *Christian Faith*, tr. MacIntosh and Stewart, §96.1, 395.

103. Ibid., §97.2, 403.

104. Ibid., §98.1, 413.

105. Ibid., §98.2, 417.

106. Ibid., §99, 417.

107. This is argument is problematic, of course, since there is no access to the pre-Easter Jesus: all the testimony in the New Testament is refracted through the lens of his resurrection. Now, rather than rejecting these doctrines altogether, Schleiermacher concedes that, since they are accepted because they are found in Scripture, they properly belong to the doctrine of Scripture rather than to christology. *Christian Faith*, of course, does not have a doctrine of Scripture; this has been replaced with the Introduction or *prolegomena*.

is based on the divine being in him, and recognizing this causes faith. That recognition happens independently of one's experience of his resurrection. Christ's cross is not the reason for our redemption, but, as Wolfgang Trillhaas points out, the "indispensable *locus* of the original verification of reconciliation."[108] Schleiermacher reinterprets the traditional metaphor of Christ sitting at the right hand of God as the peculiar dignity of Christ raised above all conflict, and he maintains that the intermediate steps of resurrection and ascension were not necessary for Christ to attain his position, and therefore stand in no relation to his redeeming efficacy.[109]

The Work of Christ

In the introduction to this second doctrine, Schleiermacher systematically distinguishes Christ's redemptive and reconciling activities. Redemption represents the completion of creation as well as the means to this goal. Since there never was a state of sinlessness in the history of the human race, nobody can escape the need for redemption. In redemption, Christ assumes persons into the power of his God-consciousness, and thus into fellowship with him, by empowering the God-consciousness to dominate any moment of their self-consciousness. In the state of grace, dominant God-consciousness influences a person's consciousness of the world. Nevertheless, human assent to Christ's activity is still conditioned in part by the consciousness of sin. Establishing a new collective life that works against the collective life of sin is an activity of Christ's sinless perfection that proceeds from the being of God in him. The relationship between the old and the new corporate life is a dynamic one in which the new life is countering sin and thus the old life. Christ's absolutely perfect God-consciousness is, as McGrath puts it, "impregnated with an assimilative power of such intensity that it is able to effect the redemption of humanity."[110] Schleiermacher explains that even though "the beginning of the kingdom of God is a supernatural thing" it "becomes natural as soon as it emerges into manifestation."[111] According to Nimmo, his influence is both "historical and historically transmitted."[112] The divine being in Christ is mediated in a natural, not in a supernatural or miraculous way, both immediately to

108. Trillhaas, "Mittelpunkt," 305.

109. See Schleiermacher, *Christian Faith*, tr. MacIntosh and Stewart, §99.1, 418.

110. McGrath, *Modern German Christology*, 43.

111. Schleiermacher, *Christian Faith*, tr. MacIntosh and Stewart, §100.3, 430.

112. Nimmo, "Mediation," 190.

his contemporaries and through the church's witness and proclamation to later generations. Eberhard Jüngel thus summarizes: "The power of Christ to communicate his own sinlessness to others has its ecclesiological correlate in the Holy Spirit, who inspirits the church as the spirit of fellowship, who impels the faithful to interact with each other and with the world in such a way that the faith is propagated and the faithful 'become . . . increasingly one' until they constitute a *Gesamtleben* that is a perfect likeness of the Redeemer."[113] The work of Christ takes place exclusively within the new collective life of the church.

Schleiermacher does not specify the precise manner of the communication of Christ's God-consciousness to other people, but he maintains that Christ communicates it by virtue of the fact that he gives himself as the source from which human beings may receive the same power. Again, he does not explain exactly how the transmission of Christ's assimilative power happens through the church's portrayal of him in the time of his physical absence.

In more general terms, states DeVries, Schleiermacher refers to Christ's activity "as a fact of inner experience mediated through the community."[114] This model requires neither any violation of the natural laws, nor does it reduce Jesus Christ to a teacher. Schleiermacher characterizes this understanding as mystical and contrasts it with what he calls magical and empirical views. The former denies the necessity of fellowship and insists on the immediate influence of the Redeemer on individuals apart from the community of faith; the latter maintains that Christ's activity consists only in bringing about increasing moral perfection through his example and thus reduces his work to teaching. As Theodore Vial explains, in the wake of the Enlightenment, "models for understanding the redemptive work of Christ seemed limited to irrational supernaturalism . . . or the deistic view that Jesus was no more than a great teacher and moral exemplar."[115]

Reconciliation consists of the Redeemer's assuming believers into the fellowship of his unclouded blessedness. This is made possible through the pre-existing human capacity for receptivity, which in turn belongs to the original perfection of the human race. Kevin Hector's assertion that "Christ makes us receptive to his pure act so that we can reproduce it as

---

113. Jüngel, "Schleiermacher," 489.

114. DeVries, "Schleiermacher," 321.

115. Vial, "Schleiermacher and the State," 273.

our action"[116] is therefore inaccurate. Receptivity is part of the original perfection of humanity and thus an anthropological constant. According to Schleiermacher, the regenerate still have a consciousness of sin because they invariably live and operate within the sphere of corporate sinfulness. However, their assumption into fellowship with Christ dissolves the connection between sin and evil. For the redeemed, all hindrances to life are simply "indications,"[117] not evils arising out of sin. Redeemed human beings are never filled with a consciousness of evil as punishment for sin. Again, Schleiermacher rejects the magical understanding of Protestant Orthodoxy and supernaturalism, which denies all naturalness in Christ's activity and attributes a transaction entirely unmediated by anything natural to him. He also rejects the empirical view of the Enlightenment that reduces Christ's reconciling activity to the level of an ordinary daily experience.

The remaining propositions of the doctrine of the work of Christ concern the prophetic, high priestly, and kingly offices of Christ. In order to safeguard the harmony between the old and new covenants, all three offices have to be present. Based on his detailed re-interpretation of the traditional treatments of the three offices, Schleiermacher concludes that the prophetic office consists of teaching, prophesizing, and performing miracles. The high priestly office includes Christ's active and passive obedience in the perfect fulfillment of the law on the one hand, and his atoning death on the other. In particular, Schleiermacher strongly refutes the doctrine of vicarious satisfaction and thus the forensic understanding of Christ's suffering and death as either substitution or sacrifice. He argues that every time people suffer evil that is not directly related to a particular actual sin they have committed, they nevertheless suffer evil, but as punishment for somebody else's sin. Thus, when Christ entered into the corporate sinful life of the human race, he suffered punishment for the sins of all others, even though he himself was sinless. Through Christ's suffering, in the corporate life of his fellowship evil is no longer regarded as punishment for sin, and such punishment is effectively abolished for the regenerate. This, Schleiermacher argues, "is the real meaning of the statements that Christ by his willing surrender of Himself to suffering and death satisfied the divine justice, as that which had ordained the connexion between sin and evil, and thus set us free from the punishment of sin."[118] But, as Nathan

116. Hector, "Schleiermacher's Christology," 319.

117. Schleiermacher, *Christian Faith*, tr. MacIntosh and Stewart, §101.2, 432.

118. Ibid., §104.2, 458.

Hieb points out, the accidental details of his suffering and death bear no direct relation to redemption.[119]

Finally, the kingly office entails that everything that the fellowship of the redeemed requires proceeds from Christ as an aspect of the divine governance of the world.

Regeneration and Sanctification

This section concerns the manner in which fellowship with the Redeemer expresses itself in human beings, or with the effects that the person and work of Christ have on the self-consciousness of those in fellowship with him. This can be represented as regeneration or the act of uniting, and as sanctification, or the state of union. As DeVries and Gerrish state, the moment of a person's regeneration is "the breakthrough of God's eternal decree for humanity into the consciousness of the individual."[120] The fellowship of believers consists precisely of the totality of all those who are sanctified, and the concept of the collective life provides the chief condition for the connection between the Redeemer and the regenerate of later generations.

Regeneration can be viewed from two different perspectives. From the point of view of the human being whose relation to God has changed, it is justification; from the point of view of a changed form of life it is conversion. Both conversion and justification are effects of the union with Christ and happen simultaneously.

For Schleiermacher, conversion makes itself known by a process of repentance and a change of heart, and then by faith in the sense of an appropriation of Christ's perfection and blessedness. Schleiermacher strongly rejects the view that conversion can be pinpointed to a particular date and place in an individual's biography as "an arbitrary and presumptuous restriction of divine grace."[121] Instead, conversion means the moment at which a person's entry into the fellowship with Christ is effected.

Justification includes the forgiveness of sin and the adoption of a person as a child of God. Forgiveness and adoption condition each other. For the individual, justification means that consciousness of sin becomes consciousness of the forgiveness of sin. Although consciousness of sin and even of penal desert is ordained by God, it is decreed exclusively and

119. See Hieb, "Resurrection," 402.
120. DeVries and Gerrish, "Schleiermacher on Justification and Election," 201.
121. Schleiermacher, *Christian Faith*, tr. MacIntosh and Stewart, §108.3, 487.

entirely in relation to redemption. Since the consciousness of guilt and evil will vanish through redemption, there is no need for a new divine decree that ordains the cessation of the consciousness of guilt and evil.

In his discussion of conversion, Schleiermacher argues that not only the ability to be received into fellowship with Christ but also the very desire for this fellowship forms part of the original perfection of the human race. That desire "is simply the ineradicable residuum in human nature of the original impartation of the divine which makes human nature what it is."[122] Indeed, this desire is an indication of "the parallel between the beginning of the divine life in us and the incarnation of the Redeemer."[123] What Helmut Thielicke calls the "infinite qualitative difference"[124] between divinity and humanity is abolished: the divine element in Christ is precisely his perfect humanity.

According to Schleiermacher, sanctification, originally a scriptural term, designates the process by which a life akin to that of Christ in terms of his perfection and blessedness is produced in the regenerate. This happens when the natural powers of a regenerate person in fellowship with Christ are put at the person's disposal.

Two aspects of sanctification are considered in more detail: the sins and the good works of the regenerate. Schleiermacher insists that in the state of sanctification, no new sins develop, but a trace of the universal sinfulness that belongs to the unregenerate nevertheless remains present in all acts of the regenerate. But these traces have no power to make regeneration nugatory, hence a fall from the state of grace is not possible. The sins of the regenerate "always carry their forgiveness with them."[125] Again, Schleiermacher insists that forgiveness of sins does not arise out of a particular decree for an individual person. Instead, it is an aspect of the single universal divine decree that ultimately emancipates the human race from the sphere of universal sinfulness.

With regard to the good works of the regenerate, finally, Schleiermacher is in full agreement with the Protestant tradition that holds that works are good *coram Deo* if they are the result of faith. By virtue of their faith, the regenerate cannot but do good works. Schleiermacher concludes that the reason why the works of the regenerate as such are objects of divine good-pleasure is that God regards the regenerate person in Christ.

122. Ibid., §108.6, 495.

123. Ibid.

124. Thielicke, *Glauben und Denken*, 252.

125. Schleiermacher, *Christian Faith*, tr. MacIntosh and Stewart, §111.1, 510.

Schleiermacher's soteriology is based on consciousness of sin, consciousness of guilt, and consciousness of forgiveness, rather than on sin, guilt, and forgiveness *per se*. Through regeneration, the guilty conscience is superseded by an ever more dominant God-consciousness. It could be argued that the emphasis on consciousness and the dependence of redemption on the perfection of Christ's God-consciousness indicates an impoverishment of the traditional doctrine of soteriology. At the very least, in comparison with the traditional doctrine of atonement, the interpretation of sin as a hindrance to the higher consciousness and redemption as its strengthening makes piety the centre of the understanding of sin and grace. Moral dimensions are ignored.

In the absence of any reciprocity between human beings and their actions on the one hand, and God on the other, claims Michael Root, salvation is only "liberation from an evil suffered rather than reconciliation for an evil committed."[126] While for Schleiermacher the effects of sin are not perceived as evil any more, they remain intact even for the regenerate. Objectively there has been no change in circumstances through regeneration, only a change in the consciousness or perception of the regenerate individual regarding the consequences of their actions.

The Christological Approach of *Christian Faith* and Election

Even though in material terms the doctrine of Christ only takes up fourteen propositions, christology is the material center of the entire structure of *Christian Faith*. Kurt Nowak described this dogmatic work with its long run up and the establishment of a new life through Christ as "a great religious drama of humankind with a salvific end"[127] and the section on the person and work of Christ as "christological panegyric."[128] Schleiermacher's doctrine of soteriology is laid out christologically: salvation in the individual takes place in a manner that is analogous to the union of the human and the divine in the person of Christ.[129] The divine decree of creation is identical with the decree to redemption, and only with Christ's incarnation is creation finally perfected. Since the completion of human nature has been ordained in Christ, he is related to both the past and the future of the human race.

126. Root, "Schleiermacher as Innovator," 100.
127. Nowak, *Schleiermacher*, 280.
128. Ibid., 279.
129. See DeVries, "Schleiermacher," 322.

In the sense that the incarnation is not contingent on human sin, Schleiermacher's Christology can be characterized as supralapsarian. From the perspective of this new creation evil, the threat of eternal damnation and everlasting death disappear. Conversely, the final existential stage of redemption, universal restoration, is possible only because of the universal sinfulness in tandem with the original perfection of the human race. Creation with universal regeneration as its goal is best understood from the theological perspective of redemption. Sin is teleologically subordinate to redemption but constitutes its temporal precondition. Despite its empirical universality, sin is ordained to disappear through redemption; the Redeemer is the theological basis for the affirmation that sin and evil are not ultimate.

Schleiermacher answers the question why Jesus of Nazareth was elected as the Redeemer with the observation that "time and place were chosen as the absolute best, that is as yielding the maximum operative effect."[130] Of course, due to eternal divine causality, God was also ultimately responsible for the occurrence of the precise situation in history in which the election of Jesus would yield this maximum effect. The election of Christ as the one in whom the divine became uniquely united with his human nature is also part of the overall divine ordination. As Richard Niebuhr stated: "The decree to create the world and to appoint Jesus of Nazareth as the inaugurator of the kingdom of spiritual men is one decree."[131]

In the person and work of Christ, the twin ideas of decree and election emerge at the surface of *Christian Faith* and expose the architectonic function of the doctrine of election.[132] Schleiermacher's contention that there is "only one eternal and universal decree, justifying men for Christ's sake"[133] is the most encompassing theological formulation of the interrelationship of the doctrines discussed in *Christian Faith*. The eternal decree that elects human beings to redemption through Christ is a summary statement concerning the complex situation of human beings in relation to God, to the world, and to each other as they are, according to Niebuhr, "simultaneously ordered anew, clarified, and interpreted by Jesus of Nazareth."[134] In Christ humanity beholds God's good-pleasure, and in

---

130. Schleiermacher, *Christian Faith*, tr. MacIntosh and Stewart, §120.2, 553.

131. Niebuhr, *Schleiermacher on Christ and Religion*, 214.

132. See ibid., 250.

133. Schleiermacher, *Christian Faith*, tr. MacIntosh and Stewart, §109.3, 501.

134. Niebuhr, *Schleiermacher on Christ and Religion*, 256.

the experience of God-consciousness mediated through him human be-ings recognize their own share in that good pleasure. "[F]aith in Christ is . . . sharing in this divine good-pleasure which abides in Christ . . . the consciousness of divine grace, or the peace of God in the redeemed heart, is . . . this quiet acceptance of the divine good-pleasure in respect of the arrangement of events which led to oneself being taken up into the sphere of redemption."[135]

Structurally, Schleiermacher infers his christology from the pres-ent impact of Christ on believers within the fellowship of the church. As McGrath notes, he thus argues "back from the observed effect to its suf-ficient cause."[136] That cause, redemption through Christ alone, has to be consistent with the Christian understanding of God, Christ, and the human race, and thus with the original divine decree that ordained that Christ is the Redeemer of sinful humanity. Creation, preservation, and redemption are all subsumed in one divine decree so that "the creation of humanity is teleologically ordered from its very inception to its perfection in Christ."[137]

Created existence provides the context for understanding redemp-tion, and redeemed existence provides the final interpretation of the origi-nal decree of creation.[138] The redemption accomplished by Christ excludes any opposition between the love and the wrath of God, which could only be assigned to a divine activity prior to and outside of redemption.

ESCHATOLOGY

Traditionally, the doctrine of the last things comprises the resurrection, the last judgment, heaven, and hell. Integral to an authentic eschatology is the union of believers with the risen and ascended Redeemer, but this union can also find expression in the doctrine of communion, as it does for instance in Calvin's *Institutio*. Scriptural references to the future ex-press the expectation that God's intentions will be revealed, but, as Fergus-son observes, the apocalyptic images used are too opaque and inconsistent to serve even as cryptic expressions of the end of the world, "Christian

---

135. Schleiermacher, *Christian Faith*, tr. MacIntosh and Stewart, §120.3, 556.

136. McGrath, *Making of Modern German Christology*, 43.

137. Mariña, "Christology and Anthropology," 161.

138. See Vance, "Sin and Self-consciousness," 197.

faith and hope . . . are predicated upon our ignorance of exactly how the future will be."[139]

Schleiermacher, who, according to Bernd Oberdorfer, "is regarded as one of the greatest demythologizers of Christian eschatology"[140] deals with eschatology as part of the wider doctrine of ecclesiology. As he observes, this positioning of the doctrine signals "the continuity of history with the *eschaton*."[141] In *Christian Faith*, the doctrine of eschatology primarily concerns the consummation of the church. It stands under the hermeneutical reservation that its explication is difficult because it discusses matters which by their very nature fall outside human experience. Further, the content of eschatology forms the *terminus ad quem* of Christian life, but the images used to describe it are no more than indicators pointing to a qualitatively different existence. Human beings "lack the vocabulary and thus the knowledge to describe it."[142] Epistemologically, the doctrine of eschatology stands on weaker ground than the rest of the dogmatic work. Robert Merrihew Adams points out that what lies behind the predictions Schleiermacher is willing to make, even if cautiously, is the teleology of the Christian life.[143]

As Oberdorfer notes, Schleiermacher's exposition demonstrates "an extraordinary subtle hermeneutics of eschatological claims."[144] For Schleiermacher, "Christian doctrines are accounts of the Christian religious affections set forth in speech"[145] and dogmatic propositions arise "solely out of logically ordered reflection upon the immediate utterances of the religious self-consciousness."[146] However, the doctrinal propositions in *Christian Faith* do not all share the same epistemological foundation. Adams observes that some "purport to express the implicit content of the feeling of absolute dependence. Others propose an empirical description of the history of that feeling and of related states of mind. . . . Others offer explanations of aspects of that history."[147] Even in the doctrines of sin and redemption, which are perhaps more expressive of personal experience

139. Fergusson, "Eschatology," 242.

140. Oberdorfer, "Schleiermacher on Eschatology and Resurrection," 166.

141. Ibid., 170.

142. Fergusson, "Eschatology," 239.

143. See Adams, "Faith and Religious Knowledge," 47.

144. Oberdorfer, "Schleiermacher on Eschatology and Resurrection," 167.

145. Schleiermacher, *Christian Faith*, tr. MacIntosh and Stewart, §15, 76.

146. Ibid., §16 postscript, 81.

147. Adams, "Faith and Religious Knowledge," 46.

than others, an element of theological interpretation remains. Nevertheless, for Schleiermacher "the doctrines in all their forms have their ultimate ground so exclusively in the emotions of the religious self-consciousness, that where these do not exist the doctrines cannot arise."[148]

As Herms argues convincingly, the difference between doctrinal propositions and eschatological statements in *Christian Faith* is that they consider the same object, the Christian determination of the immediate self-consciousness, from different points of view.[149] The other doctrinal statements deal with Christian self-consciousness from the perspective of being redeemed. The point of view of eschatology, too, is contained in the Christian self-consciousness, but it is the state of this pious self-consciousness in which the contrast between sin and grace is totally removed. In other words, eschatological propositions express the perspective of having been redeemed, and because of this future perfect point of view Schleiermacher designates them as prophetic doctrines. Thus, although their contents differ from that of the other propositions, he explicates them as statements of faith with the same topic,[150] namely the determination of human existence through redemption, but from a perspective that eludes all present experience—though not all possible experience. Nathan Hieb's contention that Schleiermacher's system of theology "is functional only for this life," and that he "oversteps the bounds of his methodology" is therefore misguided.[151]

Herms describes the structure of the relation between the doctrine of eschatology as part of ecclesiology and the doctrine of soteriology as follows:[152] the state of the world under the influence of grace is characterized by the existence of the church in the world. The doctrine of soteriology, consisting of christology as well as regeneration and sanctification, describes the individual existence of the Christian faith, whereas ecclesiology, consisting of pneumatology, ecclesiology proper, and eschatology, describes the social or corporate existence. Moreover, christology and regeneration, which describe the development of faith in the individual, correspond to eschatology, which explicates the development of the social form of faith, the church. And finally, ecclesiology proper, or

148. Schleiermacher, *Christian Faith*, tr. MacIntosh and Stewart, §15.2, 78.

149. See Herms, "Schleiermachers Eschatologie," 136–37.

150. Daniel Pedersen's claim that it is "the source of a doctrine, not the subject of a doctrine that authorizes it as an appropriate subject for Christian dogmatics" is misconceived. Pedersen, "Eternal Life," 346.

151. Hieb, "Resurrection," 412.

152. For the following see Herms, "Schleiermachers Eschatologie," 130.

the subsistence of the church in the world, has a material parallel in the sanctification of the individual. Accordingly, Herms argues, every proposition in the doctrine of soteriology has to be understood as an implication of the doctrine of ecclesiology.

Schleiermacher stakes his claims about the doctrine of the last things in three introductory paragraphs (§§157–159). The topics of the consummate state of the church and of personal immortality, which are complementary elements of the *eschaton*, are treated as a material unit. Eschatology concerns first the consummation of the church, and in a secondary sense the fate of individuals after death. It is a cosmological eschatology that emphasizes the corporate or social dimension as well as the individual one.

As Hieb rightly points out, there is an obvious tension here between the continuity necessitated by personal survival after death and the discontinuity required by the consummation of the church.[153] The actual consummation of the church, or the completion of the kingdom of God, is not a historical possibility because its realization constitutes the end of the world and thus of history. It can only come about when all influences of the world, and therefore of sin, have exhausted themselves. Hieb's suggestion that the consummation of the church could be construed as "an event that occurs at a future point in history in which humanity has learned to experience perfectly Christ's powerful God-consciousness"[154] is thus misleading. Moreover, for Schleiermacher, redemption is not a matter of learning to experience Christ's God-consciousness; it does not constitute a process that can be instigated and controlled by human beings. Instead, it is the assumption of human beings into the power of Christ's perfect God-consciousness. In traditional terms, the church militant is always involved in conflict caused by the renewed development of sin in each generation; it has to conquer the world. In contrast, the church triumphant has absorbed everything that was worldly and is in the state of consummation.[155] The sufficient reason for that state is the Holy Spirit.[156] Although this state of consummation cannot be conceived from the human perspective, its idea is rooted in the Christian self-consciousness as the continuing fellowship of human nature with Christ.

153. See Hieb, "Resurrection," 409–10.

154. Ibid., 411.

155. See Schleiermacher, *Christian Faith*, tr. MacIntosh and Stewart, §157.1, 697.

156. See ibid., 157.1, 696.

With regard to the individual, faith in the Redeemer represents the justification for belief in the continuation of personality after death. The union of the divine being with the human nature in Christ functions as the guarantor of the belief in continuing existence after death. According to Schleiermacher, Christ ascribed such a continuation of personality to himself,[157] and in virtue of the identity of his human nature with ours the same immortality must apply to all human beings. Indeed, from the beginning of creation human beings must have possessed the same immortality as that Christ was conscious of. Since faith in the Redeemer is the exclusive reason for belief in immortality, and is not, as Pedersen wrongly claims, "derived indirectly from the God-consciousness,"[158] the doctrine of the persistence of personality is grounded in christology. In fact, Schleiermacher actually argues that there is no connection between the belief in immortality and God-consciousness: "We must not continue to assert that this belief [in the survival of personality] and the God-consciousness are bound up together."[159]

Although both the consummate church and the continuing existence of personality after death are inconceivable inasmuch as a concrete idea of them cannot be developed, argues Herms, the reasons for the inconceivability of the two notions differ. The consummation of the church has no analogy because the opposition of sin disappears in the consummate state of freedom from all struggle against sin. The continuance of personality on the other hand depends on a particular cosmological determination of space and time that is not yet known, while reckoning with the continuity of the conditions for personality.[160] Nevertheless, these difficulties do not imply a denial of the possibility of the eschatological state of church and individuals.

God's being in Christ and the resulting union of the divine and the human nature completes the unchangeable divine decree of creation and redemption. In the context of the discussion on immortality, Schleiermacher asserts his universalist contention that "the Redeemer continues to be the mediator of immortality . . . for all, without exception."[161] This is not the case because human beings *per se* are immortal, but because of the union of the divine being with Christ's nature, which in this sense only

---

157. See ibid., §158.2, 700.

158. Pedersen, "Eternal Life," 347.

159. Schleiermacher, *Christian Faith*, tr. MacIntosh and Stewart, §158.1, 700.

160. See Herms, "Schleiermachers Eschatologie," 140.

161. Schleiermacher, *Christian Faith*, tr. MacIntosh and Stewart, §158.2, 702.

aims at all human beings. As Oberdorfer states, the Redeemer is "the only warrant of eschatological reality."[162]

Schleiermacher insists that the doctrine of eschatology cannot be ascribed the same "value" as all other doctrines.[163] This claim does not relate to their intrinsic worth, but to their epistemological difference from the other doctrines in *Christian Faith*. To mark this difference, Schleiermacher designated the eschatological doctrines as prophetic. They comprise the return of Christ, the resurrection of the flesh, the last judgment, eternal blessedness, and, in an appendix, eternal damnation.

The return or second coming of Christ forms the basis for the following doctrines. It is treated as a cosmological event, namely as the end of the present state of the world. The consummation of the church happens as "a leap to perfection"[164] that in turn constitutes an act of the kingly power of Christ. The cessation of development and growth is only possible under the condition that procreation and the coexistence of good and bad, or sin, cease. The return of Christ is fundamental to both the resurrection of the body and the last judgment.

The doctrine of resurrection deals with the continuity of personality after death. It oscillates between two concepts: the individual remains entirely the same as in this life, or after resurrection the totality of the human race is to be in the consummate church. In the first scenario, the consummated church grows incrementally out of the earthly life of human beings. In the second, the church triumphant arises suddenly as a complete entity at the expense of personal continuity. The latter is the more biblical view. Either way, though, human beings can expect a renewal of organic life after the resurrection of the body.

The continuation of the church is discussed in the last two prophetic doctrines, last judgment and eternal blessedness. The last judgment considers the consummation of the church as "conditioned by the fact that no further influence upon the church can now be exerted by those who form no part of the church";[165] the eternal blessedness considers the consummation of the church as excluding "all the activities of sin and all imperfection in believers."[166]

---

162. Oberdorfer, "Schleiermacher on Eschatology and Resurrection," 170.

163. See Schleiermacher, *Christian Faith*, tr. MacIntosh and Stewart, §159, 703.

164. Ibid., §160.2, 708.

165. Ibid., §159.3, 706.

166. Ibid.

The doctrine of the last judgment traditionally involves the separation of the church from the world, or the distinction of life in communion with God from that of separation from God. The consummate church will be an entirely self-enclosed body, either because evil has ceased to exist, or because any unregenerate human beings that might still exist will be excluded from all connection with the consummate church. For Schleiermacher, the last judgment simply implies the sphere of the struggle-free church, in which the separation contemplated above is "both inadequate and superfluous."[167]

The doctrine of eternal blessedness finally goes right to the heart of the doctrine of election. It designates the area into which the personal continuance falls. The state of unchangeable and untainted blessedness can be conceived either as an abrupt possession of what is most sublime, or as a gradual ascent to it. However, Schleiermacher points out, neither formulation implies the consummation of the church. He therefore leaves unanswered the question of how the church's supreme state is to be achieved.

Only in an appendix to the doctrine of eternal blessedness does Schleiermacher deal with eternal damnation. He characterizes it as a "pictorial representation" and since it "is not an anticipation of any object of our future experience, it cannot be given the form of a special doctrine."[168] It can only be treated "as the shadow of eternal blessedness or the darker side of judgment,"[169] as eschatological separation from God. He dismisses the notion of damnation taking shape as bodily pain, since the mitigating power of habit would mean that the misery inflicted was not pure. He is equally dismissive of damnation as spiritual pain on the grounds that it would only be torturous if there was a chance to actually partake in the state of blessedness. Taking up his argument from the essay on election, he concludes that eternal blessedness cannot exist alongside eternal damnation, since the empathy and compassion that the blessed would feel for the damned would diminish their own blessedness. As Adams observes, it is "more reasonable to conceive of life after death as one in which everyone will eventually be redeemed."[170] And, more importantly, the notions of God's love and eternal perdition are mutually exclusive for Schleier-

167. Ibid., §162.2, 716.
168. Ibid., §159.3, 706.
169. Ibid.
170. Adams, "Faith and Religious Knowledge," 46.

macher. Still, as already discussed,[171] he suggests only rather tentatively that "we ought at least to admit the equal rights of the milder view ... that through the power of redemption there will one day be a universal restoration of all souls."[172] As Fergusson notes, anything other than a universalist outcome would be "an affront to the love of God."[173] Oberdorfer also points out very aptly that in Schleiermacher's dogmatics, which represents an explication of the immediate self-consciousness of believers, to treat eternal perdition as an article of faith would be a contradiction in itself.[174]

With regard to the doctrine of election, the sparse reference Schleiermacher makes to the divine decree ordaining the ultimate consummation of the church is noticeable. The absence of an explicitly made connection between eschatology and election is all the more conspicuous because of a clear parallel between the two doctrines. As Schleiermacher himself pointed out, "a proposition indicative of divine decree is not as such an expression of immediate self-consciousness."[175] The same applies to the prophetic doctrines of eschatology. Both election and eschatology stand on a weak epistemological foundation because they relate to states of existence of which human beings can have no experience or consciousness; and they represent the logical start and end of the teleologically ordered and oriented divine causality. As Herms notes, Schleiermacher's doctrine of the original state of perfection could already have contained the teleological direction of creation towards its eschatological state of consummation.[176]

---

171. See chapter 7 above.

172. Schleiermacher, *Christian Faith*, tr. MacIntosh and Stewart, §163 appendix, 722.

173. Fergusson, "Eschatology," 240.

174. See Oberdorfer, "Schleiermacher on Eschatology and Resurrection," 177.

175. Schleiermacher, *Christian Faith*, tr. MacIntosh and Stewart, §90.2, 370.

176. See Herms, "Schleiermachers Eschatologie," 149.

10

Lutheran Concerns

THE CHRISTIAN MAINSTREAM HAS tended to side with Augustine's claim
that the eternal separation of the blessed and the damned is scriptural,
and that it is reflected in the empirical fact that some believe and some
do not. Augustine's account of divine grace as an unconditional gift of
God given without precondition, hence without regard to any human
merits or demerits, appears to have resonated with the experience of the
Christian majority. His doctrine of predestination has, in fact, served as an
explanation of unmerited grace. It reflects the experience that election can
only be ascertained *a posteriori*. Nevertheless, what James Wetzel called
Augustine's "relentlessly God-driven account of human redemption"[1] has
not been fully endorsed by the Christian tradition. His contention that
the human race is identical with the *massa peccatorum*, the sinful mass,
and that only God's unfathomable decree goes some way to explain why
some receive mercy and others are eternally overlooked, appears to have
all but obliterated any human part in redemption. As Schleiermacher himself observed in his essay, by his own time unconditional predestination
had been rejected by the majority of the Christian Church: "Yet, only in a
comparatively small portion of the Christian church had this [strict] formulation produced a lasting conviction ... it was rejected by the greatest
portion of the church."[2] In fact, only some of the Reformed Churches had
continued to commit to the doctrine of unconditional predestination.

The persistent problem with the Augustinian and Calvinist position
was its contention that the reprobate were eternally damned; whether they
were passed over by grace, as Augustine had carefully put it, or whether

1. Wetzel, "Predestination," 49.
2. Schleiermacher, On the Doctrine of Election, tr. Nicol and Jørgenson, 1.

they were fore-ordained to perdition, as the Calvinists claimed, was ultimately immaterial. The bone of contention for the Lutherans lay in the claim that reprobation had its source in the divine decree. Conversely, the strength of the argument in favor of the doctrine of unconditional predestination lay in the conviction that if everything happened according to God's decree, the world was intelligible, even if on a plane that surpassed human understanding.

Martin Luther did not formulate a doctrine of election as such, but his treatise *De Servo Arbitrio* ("On the Bondage of the Will") of 1525 leaves no doubt about his position. A fervent follower of Augustine, he actually went beyond him and fully subscribed to absolute double predestination. Because of Adam's fall and the ensuing total corruption of human nature, Luther argued, the judgment that everybody deserved damnation was just. Still, God in his infinite mercy had elected some individuals to salvation despite their demerits. Individuals were either elect and would invariably be saved, or they were not elect and would invariably receive just damnation. Human beings could contribute nothing whatsoever to their eternal fate: God's word creates what it requires. Luther dealt a blow to any human effort to better oneself *coram Deo* and to contribute to one's own salvation in any way: "In the sight of God those who are most devoted to the works of the law are farthest from fulfilling the law, because they lack the Spirit that is the true fulfiller of the law, and while they may attempt it by their own powers, they achieve nothing."[3]

Luther, whose uncompromising stance mellowed somewhat over the years, but who never retracted his early statements, therefore took the same position concerning the doctrine of election as Calvin in his *Institutio*. As a matter of fact, regarding the necessity of all things, Luther's position was basically congruent with Schleiermacher's stance: both insisted on the absolute necessity of everything. Thus, although no actual force is involved in the bondage of the will, the human will wills what it does with necessity. Even in worldly matters concerning issues that do not relate to salvation, Luther only reluctantly conceded human choice. And even that choice is not absolutely free, since God's will subjects everything to the necessity inherent in the conditions it has established, even though God's will, in turn, is not subject to any conditions not established by itself. In this sense, Eilert Herms argued, it is necessary and not contingent that humans willingly do what they do.[4]

---

3. Luther, *De Servo Arbitrio*, tr. Rupp and Watson, 304.
4. See Herms, "Gewißheit," 30.

The Gnesio-Lutherans emphasized the bondage of the will in sin until it is freed by the Holy Spirit. Upholding Luther's original interpretation, they taught that God's unconditional election was the sole cause of salvation. They affirmed that the human will does act, but that it turns to Christ only under the power of the Holy Spirit. At the same time they denied the theory that God is responsible for the perdition of those who reject the word of God and disdain God's means of grace. These persons, the Gnesio-Lutherans held, bring judgment upon themselves.

At first, Philipp Melanchthon accepted Luther's interpretation of the unfree will as explicated in *De Servo Arbitrio*. To him, an anthropological reason underpinned that understanding of the human will. While the will has a certain freedom in relation to external actions, human beings have no possibility of influencing their own hearts. Only a new and stronger external affect can change an existing affect. In spiritual matters, Melanchthon argued, the human will is therefore entirely unfree. He also at first agreed with Luther's understanding of the necessity of all things, because divine omnipotence entailed that everything happened according to God's governance.

However, over a period of twenty years he decisively shifted position. Robert Kolb cites three interests that combined to induce Melanchthon to that change: the Catholic accusation of stoicism, his growing concerns about a determinist interpretation of God as the ultimate author of evil, and the increasing importance he placed on responsible human decisions and actions.[5] In the first edition of his *Loci Communes Rerum Theologicarum* ("Commonplaces of Theological Matters") of 1521, he had argued that "since everything that happens, happens necessarily according to divine predestination, freedom of our will does not exist."[6] Subsequently, he came to deny this determinist doctrine of predestination and the "stoic madness"[7] of holding to the necessity of all things. Like Erasmus of Rotterdam, he also retained the humanist ideal of an ethical and virtuous life. While Melanchthon thus affirmed free will and the complete power of judgment of natural persons in secular matters and civil life, he maintained that natural human powers could do nothing to initiate faith. In the second edition of his *Loci* (1535) Melanchthon shifted position. He now argued that some contingency had to exist, and that the origin of this contingency was the freedom of the human will. For him, three causes

5. See Kolb, "Confessional Lutheranism," 74.

6. Melanchthon, *Loci Communes*, 29.

7. Kolb, *Bound Choice*, 83.

coincide to produce faith in a person: God's word, the Holy Spirit, and the human will that does not reject God's call. "It is God who draws, but he draws him who is willing."[8] Melanchthon deemed this reformulation necessary in order to repulse determinism.

In the third edition of his *Loci* (1543) he went yet another step further. As Sachiko Kusukawa put it, Melanchthon "linked his distaste for predestination to his rejection of Stoic determinism in the choices of everyday existence."[9] He now distinguished between that which depends on God's will alone and that which God does partly and the human will does partly, thus proposing a synergism of divine and human action. In an appendix to the 1548 edition of his *Loci*, which was the first to be published after Luther's death, he defined free will as a "faculty to turn towards grace"[10] and argued that, while the word of God precedes human action, it does not preclude it.

Melanchthon's followers, the Philippists, then focused firmly on moral responsibility, or on the domain of ethics. While adhering to God's total responsibility for the salvation of human beings, they took seriously the concerns that had caused Melanchthon to explore the part that the human will played in faith and continuing repentance. Their stance became orthodox Lutheran teaching. As Wolfhart Pannenberg pointed out, the Lutheran doctrine reverted to the scholastic distinction between God's general will to salvation and the particular realization of God's will in those whose faith he foreknows.[11] Lutheranism asserted that human beings were volitional and ethical creatures whose moral responsibility represented the cornerstone of civic society. The price they paid for this assertion of the freedom of the human will was the renouncement of the irresistibility of grace.

The reasons for the Lutherans' unease about unconditional reprobation ultimately revolved around their understanding of the nature of God and of human beings, which differed considerably from that of the Reformed. Their respective interpretations of the human race in the sight of God, or theological anthropology *coram Deo*, were entirely different. Lutheranism firmly believed that God's nature was love, and that God's gracious will was simply incompatible with foreordained reprobation. The

---

8. Kusukawa, "Melanchthon," 59.

9. Ibid., 60.

10. Hägglund, *Geschichte der Theologie*, 194.

11. Pannenberg, "Prädestination III," 486.

perverted will of human beings rejects and perverts the means of grace,[12] and according to Ernst Sartorius thus overrules God's universal will to salvation—though not his omnipotence, which, Sartorius asserts, limits itself.[13] The underlying assumption that God could but does not save everybody appears at first glance to be congruent with the Calvinist theory. However, the dispute is not about the universal or particular effect of salvation, but about the ultimate reason for the particularity it involves: God's hidden decree or a person's free will? This is the motivation behind Sartorius' clarification that "we shy away not from the harshness of the expression but from the harshness of the matter."[14] It is important to note in this context that foreordained eternal reprobation was also the issue on which Schleiermacher broke with the Reformed tradition to advocate a theory of universal restoration in which perdition only describes a state of being of the not yet regenerated.

With regard to the image of humanity in God's sight, or theological anthropology, orthodox Lutheranism considered a certain degree of free will to be an integral part of human nature. Although the will cannot of itself will salvation, let alone bring it about, it is free to react to God's offer of the means of grace. "Sanctification is not created but achieved,"[15] stated Johann Christian Steudel. Such optimism regarding human power is grounded in the contention that Adam's fall did not corrupt human nature to the extent that the human will subsequently became entirely unfree. While the *Formula of Concord*, Epitome II, stressed that the unregenerate will was actively averse and indeed hostile to God, desiring those things which were opposite to God's will,[16] later Lutheran theologians moved away from this interpretation and emphasized the will's ability to change the direction of its own volition and to turn towards moral improvement as admonished by Scripture.

The much more pessimistic understanding of human power characteristic of the Calvinists tradition corresponds to their view of the omnipotent, glorious majesty of God. For them, as indeed for Martin Luther

---

12. See *Formula of Concord*, Solida Declaratio XI: "Such contempt of the word is not the origin of God's predestination, but the perverted will of human beings which rejects and perverts the means and instrument of the Holy Spirit that God offers them through calling them." *Bekenntnisschriften der evangelisch-lutherischen Kirche*, 1076.

13. See Sartorius, *Die lutherische Lehre*, 163.

14. Ibid., 164.

15. Steudel, "Fortsetzung der Anzeige," 721.

16. See *Bekenntnisschriften der evangelisch-lutherischen Kirche*, 777.

himself, human nature after the fall is entirely corrupt, and God cannot be held to account for whom he graciously saves and whom he justly damns.

The unease which Schleiermacher's Lutheran contemporaries continued to feel towards the Calvinist doctrine of predestination had different aspects, including rational, ethical, and psychological arguments against the unconditional double decree. To start with, they perceived foreordained reprobation simply as irrational. As Christoph Friedrich Ammon stated, "to our reason and our conviction of God's grace those damned because of predestination are an offence."[17] This conviction was echoed by an anonymous Lutheran reviewer of Schleiermacher's essay, who maintained that "even the most faithful reason has never been able to cope"[18] with a decree that eternally condemns the reprobate.

The arbitrariness Lutherans perceived to be inherent in what the *Formula of Concord* calls "the secret, impenetrable decree of God"[19] was another cause of their unease. This can be seen, for instance, in the rather ironic description of a scene described by Steudel, where one can "just sit back, wait and watch how soon one, then another is seized by the omnipotent word of the eternal and moved across to the regenerate."[20] This criticism fails to hit home, though, since according to the Reformed understanding nobody is in the neutral position to simply sit back and watch, since the absolute decree eternally encompasses each individual.

Schleiermacher's contemporaries reiterated concerns, already expressed in the *Formula of Concord*, that the Calvinist view results either "in confidence and impenitence, or in despondency and desperation."[21] Steudel for instance makes a case for the latter scenario when he warns that those who are taught that they are nothing but what God has made them to be will lose faith both in themselves and indeed in God and become "shy and insecure."[22] The congruence of the arguments put forward by the *Formula of Concord* and by Schleiermacher's Lutheran counterparts is apparent. The *Formula of Concord* voiced them in the context of the perceived arbitrariness of a decree founded in the "mere, secret, hidden, impenetrable predestination of God,"[23] which one can only speculate

---

17. Ammon, "Abhandlung," 43.

18. Anon., *Theologische Quartalschrift*, 282.

19. *Bekenntnisschriften der evangelisch-lutherischen Kirche*, 1066.

20. Steudel, "Fortsetzung der Anzeige," 721.

21. *Bekenntnisschriften der evangelisch-lutherischen Kirche*, 1066.

22. Steudel, "Fortsetzung der Anzeige," 686.

23. *Bekenntnisschriften der evangelisch-lutherischen Kirche*, 1068.

about, rather than in the "counsel, intention and foreordination of God in Christ Jesus"[24] who has been revealed through the word. For early nineteenth-century Lutherans, the real problem was that they identified unconditional predestination with determinism, and thus with the unfree will. Of course, determinism does not deny freedom as such but, as Julia Lamm rightly argues, "the customary conception that there is no causality apart from free causes."[25] In the same way, necessity is not coterminous with coercion. Rather, it indicates the opposite of contingency. If something happens with necessity that does not mean that it is forced on agents against their will.

Schleiermacher's Lutheran contemporaries insisted on freedom of the human will as an inalienable constituent of human nature even after the fall. Steudel defined free will as "the ability to determine one's will for the good."[26] If this capacity were denied, the only alternative would be the unfree will propagated by the Reformed. For Steudel, in turn, affirming an unfree will entailed that "virtue disappears into nothing, praise and criticism of the conscience disappear in delusion, responsibility for actions in deception, and betterment or worsening into illusion."[27] That concern as such may well be valid, but it is rooted in a theological anthropology that has parted decisively from that of the underlying orthodox Lutheranism. The Lutheran confessions, and indeed the Reformed tradition as well, assert the inability of the human will to turn the direction of its own volition towards God and the good *coram Deo*. They concede that the will can change the object of its desire, but it cannot change, let alone determine, its very direction. As Gerhard Forde noted, "we are *bound* to say no and this is precisely our bondage."[28]

Rightly or wrongly, the Lutherans' main argument against the Reformed doctrine centered on the issue of moral responsibility, or the domain of ethics. As Wetzel argues, adherence to the double decree "cultivated disbelief in the validity of moral appraisal, and, therefore, disinterest in moral improvement."[29] Karl Gottlieb Bretschneider summed up various scenarios in this way: If one assumes oneself to be part of the elect, the doctrine will lead to foolishness, thoughtlessness or pride. If one feels

24. Ibid.
25. Lamm, *The Living God*, 185.
26. Steudel, "Anzeige," 412.
27. Ibid., 415.
28. Forde, *Captivation*, 50.
29. Wetzel, "Snares of Truth," 125.

torn between virtue and vice, either foolishness or despondency will be the consequence. And if one feels incapable of tearing oneself away from the bondage of sin, hopelessness will ensue.[30] Either way, any willingness to take moral responsibility is severely impaired, and either "impenitent carelessness"[31] or permanent anxiety will be the result. Scriptural admonition would be rendered useless, the Lutherans claimed, if human beings did not have the capacity for moral improvement. However, this argument is seriously flawed. As Schleiermacher pointed out in his essay, not only the Reformed doctrine asserted that the human race had lost the capacity to fulfill the moral law, but "the system of the Lutheran church does indeed affirm this loss just as decidedly and openly as does the Calvinian theory. In fact, this statement is simply another expression of that doctrine of human incapacity."[32] Both Reformed and Lutherans admit a natural freedom to act morally only in secular matters.

The following statement by Ammon encapsulates the Lutherans' main concerns about the double decree: "The inner self rebels against the coercion of predestination, which eradicates all freedom and love of God from the human heart, and instead fills it with fear and anxiety."[33] It also demonstrates in what way their criticism was misplaced. The non-elect harbor no love of God in their hearts in the first place, and the double decree only eradicates the freedom to choose one's own salvation—a possibility that does not exist according to the traditional Lutheran symbols at any rate. It remains unclear why there is so much emphasis on the human ability to reject grace, when the result of such a choice is the same as that of foreordained reprobation. Obviously, the purpose behind this theory is that if non-belief is a matter of human choice, God is vindicated from all responsibility for perdition; however, this argument fails to convince. Moreover, it was precisely in order to address the fear and anxiety about the uncertainty of grace that originally drove Martin Luther to the conclusion that salvation must be entirely and exclusively by divine grace. Schleiermacher's Lutheran contemporaries were now diametrically opposed to Luther's original teaching.

August Detlev Twesten's observation about the Calvinist doctrine and its Lutheran criticism, expressed in a letter to Schleiermacher of 1 November 1819, hit the nail right on the head. He wrote that in his essay

30. See Bretschneider, *Aphorismen*, 458.

31. Anon, "Bemerkungen," 198.

32. Schleiermacher, On the Doctrine of Election, tr. Nicol and Jørgenson, 35.

33. Ammon, "Abhandlung," 18.

Schleiermacher had shown convincingly how closely the Calvinist doctrine was related to that of humanity's inability to attain grace of its own
power. Still, Twesten predicted, even though Schleiermacher had refuted
the "prejudice of the harmful influence of this theory on morals," he would
not find many supporters "because of the Pelagian tendency of the time."[34]
Bretschneider had openly advocated relinquishing the doctrine of the irresistibility of divine grace in favor of a synergism that allowed the will
to decide for and actively bring about salvation. While other Lutherans
were more cautious about this point in their publications, their Pelagian
tendency is more than apparent in their criticism of this aspect of the Calvinist doctrine.

34. Heinrici, *Twesten*, 355.

11

Universal Restoration and Schleiermacher's Position

HISTORICAL AND SYSTEMATIC BACKGROUND

Introduction

HARTMUT ROSENAU DEFINED UNIVERSAL restoration as "the eschatological idea which assumes the reception without exception of all men or beings (including angels, demons and the devil) into eternal salvation, the kingdom of God, for eternal life."[1] A more restrictive notion of universalism, advanced by Gregory MacDonald, states "that at the end of history, all created intellects will be restored to their original condition of union with God."[2] As Thomas Torrance points out, the Christian Church throughout its history has consistently rejected universalism as "a heresy for faith and a menace to the gospel."[3] It was formally condemned at the Fifth Ecumenical Council in Constantinople in 553,[4] and therefore, strictly speaking, represents an unorthodox or heterodox stance rather than a heresy in its original sense of differentiation or exclusion. Even though a binding, profiled doctrine of universalism has not been able to assert itself, universal restoration has always been championed by a resilient minority. According

---

1. Rosenau, "Wiederbringung aller," 774.

2. MacDonald, "Introduction," 6.

3. Torrance, "Universalism or Election," 310.

4. It appears to be ambiguous whether the Council condemned all forms of universalism or simply Origenist *apokatastasis*. See MacDonald, "Introduction," 9.

to Richard Bauckham, Schleiermacher was "the first great theologian of modernity to teach universalism."[5]

No attempt is made here to give a full account of the history of universalism, the wide variety of universalist beliefs, or their representatives. Thomas Whittemore's *The Modern History of Universalism from the Era of the Reformation to the Present Time*, published in Boston in 1830, gives a historical overview of universal restoration of the three centuries between the Reformation and the early nineteenthth century,[6] and other accounts cover more recent times as well as the centuries leading up to Schleiermacher.[7] This study confines itself to the debate about universalist as opposed to particularist models of salvation, that is, to the systematic-theological context in which Schleiermacher developed his interpretation. It will also discuss some typologies of universalism and assign Schleiermacher his position within them.

The Debate about Universalism

Universalism is a cover term for a variety of beliefs, the only common denominator of which is the notion that ultimately all human beings will be saved; the rationale for that belief and its theological content vary considerably.[8] Robin Parry and Christopher Partridge have assembled a number of issues on which universalists themselves do not agree.[9] They include the following points: Is universal salvation an eschatological hope or a dogmatic certainty? Will anyone ever experience the horrors of hell or does hell remain empty? Will only human beings ultimately be saved or also demons and the devil? Is faith in Jesus Christ the *sine qua non* of salvation or are there other routes to eternal blessedness? Are human beings endowed with indeterministic freedom or not? Is God's punishment restorative or retributive? And finally, is God free to choose to save all, or is he bound by his nature to do so?

---

5. Bauckham, "Universalism," 50.

6. Schleiermacher is not mentioned in this account, probably because neither his essay On the Doctrine of Election nor *Christian Faith* were available in English at the time. Indeed, Whittemore only mentions a small handful of non-English-speaking (or -writing) universalists.

7. See for instance MacDonald, *"All Shall Be Well,"* and Ludlow, "Universalism in the History of Christianity."

8. See Bauckham, "Universalism," 49.

9. See Parry and Partridge, "Introduction," xviii–xxi.

The arguments that have been raised for and against universal restoration are very varied themselves, and in the course of time they have changed at least in focus, if not materially. Exegetical evidence both for and against universal restoration has been gathered for centuries, but remains equivocal. While some New Testament passages appear to suggest a divine judgment according to which only some are saved,[10] others seem to point to the opposite.[11] Thomas Johnson also cautions that "most of the biblical passages involved are talking about groups of people . . . [whereas] especially since the Enlightenment, we have been preoccupied with individuals. . . . The Bible, for the most part, does not reflect this preoccupation."[12] Moreover, since Scripture does not know of any symmetry between election and perdition[13] or of an umbrella term embracing both, evidence from Scripture is not conclusive.

Since the Enlightenment, anthropological arguments have replaced theocentric ones. David Fergusson observes that Augustine and the Calvinists "had recourse to the aesthetic consideration that the balance of gracious redemption and righteous damnation is a majestic testimony to the variety and order of created reality, and a *fortiori* to the glory of the creator."[14] In more recent times, the focus has shifted from the glory of God to humanity's freedom of the will. As a result, the concern that universal restoration might override the human freedom to refuse God's grace has become much more prominent.

Arguments Contra Universalism

In the systematic-theological sense, universalism minimizes or trivializes the seriousness of sin, leads to an impoverishment of atonement, and denies that faith in Jesus Christ is a necessary precondition for salvation. It conflicts with the traditional notion of eschatological dualism that envisages the ultimate separation of the redeemed from the damned. As Hartmut Rosenau points out, it also stands in contrast to the less common eschatological notion of the annihilation of the reprobate.[15] The

10. See in particular Marshall, "The New Testament Does *Not* Teach Universalism."

11. See in particular Johnson, "A Wideness in God's Mercy: Universalism in the Bible."

12. Ibid., 79.

13. See Link, "Prädestination II," col. 1531.

14. Fergusson, "Predestination: A Scottish Perspective," 460.

15. See Rosenau, "Apocatastasis," 307.

traditional doctrine of humanity's total incapacity for good, "the funda-mental anthropological principle of soteriological impotence"[16] has been questioned in its relation to civic responsibility and ethical improvement. It is claimed that, if human beings cannot contribute to their salvation, but their redemption is brought about nevertheless, they are denied a cer-tain eschatological responsibility. Obviously, this concern applies to any unconditional or absolute decree regarding predestination, and thus to double predestination as much as to universalism.

Pedagogical concerns relate to the deep-rooted belief that the threat of punishment is a necessary deterrent from immoral or unethical behav-ior and libertinism. There is some entirely anecdotal evidence against this concern, for instance from a Fr. R. Suffield who observed that such a belief can be misplaced. Fr. Suffield had made the experience that the dogma of hell never affected the right persons: it frightened and tortured innocent and virtuous people and drove them into superstitious practices, but "it never deterred from the commission of sin."[17]

Universalism also appears to fail to do justice to the reality of evil. If everybody is ultimately saved, perpetrated evil deeds, the victims of violence and injustice, and their sufferings can be seen to be essentially irrelevant. By denying a final judgment, universal restoration seems to dispense with eschatological justice. The motivation for mission and the sense of historical actions and engagements can become problematical if the ultimate salvation of everybody without distinction is already decided before their very first deed.

The universalist theory lays down the impossibility of ultimate eter-nal damnation. Yet, while the actuality of the reprobation of any human being cannot be demonstrated, neither can the possibility of reprobation simply be discarded. As Thomas Torrance argues, the possibility that all might be saved "does not and cannot carry as a corollary the impossibility of being eternally lost."[18] To turn what can at best be described as an escha-tological hope into a systematic doctrine of universal restoration is to turn possibility into necessity. In this sense, claims Torrance, universalism's at-tempt to bridge the gulf between God and guilty humanity amounts to an effort to "systematize the illogical."[19]

16. Ibid., 307.

17. Powys, *Hell*, 56.

18. Torrance, "Universalism or Election," 312.

19. Ibid., 313. Incidentally, the last point also applies to any interpretation of the doctrine of predestination, not just the universalist variety.

Arguments Pro Universal Restoration

The arguments in favor of universalism are as varied as those against it. Apart from Torrance's generic observation that "the doctrine of universalism gains its plausibility from the inconsistency of the position it attacks,"[20] they range from doctrinal reasons to the interpretation of the elect and of hell. Underlying the theory of universalism is the emphasis on the nature of God's love as "both absolutely good and absolutely sovereign."[21] As Terrence Tice puts it, "ultimately no other attribute but love can be predicted of the Supreme Being with full warrant."[22] Divine omnipotent love differentiates between deed and perpetrator. Because of the equal demerits of all human beings before God, humanity is dependent on the *sola gratia* of salvation. Christ has atoned for everyone, and all without exception are redeemed in him. It has been argued that universalism offers a soteriological and eschatological concept for comprehending the unity of all that is real. Rosenau explains that such a union depends on God's loving nature to differentiate work and person, and that it emphasizes the universal dependence on salvation through the unlimited effect of the death and resurrection of Christ.[23]

Universalism does not get entangled in the contradictions of eschatological dualism. However, even if predestination is only understood as the election of some to salvation, but not of others, as far as those outside the fellowship with Christ are concerned, Brian Gerrish states that "we have no warrant for the further inference that for them there must be a corresponding predestination to damnation."[24] John Robinson goes further than this cautious inference by suggesting that from the point of view of the doctrine of God, universal restoration has to be the ultimate outcome.[25]

It has been argued that since human beings possess only relative freedom, no absolute or eternal consequences can be derived from their exercising their free will. There is a similar argument that finite sins cannot

20. Ibid., 314.
21. Bettis, "Critique," 330.
22. Tice, *Schleiermacher*, 35.
23. See Rosenau, "Wiederbringung aller," 777.
24. Gerrish, *Tradition and the Modern World*, 117.
25. See Robinson, "Universalism—A Reply," 380.

justly be punished by infinite torment. Conversely, Daniel Strange has argued for the Calvinist side that sin committed against an infinite God does demand infinite punishment.[26]

SYSTEMATIC CONSIDERATIONS

Divine Attributes

Before attempting an assessment of Schleiermacher's particular type of universalism, it is worth exploring the theory of universalism and its premises in more detail. At the core of the debate concerning universalism as opposed to the particularism of either single or double predestination is the dichotomy on the one hand between divine love and justice, and on the other between divine omnipotence and humanity's free will. In the first case, either God's love is omnipotent and must conquer, or humanity's freedom is inviolable, in which case God's victory cannot be conceived as necessary. Here, according to Fergusson, "the triumph of the love of God is secured by limiting its scope."[27] In the second case, either the possibility that not all are saved must be shown to be compatible with God's omnipotence (God can but does not save everybody), or the necessity of all being saved must be shown not to be an infringement of human freedom (nobody is saved against their will). The first dichotomy cannot be overcome unless divine justice is seen as a substitute for love that comes into operation when love has failed to be effective.[28] The second dichotomy cannot be resolved by objective reason, which posits either divine omnipotence or human freedom,[29] but not both.

Attempts have been made, in particular by theologians following Karl Barth (1886–1968), to reconcile divine love and omnipotence. Torrance observes that the question if we can "ever get behind God's self-manifestation and action and discuss the relation of omnipotence and love in terms of the necessity of his divine nature"[30] already implies the response that this very quest violates the secret of God, who does not need to respond to human expectations or logic, and is therefore untenable. An

---

26. See Strange, "A Calvinist Response," 151.

27. Fergusson, "Will the Love of God Finally Triumph?" 188.

28. See Robinson, "Universalism – Is it Heretical?" 143.

29. Schleiermacher's subsumption of the free choice of human beings or the causality of finite agents under absolute divine causality is a special case.

30. Torrance, "Universalism or Election," 311.

even more fundamental issue, however, is whether God's love needs to be defined in terms of the salvation of human beings in the first place. In this context, Joseph Bettis notes that "God's love is not a human predicate; men are a divine predicate."[31] If it is true that the doctrine of universal restoration rests wholly on the final self-assertion of God, not on logic or human analogy, then universalism cannot be expressed in a coherent doctrine but can only be conceived as a proclamation of faith *sola gratia*.

Freedom of the Will

Freedom of the will is to be recognized as an essential and integral part of human nature, and as the ground of ethical responsibility. Therefore, any solution which compromises this freedom stands self-condemned. As a corollary, if a human being's response to God's offer of grace is indeed free, universal salvation can never be certain. So, if divine love cannot draw out the human will to a free positive response, God has no other resource and, as Fergusson points out, "it remains a possibility that some may place themselves outwith the divine grace."[32]

One of the strongest arguments against universalism has always been the assumption that it renders human choice and freedom null and void. Paul Jewett argues: "If supralapsarianism appears to make the human choice unreal, restitutionism makes it palpably unnecessary."[33] This stance is certainly indicative of one trajectory from Calvin to Schleiermacher. But is it actually true that submission to God's omnipotent love, or the irresistibility of grace, or indeed the truth, involve the abandonment of human freedom? Or is the very act of submission to God an act of freedom? After all, no human being is made more willing to be reconciled to God by being told that the salvation of all is certain. Does God violate human autonomy? Or can divine love be conceived as so strong that ultimately nobody will be able to resist and will surrender in an act of freedom to God's will to save? Is truth coercive or compulsive? Any acceptance of God's grace is mediated by the overwhelming revelation of God's love, and in this sense, the human will is never coerced to accept grace. Whether this means that it freely accept God's grace remains debatable, as Eric Reitan's argument, perhaps unwittingly, demonstrates: "If the unregenerate were forced not only to see but to experience in an unmediated way the truth about God

31. Bettis, "Critique," 337.

32. Fergusson, "Predestination: a Scottish Perspective," 475.

33. Jewett, *Election and Predestination*, 116.

and about their own relation to him, they would no longer be capable of rejecting him."[34]

The concept of human freedom is also the key to Reitan's conclusion that "the only plausible way to reject universalism is to say that we are not forever free to accept the offer of salvation."[35] Another aspect of the debate about human freedom is discussed by Bettis. He presents the universalist argument that there is no freedom in the choice between salvation or damnation, on the contrary: there is nothing but bondage "in the burden of knowing that one's eternal destiny hangs on every decision."[36] According to this argument, Christian freedom does not manifest itself in the choice for or against God, but in the spontaneity to act in the knowledge that God has already chosen all human beings.

Universalism means that the ultimate point of view is God's or, in Robinson's words, that "man's reality is taken up into God's without being destroyed."[37] This is certainly the case in Schleiermacher's system, in which divine causality subsumes the causality of free agents and human choice is thus compatible with divine determination.

Schleiermacher's interpretation of universalism identifies the elect ultimately with the entire human race. A more differentiated interpretation sees the elect not primarily as the redeemed but as those through whom God's eternal purposes are mediated. Their calling to serve a universal end implies that mission is not obsolete, but that it functions as a mediator for the message of universalism, the opening of a new, fearless perspective. It is motivated by God's salvific action, not by individuals' concern over their state of salvation.

Reprobation and Hell

Most universalists hold that death is not the decisive borderline Christian orthodoxy has taught. A person's state of grace at the time of death is not crucial, and ultimate salvation is possible posthumously and even after temporary damnation. What universalism denies is not punishment or perdition as such, but eternal torment in hell, poignantly characterized by Jürgen Moltmann as "the religious torture chamber."[38] Indeed, the notion

---

34. Reitan, "Eternal Damnation and Blessed Ignorance," 447.

35. Reitan, "Human Freedom," 140.

36. Bettis, "Critique," 334.

37. Robinson, "Universalism—A Reply," 380.

38. Moltmann, *In the End—the Beginning*, tr. Kohl, 146.

of punishment as temporary torment after death has been endorsed by many universalists, even though the question whether or not anybody will ever experience the horror of hell remains a matter of debate. The function of temporary punishment is described variously as reformative, purifying, corrective, or teleological, but it is not understood as retributive, as it is in the traditional doctrine of hell. Some theologians, not all of them universalists, combine the concept of sin being its own punishment with the idea of a divine punishment after death. Torrance suggests that to "choose our own way and yet in that choice still to be chosen by God would be hell."[39] In another twist, Stephen Davis argues that those in hell are there not against their will but because they choose to be in hell: they choose to live their lives apart from God, and will do so after death too. God continuously grants them the freedom to choose or reject him, but "the citizens of hell . . . would be unable to endure heaven."[40]

Formulated in detail by Anselm of Canterbury (1033–1109) and Thomas Aquinas (1225–1274), the doctrine of hell had become universally established as orthodox teaching by the time of the Reformation. In its classical form it states that God imposes unending torment on the reprobate as punishment: "sinners must be sent to hell because hell is what they deserve."[41] Strange defines hell as "the place where God's undiluted anger is poured out against sinners who have rebelled against him,"[42] adding that "those who are in hell continue to sin, incurring more guilt to all eternity."[43] Reitan presents what he characterizes as the progressive understanding of hell:[44] Christ's atonement is for all, but some refuse the offer of salvation. In this scenario, divine love and grace as well as the sufficiency of Christ's atonement remain intact, and the sufferings of the damned are their own choice in so far as "the reprobate persist in the rejection of God's electing grace,"[45] as Benjamin Myers puts it. However, this understanding is only universal with regard to the divine offer and the sufficient condition for universal salvation, not with regard to its result, which remains particular. While Reitan does not refer to a doctrine of predestination, this

---

39. Torrance, "Universalism or Election," 317.

40. Davis, "Universalism, Hell and Ignorance," 179.

41. Parry and Partridge, "Introduction," xxiii.

42. Strange, "A Calvinist Response," 151.

43. Ibid., 152.

44. See Reitan, "Human Freedom," 127.

45. Myers, "Predestination and Freedom," 73.

result (including its preconditions) is entirely congruent with the doctrine of election in the Lutheran sense.

When the Reformation abolished the notion of purgatory, hell was rendered particularly harshly. Purgatory had effectively widened the circle of the righteous to include those who had been cleansed, whereas the abolition of purgatory entailed that the number of the eternally damned was much larger than before, because now it included those who might have passed through purgatory to salvation. Punishment after death had no reformative aim anymore.

David Powys maintains that in Western Christianity the doctrine of hell prevailed as orthodoxy until recent times.[46] His argument that it was not substantially challenged until the nineteenth century is based entirely on its development in the English-speaking world[47] and is thus rather limited in scope. But even within the confines of Anglo-American theology the doctrine of eternal hell has in fact been challenged since early modern times. A number of late seventeenth-century English theologians, such as Jeremiah White, Peter Sterry and others, paid particular attention to the notion of punishment while defending universalism.[48] Nevertheless, Powys' contention that the doctrine was not substantially challenged, remains valid. Where opposition to the doctrine did exist, that opposition was certainly the exception rather than the rule. Questioning eternal punishment was equal to questioning the authority of Scripture and of the Church, the social and religious order, and divine justice. For this reason, opposition tended to come from outside mainstream churches. Powys ventures that, where opposition to the doctrine was voiced, it "was probably a reaction against High Calvinism's particularism."[49] This may possibly be a valid assumption as far as Anglo-American theology is concerned, but in Schleiermacher's case Powys' argument does not hold. Schleiermacher did not develop his doctrine of universal salvation, which entails the abolition of eternal perdition, as a reaction against the Calvinist doctrine; rather, he developed it from that position. Those who did oppose the Calvinist interpretation, as for instance Lutherans, did not challenge the doctrine of eternal hell, but the fore-ordination of perdition.

From the nineteenth century onwards, certainly, confidence in evolutionary development and the inevitability of progress, a belief in

46. See Powys, "Debates about Hell and Universalism," 19.

47. See ibid.

48. For more details see Ludlow, "Universal Salvation," 200.

49. Powys, "Debates about Hell and Universalism," 26.

repentance and the possibility of moral improvement coupled with a new valuing of the individual and a prevailing optimism provided an entirely new outlook. Yet, these developments brought no new answer to the question of God's active purpose regarding unregenerate individual after death.

Modern theological interpretations of judgment focus on the responsible individual with a free will rather than on a judging God. By virtue of this paradigm shift from a theocentric to an anthropological perspective, the last judgment, Jürgen Moltmann concludes, "appears to be simply the ultimate endorsement of our free will."[50] Today, fewer and fewer people are able to conceive of eternal physical punishment, and, as Richard Bauckham suggests, no other traditional Christian doctrine has been so widely abandoned as the teaching of eternal damnation in hell.[51] The era seems past "when the threat of hell can corral people into church attendance and provide an effective form of social control."[52] Those who reject the doctrine of eternal hell but want to retain the notion of immortality posit a posthumous opportunity for repentance and subsequent redemption. Temporary perdition and annihilation are acceptable to them as long as everybody will be redeemed before the end of eternity, or indeed before everybody has been consumed in hell.

Universalism clarifies what forgiveness of sin ultimately means. Within this framework, reprobation is understood as a temporary and reversible state due either to a decision of the human will or to an act of divine will. Universalism argues that the "sole possible function of judgment can be to enable men to receive the mercy which renders it superfluous."[53] To put it in more pastoral terms, as Fleming Rutledge does, "God's judgment is an instrument of his mercy. Judgment does not mean everlasting condemnation . . . , it means a course correction in the direction of salvation."[54]

This does not imply that punishment must necessarily be denied, on the contrary. The relevance of hell—but not of eternal perdition—as a consequence of human decisions is not removed, since this would mean the denial of the very possibility of genuine justification and salvation; the latter can only come through "knowing the terror of the Lord."[55] Hell

---

50. Moltmann, *In the End—the Beginning*, tr. Kohl, 141.

51. See Bauckham, "Universalism," 48.

52. Fergusson, "Will the Love of God Finally Triumph?" 188.

53. Robinson, "Universalism—Is it Heretical?" 155.

54. Rutledge, *Help My Unbelief*, 60.

55. Robinson, "Universalism—a Reply," 380.

remains eternally a live option even for universalists. According to Trevor Hart, they do not deny the reality of judgment and hell, "but simply that the judgment will find any wanting, and that hell will be occupied."[56]

SCHLEIERMACHER'S POSITION IN CONTEXT

Typologies of Universalism

All typologies are abstractions, but they provide a handy tool for the classification of different types of the same species. One of the most encompassing typologies of universalism is presented by Parry and Partridge.[57] They differentiate three types: According to multiracial universalism, all Christians could be considered universalists since the Christian Church is made up a of multicultural group of people. However, this type does not entail that all people of all races will be saved, only that those saved will include people of all races. The second type is classified as Armenian universalism. It implies that God desires to save all individuals and thus offers salvation to all human beings, but because of the human free will God will not achieve his goal. Again, "universal" only applies to the divine intention, but not to its (partial) success. The third type, strong universalism, is characterized by the congruence of God's desire to save all with the achievement of this purpose. Strong universalism, in turn, is divided into three sub-types: non-Christian versions, a pluralist form according to which all major world religions represent different paths to the same goal, and Christian universalism. The last subsumes all those interpretations that share a commitment to working within a Christian theological framework and the claim that all individuals will be saved through Christ's work. Obviously, Schleiermacher belongs to the third sub-type of Christian universalism.

A narrower typology of universalism, advanced by MacDonald, distinguishes exclusivist, inclusivist, and pluralist types.[58] Exclusivists assert that redemption happens only through faith in Jesus Christ and membership in the Christian Church, and that posthumous redemption is a reality. Inclusivists hold that Christ's atoning work also redeems those who have no explicit faith in him. Both exclusivists and inclusivists can be subsumed under Parry and Partridge's Christian universalists' sub-type. Pluralists,

56. Hart, "Universalism," 33.
57. See Parry and Partridge, "Introduction," XV–XVII.
58. See MacDonald, "Introduction," 20–21.

finally, agree that Jesus Christ represents only one of many different routes to salvation. This type corresponds to the pluralist universalism posited by Parry and Partridge above, and it implies, as Hart states, that "the significance of the Christ event is utterly relativized."[59] In MacDonald's typology, Schleiermacher would rank among the exclusivists.

A third typology, advanced by Rosenau, deals with MacDonald's exclusivist type only. Again, it differentiates between three kinds of universal restoration that are characteristic of the patristic period, the nineteenth century, and the twentieth century respectively.[60] First, a metaphysical type associated with the neo-Platonic tradition exemplified by Origen; this is characterized by its rational contemplation of the nature of God as love and grace, of human freedom to do good directed by God's providence, and of the immortality of the soul. At the end of all world eons salvation will be equally for all. The second or transcendental type is that championed by Schleiermacher. It develops universalism on the basis of an analysis of the specifically Christian self-consciousness, which claims that nobody can fully be in a state of blessedness if anybody is eternally damned. This type is thus characterized by a strong relation-ontological argument, namely sympathy or compassion, for the eschatological salvation of all human beings. Incidentally, Morwenna Ludlow makes a further distinction between two forms of universalism prevalent in the eighteenth and nineteenth centuries, which can be subsumed under MacDonald's second type. One is the purgatorial form, which emphasizes the necessity of posthumous punishment in order to reconcile all human beings to God. The other is the hyper-Calvinist form, which accepts Calvin's doctrines of predestination and atonement while asserting that they apply to all human beings, not just the small group of the elect.[61] The third type of universalism identified by Rosenau was developed in the late nineteenth and into the twentieth century. Its representatives argued christologically to suggest that the idea of restoration was compulsory. They claimed the reality of the reconciliation of the world with God through Christ according to God's election for all.

The later twentieth century has seen the emergence of a majority third way apart from doctrinal universalists and particularists. Its representatives understand universal restoration not as a binding doctrine, but as an expression of eschatological hope. Theologians such as Jürgen

59. Hart, "Universalism," 13.

60. For this and the following, see Rosenau, "Wiederbringung aller," 776.

61. See Ludlow, "Universalism in the History of Christianity," 204–5.

Moltmann, Wolfhart Pannenberg, and John Hick understand it in this way.[62] That interpretation invariably entails a problematic relation between faith and doctrine.

It is striking that none of the typologies of universalism presented makes reference to the doctrine of predestination. In a sense, this omission reflects the consideration that if all are elect, the very notion of election becomes obsolete. The notion of particular salvation today invariably involves the issue of free will to safeguard the possibility of rejecting faith rather than affirming the traditional Calvinist double decree of election and perdition. This suggests that modern universalists are not opposed by particularists arguing for a double decree, but by those insisting on the freedom of the will. Here is a clear trajectory from Schleiermacher's Lutheran opponents, who also insisted on the freedom of the will. Although they rejected the notion of a double decree rather than Schleiermacher's universalism, which they did not consider seriously, the force of their argument was directed against any divine foreordination that ignores and ultimately overrides human choice.

Between Calvinists and Lutherans

According to Ludlow, Schleiermacher was "the first really influential theologian since the Patristic period to consider universalism."[63] His intention was to formulate the doctrine of predestination in such a way that it could be acceptable to both the Reformed and to Lutherans. To reiterate: the Calvinist position asserts an unconditional divine double decree to salvation of some and perdition of the others that is based entirely on God's inscrutable decree and good-pleasure. The decree is particular in that God's grace is only for the elect.[64] In this model, grace is irresistible. Divine

62. Rosenau also mentions Wilfried Härle as one representative of this third way. See Rosenau, "Wiederbringung aller," 777. However, this observation is not accurate. In his *Dogmatik*, Härle deals with predestination explicitly as the doctrine of universal restoration. He argues from the point of view of divine love that it is integral to the nature of love not to exclude anybody but to reject everything that is irreconcilable with love. God eternally condemns sin and evil, but not sinners. Therefore, Christian theology must not teach double predestination but only eternal election to salvation. See Härle, *Dogmatik*, 506–8.

63. Ludlow, "Universalism in the History of Christianity," 207.

64. Oliver Crisp offers an unorthodox interpretation of the Calvinist or, as he calls it, traditional Augustinian doctrine of predestination, according to which "God may vindicate his justice and actualize the greater good of divine self-glorification without damning any human agent to hell" by claiming that the elect are co-extensive with all human agents. Crisp, "Augustinian Universalism," 134.

love manifests itself in the redemption of the elect, whereas divine justice manifests itself in the damnation of the reprobate. Orthodox Lutheranism maintains that God's will to salvation is universal, that there is accordingly only a single decree to salvation, but that salvation is not universally successful because humans can and do reject the gift of grace. The decree is conditional: election is based on God's foreknowledge of an individual's response to the universal offer of grace. Grace is therefore not irresistible.

Schleiermacher's compromise consisted in declaring the difference between the saved and the damned to be only temporary, and in asserting ultimate universal restoration. Election and thus redemption is not an exclusivistic, selective event relating to individuals, but what Paul Jewett calls a "cosmic concept."[65] Schleiermacher posited an unconditional, universal, single divine decree to create and redeem the entire human race through God's irresistible grace, which still operates beyond death. For him, God's governance and predestination encompass the nature system as a whole so that no individual as such is set apart or set free.

Contrary to the Reformers' and their followers' interpretation, Schleiermacher argued that humanity had to be sinful in order to need redemption in the first place. He was probably unique in giving expression to the consequence that sin was, and indeed had to be, ordained by God, albeit only in relation to redemption. As Robert Williams summarizes: "Only from the final perspective of redemption as the completion of creation can it be affirmed theologically that evil is not ultimate, and that it is a merely instrumental, defeated power which serves a more ultimate good purpose."[66] For Schleiermacher, evil belongs to the economy of salvation, or of soteriological super abundance.

Schleiermacher accepted perdition as a necessary step in the teleological development of humanity towards the kingdom of God, which Christ establishes "as a phenomenon of history."[67] The reprobate are simply the not-yet-redeemed. Schleiermacher rejected any eternal separation from God. It is my contention that he would also have rejected any notion of the annihilation of the unregenerate. It is the idea that some remain eternally separate from God rather than the precise nature of their separate fate that defies the species-consciousness posited by Schleiermacher.

The blessed must necessarily know of the condition of the damned since ignorance of something as significant as their torment in hell is

65. Jewett, *Election and Predestination*, 117.

66. Williams, "Theodicy, Tragedy, and Soteriology," 410.

67. Gerrish, "Place of Calvin," 301.

incompatible with the state of blessedness. Likewise, it is inconceivable that, due to the overwhelming bliss of salvation that the elect experience, they know of the state of the reprobate without actually being aware of it. As Reitan argues, blessedness that depends on a lack of awareness of facts "falls short of supremely worthy happiness."[68] In this view, then, the doctrine of eternal hell is incoherent.

According to Schleiermacher, human species-consciousness demands that the human race in its entirety must ultimately form God's kingdom because "the salvation of any requires the salvation of all."[69] This argument represents a modern insight. According to the traditional view, the redeemed would be sufficiently sanctified to share God's attitude towards the damned, namely that they were justly punished for their rejection of grace. As I. Howard Marshall concludes, "therefore their lot is not to be regretted."[70] For Tertullian (c. 160–c.225 AD), Cyprian (d. 258 AD), Augustine, Peter Lombard (c. 1100–1160), Thomas Aquinas, and other Church Fathers, the blessedness of the redeemed was in fact enhanced rather than marred by the contemplation of the damned, since those who are wholly at one with God would rejoice to see his justice done.[71]

With regard to scriptural tradition, it is perhaps surprising that Schleiermacher largely ignored the exegetical difficulties of his position, in particular in consideration of the fact that he was one of the leading New Testament scholars of his time. It is worth remembering in this context that he had the Chair of New Testament at the University of Berlin. Schleiermacher's neglect is even more remarkable in light of Bauckham's observation that nineteenth-century debates about predestination involved extensive exegetical discussions.[72] While Schleiermacher claims that his idea of universal restoration appears to him to be "as well supported in scripture"[73] as the doctrine of eternal perdition, and that the separatism taught by Scripture is to be understood as a temporary measure, he asserts that the matter is beyond the scope of his essay on election. At least he does concede that evidence from Scripture is not unambiguous.

---

68. Reitan, "Eternal Damnation and Blessed Ignorance," 439.

69. Ibid., 442.

70. Marshall, "The New Testament Does *Not* Teach Universal Salvation," 60.

71. See Bauckham, "Universalism," 51.

72. See ibid., 52.

73. Schleiermacher, On the Doctrine of Election, tr. Nicol and Jørgenson, 95.

EVALUATION

Schleiermacher's significant reinterpretation of the Calvinist doctrine of predestination has variously been described as a "brilliant reinterpretation of Calvin's 'horrible decree',"[74] a restatement of the doctrine,[75] a break with the traditional division of divine love and righteousness,[76] a middle way between rationalism and inflexible confessionalism,[77] and as overcoming traditional particularism.[78] Schleiermacher's interpretation of the doctrine of election certainly marked a new departure, both in the sense that it revived, invigorated and polarized the debate about the doctrine in the context of the Prussian Church Union, and in the sense that it was a genuine effort to address the old dogmatic difference that had separated Lutherans and Reformed for three centuries.

Despite the importance of Schleiermacher's contribution, both dogmatically and historically, it has largely been ignored. The minimal attention that the reviewers of his essay paid to his theory of universalism is an early indication of this neglect. As Theodor Mahlmann reports, a century after the publication of Schleiermacher's essay, it was concluded that with regard to the doctrine of predestination, he had had little influence on contemporary dogmatics.[79]

Apart from his best-known student[80] Alexander Schweizer (1808–88), a Swiss pastor and professor of divinity, hardly anybody ventured a fresh elaboration of the doctrine of universal restoration.[81] Rather uncritically, Schweizer praised Schleiermacher's version as the perfection of the

74. Gerrish, *Tradition and the Modern World*, 112.

75. See Jewett, *Election and Predestination*, 17.

76. See Gockel, "New Perspectives," 315.

77. See Gerrish, "Constructing Tradition," 163.

78. See Gockel, *Barth and Schleiermacher*, 188.

79. See Mahlmann, "Prädestination V," 143.

80. Other pupils include August Detlev Twesten (1789–1876); Friedrich Lücke (1791–1855); the minister Ludwig Jonas (1797–1859), who would act as Schleiermacher's literary executor; the Dane Henrik Nikolai Clausen (1793–1877), a professor of theology, minister, and later national liberal statesman; Matthias Schneckenburger (1804–48), whose *Vergleichende Darstellung des lutherischen und reformirten Lehrbegriffs* ("Comparative representation of the Lutheran and Reformed notion of doctrine") was published posthumously in 1855; also the divinity professor Karl Immanuel Nitzsch (1787–1868) of Bremen; the minister Karl Leopold Adolf Sydow (1800–1882), the first editor of many of Schleiermacher's sermons, which he had transcribed almost verbatim; the Biblical scholar Friedrich Bleek (1793–1859) and the Reformed theologian Karl Christian Ullmann (1796–1865).

81. See Gockel, *Barth and Schleiermacher*, 13.

Reformed understanding of the doctrine in his own *Glaubenslehre der evangelisch-reformirten Kirche dargestellt aus den Quellen belegt* ("Dogmatics of the Protestant Reformed Church Verified from the Sources"), published between 1844 and 1847. If Ernst Sartorius' contention that in the end all will be reconciled and everything lost will be restored[82] was noticed at all at the time, it certainly made no headlines then, nor is it remembered today. It is possible that Schleiermacher's solution was not taken seriously because it was a mere compromise. Perhaps the overall climate of progress, individualism, and optimism was simply not favorable to any variation on the doctrine of predestination that involved relinquishing an independent freedom of the will. Indeed, at the latest since the Enlightenment the doctrine of predestination had actually disappeared from the centre of Western theology. As Christian Link notes, Karl Barth's discussion of predestination in his *Kirchliche Dogmatik* II/12 (1942) more than a century after the publication of Schleiermacher's essay was the first to move it back into focus.[83]

The notion of universal restoration as such was not entirely ignored, however. The Lutheran pastors (father and son) Johann Christoph Blumhardt (1805–1880) and Christoph Blumhardt (1842–1919) and some liberal theologians such as Adolf von Harnack (1851–1930) and others advocated universalism,[84] but their theologies did not revolve around the doctrine of election. Perhaps the absence of any noticeable historical reception of Schleiermacher's understanding of election is one facet of the fact stated by Tice that he "never belonged to a distinct school of thought, nor did he ever attempt to form one for students to follow."[85] With its emphasis on the communal election first of nations and eventually of all humankind rather than on the election of individuals, Schleiermacher's universalism might have appeared more akin to the Jewish position than the Christian one; given its focus on an all-determining divine decree, it was actually closer to Martin Luther's theology than either to the Reformed or to the Lutheran orthodox positions. Unlike most others in the Augustinian tradition, who "were not willing to abandon all notions of reciprocal interaction,"[86] Schleiermacher, like Luther, upheld his adherence to the necessity of all things.

---

82. See Sartorius, *Die Lutherische Lehre*, 174.
83. See Link, "Prädestination II," col. 1530.
84. See Müller, "Idee einer Apokatastasis ton panton," 4–5.
85. Tice, "Schleiermacher Yesterday, Today and Tomorrow," 316.
86. Root, "Schleiermacher as Innovator," 87.

12

Appreciation

WHAT DID SCHLEIERMACHER'S RE-CONCEPTUALIZATION of predestination as universal restoration ultimately achieve? To approach this question we need to consider both the impact it had during his lifetime, and its further influence on today's theology.

The immediate context in which he conceived of his reinterpretation was the establishment of the Prussian Church Union of 1817. Schleiermacher played a vital role in the events that led to that Union as well as in its successful implementation. However, his reinterpretation of the doctrine of election had no bearing on this development since King Friedrich Wilhelm III decreed the Union without regard to doctrinal issues. Its aim was a reform of the church order, liturgical reforms, and the practical union of Lutherans and Reformed in worship and communion, but not a doctrinal consensus. In his correspondence with Christoph Friedrich Ammon, which, in turn, was a direct reaction to the establishment of the Prussian Church Union, particular doctrines as such were not at issue either. The debate raged about issues of church union and in particular the fact that Schleiermacher wanted to ignore doctrinal differences for practical purposes such as joint communion celebrations between Lutherans and Reformed, whereas Ammon wanted them to be discussed. The latent anti-Calvinist stance of confessional Lutherans, here represented by Ammon, was clearly evident in that correspondence. It was the publication of the essay *Aphorismen* by the pro-Unionist Lutheran Karl Gottlieb Bretschneider that finally concentrated Schleiermacher's mind on the issue of predestination. His response to Bretschneider took the form of an essay on election, which was published in 1819, two years after the establishment of the Prussian Church Union. This essay was further motivated by the fact that Schleiermacher, who was lecturing on dogmatics at the University of Berlin, by that time had reached that particular doctrine and was keen to put it into written form.

In his essay, Schleiermacher developed his re-interpretation of predestination as universal restoration and offered it up as a consensus to unite Lutherans and Reformed doctrinally. Ironically enough, nobody was in fact seeking a doctrinal consensus. Confessional Lutherans opposed the Union *per se* and upheld their Lutheran orthodox doctrines against any Calvinist influence. Lutheran supporters of the Union such as Bretschneider, on the other hand, held the view that in Germany a close rapprochement between the two faiths had already taken place: Lutherans had left behind their literal understanding of the communion elements and approached the more symbolic Reformed interpretation, while the Reformed, who, with very few localized exceptions[1] had never endorsed the Calvinist understanding of double predestination, approached the Lutheran doctrine of single predestination.

To put it bluntly, the doctrine of predestination simply presented no problem—until Schleiermacher's essay put the cat among the pigeons. His attempt to clarify the doctrinal differences between Lutherans and Reformed and to thus reactivate the old debate astonished his contemporaries. Schleiermacher himself took the view that the Reformed side had not had a fair hearing, and, in turn, expressed his own surprise about the fact that no other Reformed theologian had taken up the gauntlet thrown down by the Lutherans. It is not at all clear whom he might have had in mind. Nevertheless, it was this move to style himself a defender of Calvinism that provoked the numerous unfavorable reactions and reviews by Lutheran theologians, who argued vehemently against the Calvinist doctrine of predestination and its underlying anthropological premises.

It is one of the ironies of history that the Calvinist camp, which Schleiermacher set out to defend, and which the Lutherans criticized so fiercely, did not actually exist in Prussia or Germany as a whole. This also explains the complete absence of any Reformed voice apart from Schleiermacher's in the debate. German Reformed theology was not Calvinist as such, although it had, of course, been influenced by Calvinist ideas. Its doctrine of election in particular did not adhere to the Calvinist theory. The *Heidelberg Catechism* of 1563 programmatically omitted predestination, and

---

1. The *Bremen Confession* or *Confessio Ministerii Bremensis* of 1598 did endorse the double decree to salvation and perdition.

the *Brandenburg Confessions*, which were authoritative in Prussia, did not adhere to the double decree.

Schleiermacher's hope, voiced in his essay, that the Lutherans would be swayed to accept the Reformed, or at least the Augustinian doctrine, if only this position were presented truthfully, is frankly astonishing. The Lutherans held the majority view and were simply disinclined to change it generally, and in particular not in the prevailing climate of Lutheran confessionalism. Further, given their much more optimistic understanding of humanity *coram Deo*, Schleiermacher's effort to prove to them that their version was incoherent was doomed from the start: only from the point of view of the Reformed understanding of human nature as utterly corrupt is the Lutheran position inconsistent, but not according to its own premises. And finally, Schleiermacher undermined his defense of the Calvinist doctrine himself by proposing universal restoration as his favored theory.

He defended the Calvinist theory up to the point where it asserted foreordained perdition. His argument against the double decree—despite his efforts to prove its irrelevance in terms of practical consequences to the Lutherans—was that the complete happiness that salvation brings cannot be attained if anybody at all is excluded from the kingdom of God. Thus, where the Calvinist version became incompatible with his understanding of species-consciousness, he abandoned it in favor of the solution which would be consistent with his view of the human species.

Schleiermacher's claim that neither the Calvinist nor the Lutheran doctrine pushed him toward universalism any more than the other seems to me to be truthful. Universalism cannot legitimately be derived from either, even though it contains elements of both. It adopts the Reformed elements of the irresistibility of grace and the unconditional decree, and takes from the Lutherans the notion of God's universal will to salvation. To Schleiermacher, universalism presents the only way in which both God's grace and God's justice can be retained intact. The fact that Scripture does not, or not unequivocally, support that theory is glossed over and the fact that the Church has considered it as heresy is quietly ignored.

A number of motives can be advanced regarding Schleiermacher's adoption of the Calvinist stance. First of all, it is of course true that there would not have been much gain in defending the position of the German Reformed Church concerning predestination against the Lutheran stance since it had already moved relatively closely to the latter. The Calvinist doctrine, on the other hand, was diametrically opposed to the Lutheran understanding and thus a worthwhile subject for debate. Also, the consistency and logic Schleiermacher perceived in the Calvinist theory might well have had a psychological appeal to his systematic way of thinking. That interpretation, unlike the Lutheran one, also retained the crucial insight of the original Reformers concerning the irresistibility of grace, which clearly attracted the approval of the Protestant theologian. Schleiermacher probably derived a good deal of pleasure simply from the detailed systematic theological discussion of the traditional doctrine in an academic publication; this was exactly the forum in which he wanted to see the doctrinal debate taking place. His defense of the Calvinist theory may actually have served to clarify his own position. Ultimately, however, his intentions remain somewhat vague, if not altogether enigmatic. He undertook a thorough explication and defense of the Calvinist doctrine but abandoned it at the point at which it clashed with his notion of species consciousness; he then developed his theory of universal restoration, only to finally advocate the Augustinian doctrine of predestination.

The strength of Schleiermacher's theory of universal restoration as he developed it in *Christian Faith* lies in its logical stringency and consistency. He does not shy away from drawing ultimate conclusions. He argues that, if grace is truly irresistible, there can be nobody who will not at some stage be taken into the kingdom of God. As a consequence, he dispenses with the traditional view that death signals the end of the work of grace. Another example of his consistency is his rejection of the fall in order to preserve the ontological identity of the human race from the first generation onwards. He is also one of the very few theologians to draw the ultimate conclusion that God has to be the author of sin, albeit not for its own sake but only with a teleological view to redemption. Sinfulness is necessary rather than contingent because there can be no redemption without sin. Thus, in order to ensure the redemption of all, God must have ordered sin in the first place. Of course, in order to preserve the consistency of this interpretation of election, Schleiermacher reinterprets and indeed relinquishes some elements of the traditional doctrines of hamartiology, christology, and eschatology.

However, I would argue that this provocative re-conception as such is not the reason why his theory of the eschatological redemption of all human beings failed to convince his contemporaries. On a superficial level the Lutherans were never likely to abandon their position on the basis of this lone Calvinist voice—not least because that voice was highly ambiguous. It defended a position that was not at stake, then it introduced a compromise that was obviously uncalled for, and it finally tried to convince the critics that their stance was inconsistent. The fact that Lutheran confessionalism was on the rise did not help Schleiermacher's cause, either. Ultimately, it is not actually surprising that the vast majority of reviewers of Schleiermacher's essay completely ignored his universalist solution and instead attacked the Calvinist doctrine he professed to defend.

Of those reviewers who did comment on his universalism, only Ernst Sartorius conceded in general terms that ultimately all might have to be saved. Other reviewers considered the universalist doctrine to be nothing but a stopgap—a stopgap, moreover, that appeared to be borne out of the goodness of Schleiermacher's heart rather than stringent theological arguments. In the end, none of his Lutheran contemporaries took the universalist theory seriously, and apart from the much later endorsement by Alexander Schweizer there were no Reformed responses. The reactions to *Christian Faith,* many of which were negative, did not home in on Schleiermacher's interpretation of election, and indeed, he only tentatively suggested universalism as a proposition of equal merit as other interpretations of predestination. There is an obvious trajectory from there to the modern tendency to formulate universalism as a hope rather than a doctrine.

What about the impact Schleiermacher's interpretation of election has today? The debate between particularists and universalists is still ongoing. Regarding the particularist theory, there is no doubt that at least in Germany the Lutheran side has won the day: the Calvinist doctrine of double predestination has largely been forfeited. This trend was already recognized towards the end of the eighteenth century, and it has clearly continued to grow. Church unions between Lutherans and Reformed continued to be take place, and out of the twenty-two modern established Protestant Churches in Germany, eleven are united, nine are exclusively Lutheran, and only two are Reformed. One of these two, Lippe, also has a so-called class of Lutheran congregations, and indeed both a Reformed and a Lutheran confession. It can therefore be stated unequivocally that Schleiermacher's attempt to make the Calvinist or Augustinian understanding of election the default position for both Reformed and Lutherans has utterly failed.

His interpretation of election as universal restoration, however, represents one of the motives for characterizing Schleiermacher as the father of modern theology. Today's debate is still taking place between those who advocate universalism of one shade or another, and those who vigorously defend the freedom of the human will and its power to determine or at least influence one's ultimate or eschatological fate.[2] Schleiermacher

---

2. Of course, this is not to suggest that the Calvinist doctrine of double

was the first modern theologian to propagate universal restoration, and this interpretation of election has been accepted by a number of modern theologians. Moreover, his hesitation to express universal restoration as a proper doctrine in *Christian Faith* has been taken up too. Most theologians tend to advance universalism tentatively as a hope rather than dogmatically as a doctrine.

The original opposition Schleiermacher faced, namely the defenders of free will and synergism, is still intact, and its followers are still engaged in the same debate with those who adhere to universalism. This is not to suggest that nothing has changed in two centuries of debates about election, on the contrary. Schleiermacher's emphasis on the single divine decree to creation and redemption for all humanity has been eroded in two directions. On the one hand, the focus of particularists is invariably on the individual human being and his or her eschatological fate, not on the human race as a whole. A variety of reasons can be advanced for this development, including the trend toward individualization set in motion by the Enlightenment and a different approach to and better appreciation of other world religions. Conversely, those who understand universal restoration pastorally as a hope rather than systematically as a doctrine tend to concentrate on its purpose as the ultimate redemption not only of the human race, but as a cosmic event that involves the restoration of the entire creation. Furthermore, the traditional focus on the divine decree, on the foreordination that determines the ultimate fate of human beings has largely been lost. The question whether God's irresistible saving grace or the free will is ultimately going to prevail is no longer linked to the concept of predestination, that is to a divine decision that logically precedes creation. Instead, the focus of the debate has shifted to the here and now. For particularists, accepting or rejecting God's offer of grace is a matter to be decided in and for the present. For universalists, divine grace is ultimately irresistible because God's nature is love, not because he decreed universal restoration before the creation of the world.

The notion of divine election can and has served as a stringent explanation for the personal experience of receiving the gift of grace; it certainly filled exactly this role for Augustine of Hippo, Martin Luther, John Calvin, and other first and second generation Reformers. The doctrine of predestination for them served as a proclamation of the faith they professed to

---

predestination has vanished altogether—far from it. But it never played a dominant role in the German Reformed Church, and it does not now in any of the established Protestant Churches in Germany.

have received as an unmerited gift of grace. As such, the doctrine was a form of doxology. But the experience of receiving grace does not have to be explained by way of a doctrine of predestination that assumes an underlying divine decree. Indeed, it is questionable whether a doctrine presents at all an adequate form through which to express such a life-changing experience.

Friedrich Schleiermacher was the first modern theologian to propagate the interpretation that the eternal blessedness of all is a possibility that can neither be denied nor posited as a reality, but that it has at least as much value as alternative explanations.

Appendix

THE FOLLOWING LIST GIVES the sources Schleiermacher referenced or cited in his essay "On the Doctrine of Election" and in the relevant propositions of *Christian Faith*: §§115–120 on election; §§121–125 on pneumatology; §§126–156 on ecclesiology; and §§157–163 on eschatology. The source texts are listed in chronological order.

Symbolum Romanum (mid second century)
    In *Christian Faith* §§157–163

Ireneus (140–200)
    In *Christian Faith* §§126–156

Origenes (185–254)
    Commentaria in Matthaeum 11, 17
    In "On the Doctrine of Election"

Eusebius (260–340)
    In *Christian Faith* §§126–156

Nicaean Creed (325 AD)
    In *Christian Faith* §§157–163

John Chrysostom (c. 350–430)
    In Epistolam ad Hebraeos Homilia
    In "On the Doctrine of Election"

    In Epistolam ad Ephesios 2, 10 *Homilia*
    In "On the Doctrine of Election"

Appendix

Augustine of Hippo (354–430)
Enchiridion ad Laurentium de Fide et Spe et Charitate
In "On the Doctrine of Election," *Christian Faith* §§115–120

De Correptione et Gratia
In "On the Doctrine of Election," *Christian Faith* §§115–120

De Genesi adversos Manichaeos
In "On the Doctrine of Election," *Christian Faith* §§121–125

De Fide et Opp.
In *Christian Faith* §§126–156

Gottschalk (806/7–866/70)
In "On the Doctrine of Election"

Philip Melanchthon
Loci Communes Rerum Theologicarum (1521)
In "On the Doctrine of Election," *Christian Faith* §§115–120,
§§126–56

Huldrych Zwingli
De Vera et Falsa Religione Commentarius (1525)
In *Christian Faith* §§126–156

Martin Luther: *Large Catechism* (1529)
In *Christian Faith* §§126–156

Confessio Augustana (1530)
In "On the Doctrine of Election," *Christian Faith* §§126–156

Apologia (1530)
In "On the Doctrine of Election," *Christian Faith* §§126–156

Confessio Tetrapolitana (1530)
In *Christian Faith* §§126–156

Huldrych Zwingli
  Christianae Fidei Expositio (1531)
  In *Christian Faith* §§126–156

First Basel Confession (1534)
  In *Christian Faith* §§126–156

Confessio Helvetica Prior (1536)
  In *Christian Faith* §§126–156

John Calvin
  Institutio (3rd ed. 1559)
  In "On the Doctrine of Election," *Christian Faith* §§115–120

Martin Luther
  Schmalkald Articles (1537)
  In *Christian Faith* §§126–156

Saxon Confession (1551)
  In *Christian Faith* §§115–120, §§126–156

Confessio Helvetica Posterior (1556)
  In "On the Doctrine of Election," *Christian Faith* §§115–120,
  §§126–156

Confessio Gallicana (1559)
  In "On the Doctrine of Election," *Christian Faith* §§115–120,
  §§126–156

Scots Confession (1560)
  In *Christian Faith* §§126–156

Confessio Belgica (1561)
  In *Christian Faith* §§115–120, §§126–156

Heidelberg Catechism (1563)
  In *Christian Faith* §§126–156

Appendix

Thirty-nine Articles (1563)
  In *Christian Faith* §§115–120, §§126–156

Catechism of the Council of Trent (1566)
  In *Christian Faith* §§126–156

Formula of Concord (1577)
  In "On the Doctrine of Election," *Christian Faith* §§115–120

Rakauer Katechismus (1605)
  In *Christian Faith* §§126–156

Sigismund Confession (1614)
  In "On the Doctrine of Election," *Christian Faith* §§115–120,
  §§126–156

Canons of Dort (1619)
  In *Christian Faith* §§115–120

Johann Gerhard
  Loci Theologici (1610–22)
  In "On the Doctrine of Election," *Christian Faith* §§115–120,
  §§126–156

Relation of the Colloquy of Leipzig (1631)
  In "On the Doctrine of Election," *Christian Faith* §§115–120,
  §§126–156

Declaratio Thoruniensis (1648)
  In "On the Doctrine of Election," *Christian Faith* §§126–156

Robert Barclay
  Theologiae Vere Christianae Apologia (1673)
  In *Christian Faith* §§126–156

Johann Gottlieb Töllner
  Kurze vermischte Aufsätze. Frankfurt an der Oder (1766–69/70)
  In "On the Doctrine of Election"

Gottlob Christian Storr
  Doctrinae Christianae (1793)
  In "On the Doctrine of Election"

Franz Volkmar Reinhard
  Vorlesungen über die Dogmatik (1801)
  In "On the Doctrine of Election," *Christian Faith* §§115–120

Wilhelm Martin Leberecht de Wette
  Lehrbuch der christlichen Dogmatik (1813)
  In "On the Doctrine of Election"

Christoph Friedrich von Ammon
  *Über die Hoffnung einer freien Vereinigung beider protestantischen
  Kirchen. Ein Glückwunschschreiben an den Herrn Antistes Dr Heß in
  Zürich* (1818)
  In "On the Doctrine of Election"

Philipp Konrad Marheinecke
  Die Grundlehren der christlichen Dogmatik (1819)
  In "On the Doctrine of Election"

Karl Gottlieb Bretschneider
  *Aphorismen über die Union der beiden evangelischen Kirchen in
  Deutschland* (1819)
  In "On the Doctrine of Election"

Gustav Friedrich Wiggers
  Manuscript of *Versuch einer pragmatischen Darstellung des Augus-
  tinismus und Pelagianismus* (1821)
  In "On the Doctrine of Election"

Bibliography

Adams, Robert Merrihew. "Faith and Religious Knowledge." In *Cambridge Companion to Friedrich Schleiermacher*, edited by Jaqueline Mariña, 35–51. Cambridge: Cambridge University Press, 2005.

Albrecht, Christian. "Schleiermachers Predigtlehre: Eine Skizze vor dem Hintergrund seines philosophisch-theologischen Gesamtsystems." In *Klassiker der protestantischen Predigtlehre*, edited by Christian Albrecht and Martin Weeber, 93–119. Tübingen: Mohr Siebeck, 2002.

Ammon, Christoph Friedrich. "Abhandlung über die Folgerichtigkeit des evangelischen Lehrbegriffes von der sittlichen Unvollkommenheit des Menschen und seiner Erwählung zur Seligkeit." *Magazin für christliche Prediger* 4 (1820) 1–48.

———. *Antwort auf die Zuschrift des Herrn D. Fr. Schleiermacher, ordentlichen oeffentlichen Lehrers der Theologie an der Universität zu Berlin, über die Prüfung der Harmsischen Sätze.* Hannover: In der Hahnischen Buchhandlung, 1818.

———. "Bittere Arznei für die Glaubensschwäche der Zeit: Verordnet von Herrn Claus Harms, Archidiaconus an der Nicolaikirche in Kiel, und geprüft von dem Herausgeber des *Magazins für christliche Prediger*." *Magazin für christliche Prediger* 2 (1817) 3–32. Reprint *Friedrich Daniel Ernst Schleiermacher: Theologisch-dogmatische Abhandlungen und Gelegenheitsschriften*. Kritische Gesamtausgabe I/10, edited by Hans-Friedrich Traulsen and Martin Ohst, 429–43. Berlin: de Gruyter, 1990.

———. *Summa Theologiae Christianae.* 3rd ed. Leipzig: Hartknoch, 1816.

Anonymous. "Allgemeiner Bericht über die evangelische Kirchenvereinigung in unserer Zeit und die dadurch entstandenen Streitigkeiten." *Allgemeine Kirchenzeitung* 3 (1824) cols. 1185–92.

Anonymous. "Bemerkungen über die Lehre von der Gnadenwahl, in Beziehung auf D. Schleiermacher's Abhandlung im 1. Heft der von ihm, de Wette u. a. herausgegebenen Zeitschrift." *Studien der evangelischen Geistlichkeit Wirtembergs* 1 (1827) 157–220.

Anonymous. "[Review of *Theologische Zeitschrift*]." *Theologische Quartalschrift* 2 (1820) 278–90.

Anonymous. "[Review of *Theologische Zeitschrift*]." *Allgemeines Repertorium der neuesten in- und ausländischen Literatur* 23 (1819) 292–93.

Bader, Günter. "Sünde und Bewusstsein der Sünde: Zu Schleiermachers Lehre von der Sünde." *Zeitschrift für Theologie und Kirche* 79 (1982) 60–79.

Badham, Roger A. "Redeeming the Fall: Hick's Schleiermacher versus Niebuhr's Kierkegaard." *Journal of Religion* 78 (1998) 547–70.

Barth, Karl. *Protestant Theology in the Nineteenth Century: Its Background and History.* Translated by Brian Cozens and John Bowden. London: SCM, 1972.

Bibliography

Bauckham, Richard. "Universalism: A Historical Survey." *Themelios* 4 (1979) 49–54.

Baur, Jörg. "Johann Gerhard." In *Gestalten der Kirchengeschichte 7: Orthodoxie und Pietismus*, edited by Martin Greschat, 99–119. Stuttgart: Kohlhammer, 1984.

Die Bekenntnisschriften der evangelisch-lutherischen Kirche, herausgegeben im Gedenkjahr der Augsburgischen Konfession 1930. 10th ed. Göttingen: Vandenhoeck & Ruprecht, 1986.

Besier, Gerhard. "Das Luthertum innerhalb der Preussischen Union (1808–1918): Ein Überblick." In *Das deutsche Luthertum und die Unionsproblematik im neunzehnten Jahrhundert*, edited by Wolf-Dieter Hauschild, 11–27. Gütersloh: Mohn, 1991.

Bettis, Joseph D. "A Critique of the Doctrine of Universal Salvation." *Religious Studies* 6 (1970) 329–44.

Blocher, Henri. "Everlasting Punishment and the Problem of Evil." In *Universalism and the Doctrine of Hell: Papers Presented at the Fourth Edinburgh Conference on Christian Dogmatics, 1991*, edited by Nigel M. de S. Cameron, 283–312. Carlisle, UK: Paternoster, 1992.

Boettner, Loraine. *The Reformed Doctrine of Predestination*. 1932. Reprinted, Philipsburg, NJ: Presbyterian and Reformed Publishing Company, [n.d.].

Bretschneider, Karl Gottlieb. *Aphorismen über die Union der beiden evangelischen Kirchen in Deutschland, ihre gemeinschaftliche Abendmahlsfeier, und den Unterschied ihrer Lehre*. 1819. Reprinted in excerpts *Friedrich Daniel Ernst Schleiermacher. Theologisch-dogmatische Abhandlungen und Gelegenheitsschriften. Kritische Gesamtausgabe I/10*, edited by Hans-Friedrich Traulsen and Martin Ohst, 444–68. Berlin: de Gruyter, 1990.

———. "Die Lehre Calvins und der reformirten Kirche von der göttlichen Vorherbestimmung dargestellt, nach der neuesten Vertheidigung derselben durch Herrn Doctor Schleiermacher beleuchtet." *Zeitschrift für Christenthum und Gottesgelahrtheit* 4 (1820) 1–96.

———. "Ueber die Grundansichten der theologischen Systeme in den dogmatischen Lehrbüchern der Herren Professoren Schleiermacher und Marheinecke, so wie über die des Herrn Dr. Hase." In *Handbuch der Dogmatik der evangelisch-lutherischen Kirche 1*, 1–71. 3rd ed. Leipzig: Barth, 1828. Reprinted in excerpts *Friedrich Daniel Ernst Schleiermacher. Theologisch-dogmatische Abhandlungen und Gelegenheitsschriften. Kritische Gesamtausgabe I/10*, edited by Hans-Friedrich Traulsen and Martin Ohst, 468–85. Berlin: de Gruyter, 1990.

———. *Versuch einer systematischen Entwickelung aller in der Dogmatik vorkommenden Begriffe nach den symbolischen Büchern der protestantisch-lutherischen Kirche: nebst der Literatur, vorzüglich der neuern, über alle Theile der Dogmatik*. Leipzig: Barth, 1805.

Calvin, John. *Concerning the Eternal Predestination of God*. 1552. Translated by John K. S. Reid. London: James Clarke, 1961.

———. *Institutes of the Christian Religion*. 1559. Translated by Henry Beveridge. Grand Rapids: Eerdmans, 1989.

Clark, Christopher. *Iron Kingdom: The Rise and Downfall of Prussia 1600–1947*. London: Penguin, 2007.

Clarke, F. Stuart. "Christocentric Developments in the Reformed Doctrine of Predestination." *Churchman* 98 (1984) 229–43.

Cochrane, Arthur C. *Reformed Confessions of the Sixteenth Century*. Philadelphia: Westminster, 2003.

Colloquium Lipsiense, das ist die Unterredung deren zu Leipzig im Jahr 1631 *anwesenden Chur-Sächsischen Chur-Brandenburgischen und Fürstlichen hessischen Theologen, von denen zwischen den evangelischen streitigen Religionspuncten.* Frankfurt an der Oder: Koch, 1640.

Crisp, Oliver. "Augustinian Universalism." *International Journal for Philosophy of Religion* 53 (2003) 127–45.

Cuncliffe-Jones, Hubert. "Is the Use of the Word Predestination Really Necessary in Theology?" *Scottish Journal of Theology* 3 (1950) 409–15.

Davis, Stephen T. "Universalism, Hell, and the Fate of the Ignorant." *Modern Theology* 6 (1990) 173–86.

DeVries, Dawn. "Schleiermacher." In *Blackwell Companion to Modern Theology*, edited by Gareth Jones, 311–26. Oxford: Blackwell, 2007.

DeVries, Dawn, and B. A. Gerrish. "Providence and Grace: Schleiermacher on Justification and Election." In *Cambridge Companion to Friedrich Schleiermacher*, edited by Jacqueline Mariña, 189–207. Cambridge: Cambridge University Press, 2005.

De Wette, Wilhelm Martin Leberecht. *Lehrbuch der christlichen Dogmatik in historischer Entwickelung dargestellt.* Zweyter Theil, *Die Dogmatik der lutherischen Kirche enthaltend.* Berlin: Realschulbuchhandlung, 1816.

———. "Über die Lehre von der Erwählung, in Beziehung auf Herrn Dr. Schleiermachers Abhandlung darüber in dieser Zeitschrift 1. Heft." *Theologische Zeitschrift* 2 (1820) 83–181.

Dibelius, Franz Wilhelm. "Ammon, Christoph Friedrich von." In *Realencyclopädie für protestantische Theologie und Kirche*, edited by Albert Hauck, 1:453–5. 3rd ed. Leipzig: Hinrichs, 1896.

Dilthey, Wilhelm. *Aus Schleiermacher's Leben: In Briefen.* 4 vols. Berlin: Reimer, 1860–63.

———. "Drei Briefe an Gass." In *Literarische Mitteilungen: Festschrift zum zehnjährigen Bestehen der Literatur-Archiv-Gesellschaft in Berlin*, 37–50. Berlin: Literatur-Archiv-Gesellschaft, 1901.

———. *Leben Schleiermachers.* Edited by Hermann Mulert. 2nd ed. Berlin: de Gruyter, 1922.

Dorwart, Reinhold A. "Church Organization in Brandenburg-Prussia from the Reformation to 1740." *Harvard Theological Review* 31 (1938) 275–90.

Duke, David Nelson. "Schleiermacher: Theology without a Fall." *Perspectives in Religious Studies* 9 (1982) 21–37.

Erdmann, David. "Sartorius, Ernst Wilhelm Christian." In *Allgemeine Deutsche Biographie*, edited by Historische Commission bei der königlichen Akademie der Wissenschaften, 30:382–87. Leipzig: Duncker & Humblot, 1890.

Fergusson, David. "Eschatology." In *Cambridge Companion to Christian Doctrine*, edited by Colin E. Gunton, 226–44. Cambridge: Cambridge University Press, 1997.

———. "Predestination: A Scottish Perspective." *Scottish Journal of Theology* 46 (1993) 479–96.

———. "Will the Love of God Finally Triumph?" In *Nothing Greater, Nothing Better: Theological Essays on the Love of God: Papers from the 6th Edinburgh Dogmatics Conference*, edited by Kevin J. Vanhoozer, 186–202. Grand Rapids: Eerdmans, 2001.

Forde, Gerhard O. *The Captivation of the Will: Luther vs. Erasmus on Freedom and Bondage.* Grand Rapids: Eerdmans, 2005.

Fronmüller, G. F. C., and Julius August Wagenmann. "Töllner, Johann Gottlieb." In *Realencyclopädie für protestantische Theologie und Kirche* 19, 814–17. 3rd ed. Leipzig: Hinrichs, 1907.

Gass, Wilhelm. *Fr. Schleiermacher's Briefwechsel mit J. Chr. Gass: Mit einer bibliographischen Vorrede*. Berlin: Reimer, 1852.

Gerdes, Hayo. "Anmerkungen zur Christologie der Glaubenslehre Schleiermachers." (edited by Joachim Ringleben) *Neue Zeitschrift für systematische Theologie und Religionsphilosophie* 25 (1983) 112–25.

Gerhard, Johann. *Loci Theologici cum pro Adstuenda Veritate Tum pro Destruenda Quorumuis Contradicentium Falsitate per Theses Neruose Solide & Copiose Explicatorum*. Geneva: Gamoneti, 1639.

Gerlach, Gottlob Benjamin. *Ammon und Schleiermacher oder Präliminarien zur Union zwischen Glauben und Wissen, Religion und Philosophie, Supernaturalismus und Rationalismus*. Berlin: Mauersche Buchhandlung, 1821.

Gerrish, B. A. "Constructing Tradition: Schleiermacher, Hodge and the Theological Legacy of John Calvin." In *The Legacy of John Calvin*, edited by David Foxgrover, 158–75. Grand Rapids: Calvin Studies Society, 2000.

———. *Continuing the Reformation: Essays on Modern Religious Thought*. Chicago: University of Chicago Press, 1993.

———. "The Place of Calvin in Christian Theology." In *Cambridge Companion to John Calvin*, edited by Donald K. McKim, 289–304. Cambridge: Cambridge University Press, 2004.

———. *A Prince of the Church: Schleiermacher and the Beginnings of Modern Theology*. London: SCM, 1984.

———. "Schleiermacher and the Reformation: A Question of Doctrinal Development." In *The Old Protestantism and the New: Essays on the Reformation Heritage*, 179–95. Edinburgh: T. & T. Clark, 1982.

———. *Tradition and the Modern World: Reformation Theology in the Nineteenth Century*. Chicago: University of Chicago Press, 1978.

Gockel, Matthias. *Barth and Schleiermacher on the Doctrine of Election: A Systematic-Theological Comparison*. Oxford: Oxford University Press, 2006.

———. "New Perspectives on an Old Debate: Friedrich Schleiermacher's Essay on Election." *International Journal of Systematic Theology* 6 (2004) 301–18.

Goeters, J. F. Gerhard. "Der Anschluss der neuen Provinzen von 1815." In *Die Geschichte der Evangelischen Kirche der Union, Band 1: Die Anfänge der Union unter landesherrlichem Kirchenregiment (1817–1850)*, edited by J. F. Gerhard Groeters and Rudolf Mau, 77–82. Leipzig: Evangelische Verlagsanstalt, 1992.

———. "Einleitung." In *Die Geschichte der Evangelischen Kirche der Union Band 1: Die Anfänge der Union unter landesherrlichem Kirchenregiment (1817–1850)*, edited by J. F. Gergard Groeters and Rudolf Mau, 27–40. Leipzig: Evangelische Verlagsanstalt, 1992.

———. "Die kirchliche Reformdiskussion." In *Die Geschichte der Evangelischen Kirche der Union Band 1: Die Anfänge der Union unter landesherrlichem Kirchenregiment (1817–1850)*, edited by J. F. Gerhard Groeters and Rudolf Mau, 83–87. Leipzig: Evangelische Verlagsanstalt, 1992.

———. "Religiöse Züge der vaterländischen Erhebung 1813–1815." In *Die Geschichte der Evangelischen Kirche der Union Band 1: Die Anfänge der Union unter landesherrlichem Kirchenregiment (1817–1850)*, edited by J. F. Gerhard Groeters and Rudolf Mau, 67–76. Leipzig: Evangelische Verlagsanstalt, 1992.

————. "Die Reorganisation der staatlichen und kirchlichen Verwaltung in den Stein-Hardenbergschen Reformen: Verwaltungsunion der kirchenregimentlichen Organe." In *Die Geschichte der Evangelischen Kirche der Union Band 1: Die Anfänge der Union unter landesherrlichem Kirchenregiment (1817–1850)*, edited by J. F. Gerhard Groeters and Rudolf Mau, 54–7. Leipzig: Evangelische Verlagsanstalt, 1992.

————. "Das Staatsgebiet der Preussischen Monarchie, seine kirchenorganisatorische und konfessionelle Gliederung." In *Die Geschichte der Evangelischen Kirche der Union Band 1: Die Anfänge der Union unter landesherrlichem Kirchenregiment (1817–1850)*, edited by J. F. Gergard Groeters and Rudolf Mau, 41–45. Leipzig: Evangelische Verlagsanstalt, 1992.

Goroncy, Jason A. "Review of 'Barth and Schleiermacher on the Doctrine of Election'. By Matthias Gockel. Oxford: OUP 2006." *Journal of Theological Studies* 59 (2008) 415–19.

————. "That God May Have Mercy upon All: A Review-Essay of Matthias Gockel's *Barth and Schleiermacher on the Doctrine of Election*." *Journal of Reformed Theology* 2 (2008) 113–30.

Gräb, Wilhelm. "Predigt als kommunikativer Akt. Einige Bemerkungen zu Schleiermachers Theorie religiöser Mitteilung." In *Internationaler Schleiermacher-Kongress Berlin 1984*, edited by Kurt Victor Selge, 643–59. Berlin: de Gruyter, 1985.

Graf, Friedrich Wilhelm. "'Restaurationstheologie' oder neulutherische Modernisiering des Protestantismus?" In *Das deutsche Luthertum und die Unionsproblematik im neunzehnten. Jahrhundert*, edited by Wolf-Dieter Hauschild, 64–109. Gütersloh: Mohn, 1991.

Grass, Hans. "Grund und Grenzen der Kirchengemeinschaft." In *Friedrich Schleiermacher 1768–1834. Theologe—Philosoph—Pädagoge*, edited by Dietz Lange, 217–35. Göttingen: Vandenhoeck & Ruprecht, 1984.

————. "Schleiermacher und das Bekenntnis." In *Internationaler Schleiermacher-Kongress Berlin 1984*, edited by Kurt Victor Selge, 1053–60. Berlin: de Gruyter, 1985.

Greschat, Martin. "Orthodoxie und Pietismus. Einleitung." In *Gestalten der Kirchengeschichte 7: Orthodoxie und Pietismus*, edited by Martin Greschat, 7–35. Stuttgart: Kohlhammer, 1984.

Gunton, Colin. "Election and Ecclesiology in the Post-Constantinian Church." *Scottish Journal of Theology* 53 (2000) 212–27.

Hägglund, Bengt. *Geschichte der Theologie. Ein Abriss*. Translated by A. O. Schwede. 2nd ed. Munich: Kaiser, 1990.

Härle, Winfried. *Dogmatik*. Berlin: de Gruyter, 1995.

Hart, Trevor. "Redemption and Fall." In *Cambridge Companion to Christian Doctrine*, edited by Colin E. Gunton, 189–206. Cambridge: Cambridge University Press, 1997.

————. "Universalism: Two Distinct Types." In *Universalism and the Doctrine of Hell: Papers Presented at the Fourth Edinburgh Conference on Christian Dogmatics, 1991*, edited by Nigel M. de S. Cameron, 1–34. Carlisle: Paternoster, 1992.

Hauck, Albert. "Union, kirchliche." In *Realencyclopädie für protestantische Theologie und Kirche*, edited by Albert Hauck, 20:253–61. 3rd ed. Leipzig: Hinrichs, 1908.

Hector, Kevin W. "Actualism and Incarnation: The High Christology of Friedrich Schleiermacher." *International Journal of Systematic Theology* 8 (2006) 307–22.

Bibliography

———. "The Mediation of Christ's Normative Spirit: A Constructive Reading of Schleiermacher's Pneumatology." *Modern Theology* 24 (2008) 1–22.

Heinrici, Carl Friedrich Georg. D. *August Twesten nach Tagebüchern und Briefen.* Berlin: Hertz, 1889.

———. "Twesten, August Detlev Christian." In *Realencyclopädie für protestantische Theologie und Kirche,* edited by Albert Hauck, 20:171–77. 3rd ed. Leipzig: Hinrichs, 1908.

Heppe, Heinrich. *Die Bekenntnisschriften der reformirten Kirche Deutschlands.* Elberfeld: Friderichs, 1860.

Herms, Eilert. "Der christliche Glaube." In *Lexikon der theologischen Werke,* edited by Michael Eckert et al., 86–88. Stuttgart: Körner, 2003.

———. "Freiheit Gottes—Freiheit des Menschen." In *Denkraum Katechismus. Festschrift für Oswald Bayer zum 70. Geburtstag,* edited by Johannes von Lüpke and Edgar Thaidigsmann, 197–228. Tübingen: Mohr Siebeck, 2009.

———. "Gewissheit in Martin Luthers *De servo arbitrio.*" *Lutherjahrbuch* 67 (2000) 23–50.

———. "Schleiermachers Eschatologie nach der zweiten Auflage der Glaubenslehre." In *Menschsein im Werden. Studien zu Schleiermacher,* 125–49. Tübingen: Mohr Siebeck, 2003.

———. "Willensfreiheit V: Dogmatisch." In *Religion in Geschichte und Gegenwart,* edited by Hans Dieter Betz et al., 8:1574–76. 4th ed. Tübingen: Mohr Siebeck, 2005.

Hesselink, I. John. "Calvin's Theology." In *Cambridge Companion to John Calvin,* edited by Donald K. McKim, 74–92. Cambridge: Cambridge University Press, 2004.

Heussi, Karl. *Kompendium der Kirchengeschichte.* 18th ed. Tübingen: Mohr Siebeck, 1991.

Hieb, Nathan D. "The Precarious Status of Resurrection in Friedrich Schleiermacher's *Glaubenslehre.*" *International Journal of Systematic Theology* 9 (2007) 398–414.

Hillerbrand, Hans J. "The Legacy of Martin Luther." In *Cambridge Companion to Martin Luther,* edited by Donald K. McKim, 227–39. Cambridge: Cambridge University Press, 2003.

Jacobs, Manfred. "Entstehung und Wirkung des Neukonfessionalismus im Luthertum des neunzehnten Jahrhunderts." In *Das deutsche Luthertum und die Unionsproblematik im neunzehnten Jahrhundert,* edited by Wolf-Dieter Hauschild, 28–63. Gütersloh: Mohn, 1991.

Jewett, Paul K. *Election and Predestination.* Grand Rapids: Eerdmans, 1985.

Johnson, Thomas. "A Wideness in God's Mercy: Universalism in the Bible." In *Universal Salvation? The Current Debate,* edited by Robin A. Parry and Christopher H. Partridge, 77–102. Grand Rapids: Eerdmans, 2003.

Jüngel, Eberhard. "Schleiermacher." In *Religion Past and Present: Encyclopedia of Theology and Religion,* edited by Hans Dieter Betz et al., 11:482–91. Leiden: Brill, 2012.

Kantzenbach, Friedrich Wilhelm. *Friedrich Daniel Ernst Schleiermacher.* Reinbek: Rororo, 1967.

Kawerau, G. "Sigismund, Johann und die Einführung des reformierten Bekenntnisses in der Mark Brandenburg." In *Realencyclopädie für protestantische Theologie und Kirche,* 18:331–38. 3rd ed. Leipzig: Hinrichs, 1906.

Kelsey, Catherine L. *Schleiermacher's Preaching, Dogmatics, and Biblical Criticism. The Interpretation of Jesus Christ in the Gospel of John.* Princeton Theological Monograph Series 68. Eugene, OR: Pickwick Publications, 2007.

Klän, Werner. "Die altlutherische Kirchenbildung in Preussen." In *Das deutsche Luthertum und die Unionsproblematik im 19. Jahrhundert*, edited by Wolf-Dieter Hauschild, 153–70. Gütersloh: Mohn, 1991.

Kolb, Robert. *Bound Choice, Election, and Wittenberg Theological Method: From Martin Luther to the Formula of Concord*. Grand Rapids: Eerdmans, 2005.

———. "Confessional Lutheran Theology." In *Cambridge Companion to Reformation Theology*, edited by David Bagchi and David C. Steinmetz, 68–79. Cambridge: Cambridge University Press, 2004.

———. "Luther's Function in an Age of Confessionalism." In *Cambridge Companion to Martin Luther*, edited by Donald K. McKim, 209–26. Cambridge: Cambridge University Press, 2003.

Kusukawa, Sachiko. "Melanchthon." In *Cambridge Companion to Reformation Theology*, edited by David Bagchi and David C. Steinmetz, 57–67. Cambridge: Cambridge University Press, 2004.

Lamm, Julia A. *The Living God: Schleiermacher's Theological Appropriation of Spinoza*. University Park: Pennsylvania State University Press, 1996.

Lange, Dietz. "Neugestaltung christlicher Glaubenslehre." In *Friedrich Schleiermacher 1768–1834. Theologe—Philosoph—Pädagoge*, edited by Dietz Lange, 85–105. Göttingen: Vandenhock & Ruprecht, 1985.

Lessing, Eckhard. "Schul- und Hochschulreformen. Die neuen theologischen Fakultäten. Friedrich Schleiermacher" In *Die Geschichte der Evangelischen Kirche der Union Band 1: Die Anfänge der Union unter landesherrlichem Kirchenregiment (1817–1850)*, edited by J. F. Gerhard Groeters and Rudolf Mau, 58–66. Leipzig: Evangelische Verlagsanstalt, 1992.

Link, Christian. "Prädestination II: Dogmengeschichtlich. III: Dogmatisch." In *Religion in Geschichte und Gegenwart*, edited by Hans Dieter Betz et al., 6:1526–32. 4th ed. Tübingen: Mohr, 2003.

Lindsay, James. "Friedrich Daniel Ernst Schleiermacher: The Representative Theologian of the Nineteenth Century." *Presbyterian and Reformed Review* 10 (1899) 58–69.

Lucas, J. R. "Foreknowledge and the Vulnerability of God." In *The Philosophy in Christianity*, edited by G. Versey, 119–28. Cambridge: Cambridge University Press, 1989.

Ludlow, Morwenna. "Universal Salvation and a Soteriology of Divine Punishment." *Scottish Journal of Theology* 53 (2000) 449–71.

———. "Universalism in the History of Christianity." In *Universal Salvation? The Current Debate*, edited by Robin A. Parry and Christopher H. Partridge, 191–218. Grand Rapids: Eerdmans, 2003.

Luther, Martin. *De servo arbitrio*, 1525. Translated in *Luther and Erasmus: Free Will and Salvation. Library of Christian Classics XVII*, edited by E. Gordon Rupp and Philip S. Watson. London: SCM, 1969.

MacCulloch, Diarmid. *Reformation: Europe's House Divided 1490–1700*. London: Penguin, 2004.

MacDonald, Gregory. "Introduction: Between Heresy and Dogma." In *"All Shall Be Well": Explorations in Universal Salvation and Christian Theology, from Origen to Moltmann*, edited by Gregory MacDonald, 1–25. Eugene, OR: Cascade Books, 2011.

Mackintosh, H. R. "Studies in Christian Eschatology VII: Universal Restoration." *The Expositor* 8 (1914) 128–43.

Bibliography

Mager, Inge. "Georg Calixt." In *Gestalten der Kirchengeschichte 7: Orthodoxie und Pietismus*, edited by Martin Greschat, 137–48. Stuttgart: Kohlhammer, 1984.

Mahlmann, Theodor. "Prädestination V: Reformation bis Neuzeit." In *Theologische Realenzyklopädie*, 27:118–56. Berlin: de Gruyter, 1997.

Mann, William E. "Augustine on Evil and Original Sin." In *Cambridge Companion to Augustin*, edited by Eleonore Stump and Norman Kretzmann, 40–48. Cambridge: Cambridge University Press, 2001.

Marheinecke, Philipp. *Die Grundlehren der christlichen Dogmatik*. Berlin: Dümmler, 1819.

Mariña, Jaqueline. "Christology and Anthropology." In *Cambridge Companion to Friedrich Schleiermacher*, edited by Jaqueline Mariña, 151–70. Cambridge: Cambridge University Press, 2005.

———. "Schleiermacher's Christology Revisited. A Reply to His Critics." *Scottish Journal of Theology* 49 (1996) 177–200.

Markschies, Christoph. "Willensfreiheit III: Kirchengeschichtlich." In *Religion in Geschichte und Gegenwart*, edited by Hans Dieter Betz et al., 8:1569–73. 4th ed. Tübingen: Mohr Siebeck, 2005.

Marshall, I. Howard. "The New Testament Does *Not* Teach Universal Salvation." In *Universal Salvation? The Current Debate*, edited by Robin A. Parry and Christopher H. Partridge, 55–76, Grand Rapids: Eerdmans, 2003.

McGrath, Alister. *Justitia Dei. A History of the Christian Doctrine of Justification*. 3rd ed. Cambridge: Cambridge University Press, 2005.

———. *The Making of Modern German Christology* 1750–1990. 2nd ed. Grand Rapids: Apollos, 1994.

Mehlhausen, Joachim. "Theologie zwischen Politik und Kirche im neunzehnten Jahrhundert." In *Das deutsche Luthertum und die Unionsproblematik im neunzehnten Jahrhundert*, edited by Wolf-Dieter Hauschild, 11–27. Gütersloh: Mohn, 1991.

Meisner, Heinrich. *Schleiermacher als Mensch. Sein Wirken. Familien- und Freundesbriefe 1804 bis 1834*. Stuttgart: Perthes, 1923.

Melanchthon, Philipp. *Loci Communes 1521. Lateinisch—Deutsch*. Translated by Horst Georg Pöhlmann. Gütersloh: Gerd Mohn, 1993.

Melzer, Friso. "Zu der Frage nach dem dogmatischen Gehalt von Schleiermachers Predigten." *Theologische Studien und Kritiken* 102 (1930) 382–424.

Moltmann, Jürgen. *In the End—the Beginning: The Life of Hope*. Translated by Margaret Kohl. London: SCM, 2004.

———. *Prädestination und Perseveranz: Geschichte und Bedeutung der reformierten Lehre "De Perseverantia Sanctorum."* Neukirchen-Vluyn: Neukirchener Verlag, 1961.

Moore, Walter L. "Schleiermacher as a Calvinist: a Comparison of Calvin and Schleiermacher on Providence and Predestination." *Scottish Journal of Theology* 24 (1971) 167–83.

Mühlenberg, Ekkehard. "Der Universitätslehrer." In *Friedrich Schleiermacher 1768–1834. Theologe—Philosoph—Pädagoge*, edited by Dietz Lange, 24–46. Göttingen: Vandenhock & Ruprecht, 1985.

Müller, Gotthold. "Die Idee einer *Apokatastasis ton panton* in der europäischen Theologie von Schleiermacher bis Barth." *Zeitschrift für Religion und Geistesgeschichte* 16 (1964) 1–22.

Mulert, Hermann. "Die Aufnahme der Glaubenslehre Schleiermachers." *Zeitschrift für Theologie und Kirche* 18 (1908) 107–39.

Muller, Richard. "John Calvin and Later Calvinism: The Identity of the Reformed Tradition." In *Cambridge Companion to Reformation Theology*, edited by David Bagchi and David C. Steinmetz, 130–49. Cambridge: Cambridge University Press, 2004.

———. "The Placement of Predestination in Reformed Theology: Issue or Non-issue?" *Calvin Theological Journal* 40 (2005) 184–210.

Myers, Benjamin. "Predestination and Freedom in Milton's *Paradise Lost*." *Scottish Journal of Theology* 59 (2006) 64–80.

Neuser, Wilhelm H. "Agende, Agendenstreit und Provinzialagenden." In *Die Geschichte der Evangelischen Kirche der Union Band 1: Die Anfänge der Union unter landesherrlichem Kirchenregiment (1817–1850)*, edited by J. F. Gerhard Groeters and Rudolf Mau, 134–58. Leipzig: Evangelische Verlagsanstalt, 1992.

———. "*Confessio Augustana* von 1540/1542." In *Reformierte Bekenntnisschriften Band 1 / 2 1535–49*, edited by Mihály Bucsay et al., 137–49. Neukirchen-Vluyn: Neukirchener Verlag, 2006.

Niebergall, Alfred. "Agende 18.1: Der Kampf um die Preussische Agende." In *Theologische Realenzyklopädie*, 2:55–60. Berlin: de Gruyter, 1978.

Niebuhr, Richard R. *Schleiermacher on Christ and Religion*. New York: Scribner, 1964.

Niesel, Wilhelm. "Schleiermachers Verhältnis zur reformatorischen Tradition." *Zwischen den Zeiten* 8 (1930) 511–25.

Nimmo, Paul. "The Mediation of Redemption in Schleiermacher's *Glaubenslehre*." *International Journal of Systematic Theology* 5 (2003) 187–99.

Nischan, Bodo. "Calvinism, the Thirty Years' War, and the Beginning of Absolutism in Brandenburg: The Political Thought of John Bergius." *Central European History* 15 (1982) 203–23.

———. "The *Fractio Panis*: A Reformed Communion Practice in Late Reformation Germany." *Church History* 53 (1984) 17–29.

———. "John Bergius: Irenicism and the Beginning of Official Religious Toleration in Brandenburg-Prussia." *Church History* 51 (1982) 389–404.

———. "Reformed Irenicism and the Leipzig Colloquy of 1631." *Central European History* 9 (1976) 3–26.

———. "The Second Reformation in Brandenburg: Aims and Goals." *Sixteenth Century Journal* 14 (1983) 173–86.

Nixdorf, Wolfgang. "Die lutherische Separation. Union und Bekenntnis (1834)." In *Die Geschichte der Evangelischen Kirche der Union Band 1: Die Anfänge der Union unter landesherrlichem Kirchenregiment (1817–1850)*, edited by J. F. Gerhard Groeters and Rudolf Mau, 220–40. Leipzig: Evangelische Verlagsanstalt, 1992.

Nowak, Kurt. "Schleiermacher als Prediger am Charité Krankenhaus in Berlin (1796–1802)." *Theologische Zeitschrift* 41 (1985) 391–411.

———. *Schleiermacher: Leben, Werk und Wirkung*. Göttingen: Vandenhoek & Ruprecht, 2001.

Oberdorfer, Bernd. "Schleiermacher on Eschatology and Resurrection." In *Resurrection: Theological and Scientific Assessment*, edited by Robert John Russell and Michael Welker, 165–82. Grand Rapids: Eerdmans, 2002.

Ohst, Martin. *Schleiermacher und die Bekenntnisschriften. Eine Untersuchung zu seiner Reformations- und Protestantismusdeutung*. Tübingen: Mohr Siebeck, 1989.

Pannenberg, Wolfhart. "Prädestination III: Dogmengeschichtlich. IV: Dogmatisch." In *Religion in Geschichte und Gegenwart*, edited by Hans von Campenhausen, 5:483–89. 3rd ed. Tübingen: Mohr, 1961.

Bibliography

Parry, Robin, and Christipher H. Partridge. "Introduction." In *Universal Salvation? The Current Debate*, edited by Robin A. Parry and Christopher H. Partridge, xv–xxvii. Grand Rapids: Eerdmans, 2003.

Partree, Charles B. "Calvin on Universal and Particular Providence." In *Readings in Calvin's Theology*, edited by Donald K. McKim, 69–88. 1984. Reprinted, Eugene, OR: Wipf & Stock, 1998.

Pedersen, Daniel. "Eternal Life in Schleiermacher's *The Christian Faith*." *International Journal of Systematic Theology* 13 (2011) 340–57.

Plasger, Georg, and Matthias Freudenberg. *Reformierte Bekenntnisschriften. Eine Auswahl von den Anfängen bis zur Gegenwart*. Göttingen: Vandenhoeck & Ruprecht, 2005.

Powys, David J. *'Hell': a Hard Look at a Hard Question*. Carlisle, UK: Paternoster, 1997.

———. "The Nineteenth- and Twentieth-Centuries Debates about Hell and Universalism." In *Universalism and the Doctrine of Hell: Papers Presented at the Fourth Edinburgh Conference on Christian Dogmatic, 1991*, edited by Nigel M. de S. Cameron, 93–138. Carlisle: Paternoster, 1993.

Rae, Murray. "Salvation-in-Community: The Tentative Universalism of Friedrich Schleiermacher." In *"All Shall Be Well": Explorations in Universal Salvation and Christian Theology, from Origen to Moltmann*, edited by Gregory MacDonald, 171–97. Eugene, OR: Cascade Books, 2011.

Redeker, Martin. *Friedrich Schleiermacher: Leben und Werk*. Berlin: de Gruyter, 1968.

Reid, John K. S. "The Office of Christ in Predestination." *Scottish Journal of Theology* 1 (1948) 5–18.

Reinhard, Franz Volkmar. *Vorlesungen über die Dogmatik mit literarischen Zusätzen herausgegeben von Johann Gottfried Immanuel Berger, . . . mit neuen literarischen Zusätzen versehen von D. Heinrich August Schott*. 4th ed. Sulzbach: Seidel, 1818.

Reist, John S. "Continuity, Christ, and Culture: A Study of F. Schleiermacher's Christology." *Journal of Religious Thought* 26 (1969) 18–40.

Reitan, Eric. "Eternal Damnation and Blessed Ignorance: Is the Damnation of Some Incompatible with the Salvation of Any?" *Religious Studies* 38 (2002) 429–50.

———. "Human Freedom and the Impossibility of Eternal Damnation." In *Universal Salvation? The Current Debate*, edited by Robin A. Parry and Christopher H. Partridge, 125–42. Grand Rapids: Eerdmans, 2003.

Rendtorff, Trutz. "Kirchlicher und freier Protestantismus in der Sicht Schleiermachers." *Neue Zeitung für systematische Theologie und Religionsphilosophie* 10 (1968) 18–30.

Robinson, John A. T. "Universalism—Is It Heretical?" *Scottish Journal of Theology* 2 (1949) 139–55.

———. "Universalism—A Reply." *Scottish Journal of Theology* 2 (1949) 378–80.

Rohls, Jan. *Reformed Confessions. Theology from Zurich to Barmen*. Translated by John Hoffmeyer. Louisville: Westminster John Knox, 1997.

Root, Michael. "Schleiermacher as Innovator and Inheritor: God, Dependence and Election." *Scottish Journal of Theology* 43 (1990) 87–110.

Rosenau, Hartmut. "Apocatastasis." In *Religion Past and Present: Encyclopedia of Theology and Religion*, edited by Hans Dieter Betz et al., 1:307. Leiden: Brill 2007.

———. "Wiederbringung aller." In *Theologische Realenzyklopädie*, 35:774–80, Berlin: de Gruyter, 2003.

Rutledge, Fleming. *Help My Unbelief*. Grand Rapids: Eerdmans, 2000.

Sartorius, Ernst Wilhelm Christian von. *Die lutherische Lehre vom Unvermögen des freyen Willens zur höheren Sittlichkeit, in Briefen, nebs einem Anhang gegen Herrn D. Schleiermacher's Abhandlung über die Lehre von der Erwählung*, 135–76. Göttingen: Schneider, 1821.

Schaede, Stephan. "*Institutio Christianae Religionis*." In *Lexikon der theologischen Werke*, edited by Michael Eckart et al., 399–401. Stuttgart: Kröner, 2003.

Schaff, Philip. *The Creeds of Christendom*. New York: Harper & Brothers, 1877–78.

Scheible, Heinz. "Philip Melanchthon." In *Gestalten der Kirchengeschichte 6: Reformationszeit II*, edited by Martin Greschat, 75–101. Stuttgart: Kohlhammer, 1984.

Schindler, Alfred. "Augustin / Augustanismus I." In *Theologische Realenzyklopädie*, 4:646–98. Berlin: de Gruyter, 1979.

Schleiermacher, Friedrich. *The Christian Faith*. Translated by H. R. MacIntosh and J. S. Stewart. 1928. Reprinted, Edinburgh: T. & T. Clark, 1999.

———. *Der christliche Glaube nach den Grundsätzen der evangelischen Kirche im Zusammenhang dargestellt*. 1830. Auf Grund der 2. Auflage neu herausgegeben von Martin Redeker. 7th ed. Berlin: de Gruyter, 1960.

———. *Friedrich Schleiermacher On Creeds, Confessions and Church Union: "That They May Be One."* Translated with an Introduction and Notes by Iain C. Nicol. Schleiermacher Studies and Translations 24. Lewiston, NY: Mellen, 2004.

———. *The Life of Schleiermacher as Unfolded in His Autobiography and Letters*. Translated by Frederica Rowan. London: Smith & Elder, 1890.

———. On the Doctrine of Election, with Special Reference to the Aphorisms of Dr Bretschneider. Translated with Introduction and Notes by Iain C. Nicol and Allen G. Jørgenson. Typescript. (Forthcoming: Louisville: Westminster John Knox Press, 2012)

———. *Predigten*. Edited by Hans Urner. Göttingen: Vandenhoeck & Ruprecht, 1969.

———. *Predigten*. New ed. 4 vols. Berlin: Reimer, 1843–44.

———. *Predigten. Sämmtliche Werke zweite Abtheilung*, vols. 5–10. Berlin: Reimer, 1835–56.

———. *Über das liturgische Recht evangelischer Landesfürsten*. Göttingen: Vandenhoeck & Ruprecht, 1824. Reprinted in *Friedrich Schleiermacher, Schriften zur Kirchen- und Bekenntnisfrage*, edited by Hayo Gerdes, 167–219. Berlin: de Gruyter, 1969.

———. "Über den eigenthümlichen Werth und das bindende Ansehen symbolischer Bücher." In *Reformationsalmanach auf das Jahr 1819*, edited by Friedrich Keyser, 423–54. Erfurt: Keysers, 1819. Reprinted in *Friedrich Schleiermacher, Schriften zur Kirchen- und Bekenntnisfrage*, edited by Hayo Gerdes, 137–66. Berlin: de Gruyter, 1969.

———. "Über die Glaubenslehre: Zwei Sendschreiben an Lücke." *Theologische Studien und Kritiken* (1829), 255–84 and 481–532. Reprint in *Friedrich Daniel Ernst Schleiermacher. Theologisch-dogmatische Abhandlungen und Gelegenheitsschriften. Kritische Gesamtausgabe I/10*, edited by Hans-Friedrich Traulsen and Martin Ohst, 307–94. Berlin: de Gruyter, 1990.

———. "Über die Lehre von der Erwählung besonders in Beziehung auf Herrn Dr. Bretschneiders *Aphorismen*. 1819." In Friedrich Schleiermacher, *Sämmtliche Werke* I/2, 393–484. Berlin: Reimer, 1836.

———. "Vorrede zu den Predigten in Bezug auf die Feier der Uebergabe der Augsburgischen Confession." In *Predigten 6. Sammlung*, III–XXXIV. Berlin: Reimer, 1831. Reprinted in *Friedrich Schleiermacher, Schriften zur Kirchen- und Bekenntnisfrage*, edited by Hayo Gerdes, 255–57. Berlin: de Gruyter, 1969.

———. "Vorschlag zu einer neuen Verfassung der protestantischen Kirche im preussischen Staate." *Zeitschrift für Kirchenrecht* 1861, 327–41. Reprinted in *Friedrich Schleiermacher, Schriften zur Kirchen- und Bekenntnisfrage*, edited by Hayo Gerdes, 113–36. Berlin: de Gruyter, 1969.

———. *Zwei unvorgreifliche Gutachten in Sachen des protestantischen Kirchenwesens zunächst in Beziehung auf den Preussischen Staat*. Berlin: Realschulbuchhandlung, 1804. Reprinted in *Friedrich Schleiermacher, Schriften zur Kirchen- und Bekenntnisfrage*, edited by Hayo Gerdes, 21–112. Berlin: de Gruyter, 1969.

Schott, Theodor. "Steudel, Johann Christian Friedrich." In *Allgemeine Deutsche Biographie* 36, edited by Historische Commission bei der königlichen Akademie der Wissenschaften, 152–55. Leipzig: Duncker & Humblot, 1893.

———. "Storr, Gottlob Christian." In *Allgemeine Deutsche Biographie* 36, edited by Historische Commission bei der königlichen Akademie der Wissenschaften, 456–58. Leipzig: Duncker & Humblot, 1893.

Schütte, Hans Walter. "Die Ausscheidung der Lehre vom Zorn Gottes in der Theologie Schleiermachers und Ritschls." *Neue Zeitschrift für Systematische Theologie und Religionsphilosophie* 10 (1968) 387–97.

Smend, Rudolf. "Wilhelm Martin Leberecht de Wette." In *Theologen des Protestantismus im neunzehnten und zwanzigsten Jahrhundert*, edited by Martin Greschat, 1:44–58. Stuttgart: Kohlhammer, 1978.

Sommer, Wolfgang. "Schleiermachers Stellung zu den reformatorischen Bekenntnisschriften, vor allem nach seiner Schrift *Über den eigentümlichen Wert und das bindende Ansehen symbolischer Bücher*, 1819." In *Internationaler Schleiermacher-Kongress Berlin 1984*, edited by Kurt Victor Selge, 1061–74. Berlin: de Gruyter, 1985.

Stäudlin, Carl Friedrich. *Kirchliche Geographie und Statistik*. Tübingen: In der Cotta'schen Buchhandlung, 1804.

Steudel, Johann Christian Friedrich. "Anzeige mehrerer seit einiger Zeit erschienenen Schriften, welche die Lehre von der Gnadenwahl betreffen." *Archiv für Theologie und ihre neueste Literatur* 5 (1822) 404–51.

———. "Fortsetzung der Anzeige mehrerer seit einiger Zeit erschienenen Schriften über die Frage von der Gnadenwahl." *Archiv für Theologie und ihre neueste Literatur* 5 (1822) 666–743.

———. "Fortsetzung und Beschluss der Anzeige mehrerer seit einiger Zeit erschienenen Schriften über die Frage von der Gnadenwahl." *Archiv für Theologie und ihre neueste Literatur* 6 (1824) 620–732.

Stiewe, Martin. "Unionen IV: Innerprotestantische Unionen und Unionen zwischen protestantischen und anglikanischen Kirchen / I: Deutschland." In *Theologische Realenzyklopädie*, 34:323–27. Berlin: de Gruyter, 2002.

———. *Das Unionsverständnis Friedrich Schleiermachers. Der Protestantismus als Konfession in der Glaubenslehre*. Unio und Confessio 4. Witten: Luther-Verlag, 1969.

Storr, Gottlob Christian. *An Elementary Course of Biblical Theology: Translated from the Work of Professors Storr and Flatt, with Additions by S. S. Schmucker*. London: Ward, 1840.

Strange, Daniel. "A Calvinist Response to Talbott's Universalism." In *Universal Salvation? The Current Debate*, edited by Robin A. Parry and Christopher H. Partridge, 145–68. Grand Rapids: Eerdmans, 2003.

Thadden, Rudolf von. "Schleiermacher und Preussen." In *Internationaler Schleiermacher-Kongress Berlin 1984*, edited by Kurt Victor Selge, 1099–106. Berlin: de Gruyter, 1985.

Thees, Frauke. "Catechismus oder Christlicher Vnderricht wie der in Kirchen vnnd Schulen der Churfürstlichen Pfaltz getrieben wird: Samt deren Kirchenceremonien vnd Gebetten." In *Lexikon der theologischen Werke*, edited by Eilert Herms et al. 67–69. Stuttgart: Kröner, 2003.

Thielicke, Helmut. *Glauben und Denken in der Neuzeit*. Tübingen: Mohr Siebeck, 1983.

Thompson, Bard. "The Palatinate Church Order of 1573." *Church History* 23 (1954) 239–54.

Tice, Terrence N. *Schleiermacher*. Nashville: Abingdon, 2006.

———. "Schleiermacher Yesterday, Today and Tomorrow." In *Cambridge Companion to Schleiermacher*, edited by Jacqueline Mariña, 307–17, Cambridge: Cambridge University Press, 2005.

Torrance, Thomas. F. "Universalism or Election." *Scottish Journal of Theology* 2 (1949) 310–18.

Trillhaas, Wolfgang. "Der Berliner Prediger." In *Friedrich Schleiermacher 1768–1834. Theologe—Philosoph—Pädagoge*, edited by Dietz Lange, 9–23. Göttingen: Vandenhoeck & Ruprecht, 1985.

———. "Der Mittelpunkt der Glaubenslehre Schleiermachers." *Neue Zeitschrift für Systematische Theologie und Religionsphilosophie* 10 (1968) 289–309.

Tschackert, P. "Thorn, Religionsgespräch." In *Realencyclopädie für protestantische Theologie und Kirche* 19:746–51. 3rd ed. Leipzig: Hinrichs, 1907.

Urner, Hans. "Schleiermacher als Prediger." In *Friedrich Schleiermacher Predigten*, edited by Hans Urner, 9–20. Göttingen: Vandenhoeck & Ruprecht, 1969.

Van Driel, Edwin. "Schleiermacher's Supralapsarian Christology." *Scottish Journal of Theology* 60 (2007) 251–70.

Vance, Robert Lee. *Sin and Self-consciousness in the Thought of Friedrich Schleiermacher*. NABPR Dissertation Series 11. Lewistown, NY: Mellen, 1995.

Vial, Theodore. "Schleiermacher and the State." In *Cambridge Companion to Friedrich Schleiermacher*, edited by Jacqueline Mariña, 269–85. Cambridge: Cambridge University Press, 2005.

Wagenmann, Julius August. "Marheinecke, Philipp Konrad." In *Allgemeine Deutsche Biographie* 20, edited by Historische Commission bei der königlichen Akademie der Wissenschaften, 338–40. Leipzig: Duncker & Humblot, 1884.

Wallmann, Johannes. *Kirchengeschichte Deutschlands seit der Reformation*. 3rd ed. Tübingen: Mohr Siebeck, 1988.

Wappler, Klaus. "Reformationsjubiläum und Kirchenunion (1817)." In *Die Geschichte der Evangelischen Kirche der Union Band 1: Die Anfänge der Union unter landesherrlichem Kirchenregiment (1817–1850)*, edited by J. F. Gerhard Groeters and Rudolf Mau, 93–114. Leipzig: Evangelische Verlagsanstalt, 1992.

Warfield, Benjamin Breckinridge. "Predestination in the Reformed Confessions." *Presbyterian and Reformed Review* 12 (1901) 49–128.

Weeber, Martin. "Die christliche Glaubenslehre nach protestantischen Grundsätzen." In *Lexikon der theologischen Werke*, edited by Michael Eckert et al., 90. Stuttgart: Kröner, 2003.

———. "Die Grundlehren der christlichen Dogmatik als Wissenschaft." In *Lexikon der theologischen Werke*, edited by Michael Eckert et al., 358–9. Stuttgart: Kröner, 2003.

Bibliography

————. *Schleiermachers Eschatologie. Eine Untersuchung zum theologischen Spätwerk.* Gütersloh: Kaiser, 2000.

Wendel, François. "Justification and Predestination in Calvin." In *Readings in Calvin's Theology,* edited by Donald K. McKim, 153–78. 1984. Reprinted, Eugene, OR: Wipf & Stock, 1998.

Wetzel, James. "Predestination, Pelagianism, and Foreknowledge." In *Cambridge Companion to Augustine,* edited by Eleonore Stump and Norman Kretzmann, 49–58. Cambridge: Cambridge University Press, 2001.

————. "Snares of Truth: Augustine on Free Will and Predestination." In *Augustine and His Critics: Essays in Honor of Gerald Bonner,* edited by Robert Dodaro and George Lawless, 124–41. London: Routledge, 2000.

Whittemore, Thomas. *The Modern History of Universalism, from the Era of the Reformation to the Present Time.* Boston: Published by the Author, 1830.

Williams, Robert R. "Theodicy, Tragedy, and Soteriology: The Legacy of Schleiermacher." *Harvard Theological Review* 77 (1984) 395–412.

Wright, N. T. "Towards a Biblical View of Universalism." *Themelios* 4 (1979) 54–58.

Wyman, Walter. "Rethinking the Christian Doctrine of Sin: Friedrich Schleiermacher and Hick's Irenaean Type." *Journal of Religion* 74 (1994) 199–217.

————. "The Role of the Protestant Confessions in Schleiermacher's *The Christian Faith.*" *Journal of Religion* 87 (2007) 355–85.

————. "Sin and Redemption." In *Cambridge Companion to Friedrich Schleiermacher,* edited by Jaqueline Mariña, 129–49. Cambridge: Cambridge University Press, 2005.

Index of Names

Index of Symbolic Books, Confessions, and Catechisms